Heterosexuality in Question

Heterosexuality in Question

Stevi Jackson

SAGE Publications
London · Thousand Oaks · New Delhi

First published 1999

SAGE Publications Ltd
6 Bonhill Street
London EC2A 4PU

SAGE Publications Inc
2455 Teller Road
Thousand Oaks, California 91320

SAGE Publications India Pvt Ltd
32, M-Block Market
Greater Kailash - I
New Delhi 110 048

British Library Cataloguing in Publication data

A catalogue record for this book is
available from the British Library

ISBN 0 7619 5342 6
ISBN 0 7619 5343 4 (pbk)

Library of Congress catalog card number available

Typeset by Type Study, Scarborough, North Yorkshire
Printed and bound in Great Britain by Athenaeum Press,
Gateshead

For Sue

Contents

Preface and Acknowledgements

The bulk of this volume comprises previously published work, framed by introductory and concluding chapters written specifically for the book, situating the contents within ongoing debates in heterosexuality. Chapters 2–11 have been edited for continuity and to avoid excessive repetition, but only Chapter 2 has been substantially abridged. I have avoided the use of ellipses to indicate cuts in the interests of fluency. I have also resisted the urge to rewrite earlier work in more contemporary language. Each of the previously published chapters is preceded by a short editorial commentary, which explains the context in which the work was produced and provides an opportunity for a retrospective critical reflection on it; since both contextualization and reflexive critique are more necessary in relation to my earlier work, the commentaries in Part Two are longer than those in Part Three.

Bringing this work together has not only been an opportunity to think about the development of my own work, but also about the people who have been important to me intellectually, professionally and personally. Since these writings span most of my adult life, I cannot possibly acknowledge everyone who has influenced or supported me, but I will do my best. I should begin with my first mentor, Laurie Taylor, who supervised my Master's dissertation, edited the series in which my first book was published, helped me find an authorial voice and encouraged me in very many ways. The other major influence at the beginning of my career was Diana Leonard, who was instrumental in getting most of my early work published and in drawing me into a community of feminist scholars. She has continued to be a presence in my life ever since, and I owe her a great many intellectual and personal debts. My oldest friend, Jean Thirtle, deserves a mention not simply for being there for 30 years, but also for the innumerable personal and political discussions we have had about sexuality – and so too does Chris Jones, who has been a participant in those discussions and a friend for almost as long. My first academic job was in a decidedly non-elite institution in a small North Wales town. Here Peter Rushton helped keep my brain alive through debate and collaborative work, while Dave and Louise Carpenter, Glyn Watson and Mary Dalton provided other forms of support. When I moved on to the Polytechnic of Wales – subsequently the University of Glamorgan – I was again grateful to those friends and colleagues both within and outside the institution who sustained me intellectually and personally through the depressing 1980s and into the 1990s, especially to Deirdre Beddoe, Pauline Young, David Adamson,

Peter Brunsdon, Teri Bewer, Jane Prince, Rose Pearson, David Hillier, Tia DeNora, Brendan Young and Shaun Moores. At the University of Strathclyde I would like to thank all those colleagues both from the Department of Government and from Women's Studies, who helped to make my five years there both intellectually productive and personally enjoyable, especially Catherine Grant, Anne Witz, Debbie Cameron, Hazel Croall, Tom Mackie, David Judge, Terry Cox, Momin Rahman and Magdalene Ang. I would also like to thank all the women I have worked with on the Trouble & Strife collective who, in addition to two already mentioned in other contexts (Diana Leonard and Debbie Cameron), include Sophie Laws, Lisa Adkins, Dianne Butterworth, Liz Kelly and Joan Scanlon. Not only have I received from them incisive and constructive criticism of my writing, but they have also helped keep me in touch with feminism's activist roots and ensured that I do not forget that theory has a political purpose. There are a number of individuals who have been particularly important to me in the last few years. Christine Delphy's ideas have long had a strong influence on mine, but since I have come to know her personally I have been grateful for her interest in, and support for, my work as well as for challenging discussions of feminist theory. In Gabriele Griffin and Sasha Roseneil I have found not only the stimulation of productive collaboration but valued friends. Kathryn Backett-Milburn and Sue Scott have provided both intellectual and emotional support. Sue, in particular, has been both a co-author and close friend with whom I have shared the vicissitudes and contradictions of living as a heterosexual feminist. Writing with her has been inspirational, fruitful and, above all, fun. Sue has had more influence on this book than she is likely to be aware of. Not only are many of the ideas developed in the more recent chapters derived from our collaboration, but her support for the project kept me going when my enthusiasm flagged. I doubt I could have finished it had she not seen me through some tough times and given me a well aimed kick (metaphorically speaking) in the closing stages. Finally, I would like to thank Karen Phillips, my editor at Sage, who has displayed patience above and beyond the call of duty and who has been consistently supportive and encouraging.

Sources

Chapter 2 is taken from *The Social Construction of Female Sexuality*, London: Women's Research and Resources Centre (1978). Chapter 3, 'The social context of rape: sexual scripts and motivation' was originally published in *Women's Studies International Quarterly*, 1(1), 1978, pp. 27–38. Chapter 4, 'How to make babies: sexism in sex education' was originally published in *Women's Studies International Quarterly*, 1(4), 1978, pp. 341–52. Chapters 3 and 4 are reproduced by permission from Elsevier Science Ltd, Pergamon Imprint, Oxford. Chapter 5, 'Femininity, masculinity and sexuality' is from *On the Problem of Men: Two Feminist Conferences*, edited by Scarlet Friedman and Elizabeth Sarah, first published in 1982 by The Women's Press Ltd, 34 Great Sutton Street, London EC1V 0LQ, and is reproduced with their agreement. Chapter 6, 'The desire for Freud', was published in *Trouble & Strife*, 1 (1983). Chapter 7, 'Even sociologists fall in love: an exploration in the sociology of emotions' appeared in *Sociology*, 27(2), 1993, pp. 201–20, and is reproduced with the permission of BSA Publications Ltd. Chapter 8, 'Women and heterosexual love: complicity, resistance and change' is taken from L. Pearce and J. Stacey (eds) *Romance Revisited*, London: Lawrence and Wishart and is reproduced by arrangement with the publishers. Chapter 9, 'Gender and heterosexuality: a materialist feminist analysis' appeared in M. Maynard and J. Purvis (eds) *(Hetero)sexual Politics*, London: Taylor & Francis (1995) and is reproduced by permission of Taylor & Francis. Chapter 10 appeared as 'Ignorance is Bliss when you're Just Seventeen' in *Trouble & Strife*, 33 (1996) and Chapter 11 as 'Taking liberties' in *Trouble & Strife*, 34 (1997).

PART I

THE CONTEXT

---

1 Querying Heterosexuality: A Personal History of Feminist and Sociological Theorizing

The chapters gathered together here were written over a period of 25 years and represent my attempts to theorize sexuality as a feminist and a sociologist. They do not all foreground heterosexuality as such, but all address aspects of heterosexual desire and practice. The two new chapters which introduce and conclude the collection are directly informed by the renewed interest in problematizing heterosexuality evident during the 1990s. Indeed, it is this which provided the inspiration for the volume as a whole and for the critical reflection on my own work which it entails. Today heterosexuality is being queried more radically and more rigorously than ever before, but it began to be called into question as long ago as the 1970s. This first chapter traces the critique of heterosexuality back to these early origins and maps out some of the diverse approaches to sexuality which have since developed. The final chapter engages with more recent theorizing, specifically the arrival of queer theory on the academic scene and the revival of feminist debates on heterosexuality.

There are a number of reasons for beginning with a historical contextualization of feminist and sociological analyses of heterosexuality. The first and most obvious of these is that this is a history in which my own work is located. The fact that I began writing on sexuality in 1973 had much to do with the rise of the Women's Liberation Movement and my engagement with it. The ways in which I wrote about it were influenced both by my training as a sociologist and the new critical perspectives circulating among feminists. My work continues to bear the marks of this dual influence, and hence of changes and developments in feminist and social theory. There is, however, more at stake in this history than my personal intellectual biography, for some of the theoretical perspectives which have gained currency over the last two decades have had the effect of obliterating earlier insights into sexuality. Those who have come to the study of sexuality through

Foucault, queer theory and postmodern feminism are all too often ignorant of the earlier origins of social construction theory.[1]

One of my concerns here is the eclipsing of specifically sociological perspectives – a concern shared by others (Epstein, 1996; Stein and Plummer, 1996; Seidman, 1996b). However, feminism's contribution to the genesis of social constructionist thought is even less likely to be acknow-ledged by later writers. This dual erasure of sociological and feminist work on sexuality is not coincidental. Within feminist theory much early work was informed by sociological thinking, but with the 'cultural turn' of the 1980s (Barrett, 1992) sociology was displaced by cultural, literary and philosophical perspectives. It was in the context of this changing disciplin-ary hierarchy that postmodern feminisms developed and, in parallel, shifts occurred in lesbian and gay studies with the emergence of queer theory.

Reaffirming the importance of early feminist and sociological theorizing is not merely a case of establishing an accurate chronology or ensuring that particular theorists are given due credit for their work. If we forget these earlier contributions we risk re-inventing the wheel and deprive ourselves of the opportunity of building on past work (Allen and Leonard, 1996; Epstein, 1996). Moreover, I also wish to argue that a sociologically informed feminism has much to contribute to current debates on sexuality. Where queer theorists have tended to concentrate on texts, discourses and cultural practices, there is clearly a space for approaches which pay atten-tion to social structures, to the socially situated contexts of everyday sexual practice and experience, to the material conditions under which our sexu-alities are lived.

My more specific aim is to demonstrate that critical analyses of hetero-sexuality are not new, that they have a history dating back to the early years of second wave feminism. This is not to say that a radical critique came into being fully formed in the 1970s. Indeed, much feminist work at that time failed fully to problematize heterosexuality and was framed within what Chrys Ingraham has called 'the heterosexual imaginary' – a mode of thought which 'conceals the operation of heterosexuality in structuring gender and closes off any critical analysis of heterosexuality as an organiz-ing institution' (Ingraham, 1996: 169). Nonetheless, there was work at this time which provided an implicit critique of heterosexuality and laid foundations for more radical questioning. Moreover, lesbian feminists began, early in the 1970s, to mount an attack on heterosexuality as a patriarchal institution.

My focus here is on feminist critiques of heterosexuality and, in this chapter, gay and queer theorizing will only be considered in passing. I am particularly interested in problematizing heterosexuality from within and hence in the ways in which straight feminists have engaged with – or distanced themselves from – this project. I cannot, however, discuss this without also talking about lesbian feminisms, since straight feminists have often needed considerable prodding before we have been willing to ques-tion our own sexual practice. Heterosexuals do not generally expect to be asked to explain themselves. Lesbian and gay sexualities are marked categories, routinely named and made visible as 'other', while heterosexuality has usually been unmarked as the unexamined norm which needs no name and no justification for its existence. The process of querying heterosexuality has entailed making it visible, divesting it of its cloak of neutrality and normality.

Where I stand

In this introduction I will outline the historical antecedents of current debates and trace some lines of development from early theorizing on sexuality, concentrating on feminist engagements with wider social theory. Before doing so, however, I will say something about the theoretical and political stance from which I am writing and the ways in which I am using the key terms 'gender' and 'sexuality'. I am situating myself within this narrative as a heterosexual feminist, although that label is in some ways problematic; like others in the same position, I would not want to define my feminism by my heterosexuality (see Rowland, 1993; Swindells, 1993). I have, at times, felt acute disjunctions between my feminist politics and my heterosexual practice and experience. Some, notably Lynne Segal, are liable to interpret statements of this kind as a guilty defensiveness resulting from the 'self-righteous' moralism of radical lesbian feminists (1994: 213–14). I would suggest, however, that it is impossible to live in a patriarchal society as both a feminist and a heterosexual without being aware of contradictions – unless one is totally without reflexive capacities. Owning my heterosexuality and being willing to subject it to critical scrutiny is not a form of self-abjection but a necessary step in the process of theorizing sexuality from a position which is both feminist and anti-homophobic.

I define myself as a materialist feminist, in the sense that I see gender divisions (and indeed all social divisions and inequalities) as rooted in material social structures and embedded in everyday social practices. Privileging the material in this way does not mean ignoring issues of culture, discourse or subjectivity – much of my writing has been concerned with precisely these issues – but it does entail keeping in mind the material social contexts in which cultural products and practices emerge, in which discourses are deployed and subjectivities are constituted. This is not to say that I have always successfully maintained my hold on these different strands of analysis, and only in my most recent work have I really begun to tie gender and sexuality to social structural factors. I have certainly never attempted anything so ambitious as a coherent theorization of the relationship between structure, discourse, agency and subjectivity or between the social and the cultural. Indeed, I do not think such totalizing theory is either possible or desirable: the best we can do is to try to appreciate the complexity of social life without losing sight of its regularities. Here my materialism serves as a guiding thread, a reminder to myself that there are observable, 'real' material social relations, institutions and practices out there in the world which need to be taken into account.

My materialist feminism derives primarily from the French tradition associated with Christine Delphy, Colette Guillaumin, Monique Wittig and others. This is a form of radical feminism in that these theorists see the relative social positions of women and men not merely as unequal, but as a hierarchical power relation. In other words, it is not possible to change the situation of women without changing that of men, without fundamentally transforming the gendered social order. This is not the radical feminism so frequently caricatured as essentialist, as preoccupied exclusively with male violence or as reducing male domination to the appropriation of women's sexuality. On the contrary, materialist feminism has consistently held to a 'strong' anti-essentialist position within which gender and sexuality are taken to be social, not natural, phenomena and has always resisted the reduction of women's oppression to any single cause (see, for example, Delphy, 1984: 21–5).

It follows from this that, despite my long-standing interest in sexuality, I do not accord it any causal priority in explaining women's subordination. Indeed, I have consistently argued that one of the pervasive features of the social organization of sexuality within the modern world is the extraordinary weight and significance accorded to the sexual, the way in which it is singled out as a 'special' area of life whether it is seen as requiring specific and stringent moral controls or celebrated as a route to self-fulfilment and radical social change (see especially Jackson, 1982a; Jackson and Scott, 1996, 1997). Feminists should, in my view, question this over-privileging of sexuality rather than buying into it. As I point out in Chapter 9, paraphrasing Delphy (1992), men may say women are 'only good for one thing', but there is no reason why we should believe them – and there is even less reason to make this patriarchal maxim central to feminist theory. This does not mean that sexuality is unimportant, but that its place in women's lives and its salience for the perpetuation of gender inequality must be understood in the context of other, equally gendered, social institutions, relationships and practices. Heterosexuality itself is not merely a matter of specifically sexual desires and practices, but also entails divisions of labour, power and resources.

Sexuality cannot be understood as an essential human attribute, as a presocial proclivity to be contained, controlled, repressed or, alternatively, to be liberated and encouraged to flourish. Sexuality per se is neither inherently oppressive to women nor inherently liberating. It has no intrinsic qualities – good or bad. Since it is a social phenomenon, it is particular, culturally and historically rooted, forms of sexuality which are oppressive. Thus for social constructionists sexuality is not definable as a fixed object of analysis. It encompasses all those acts, desires, identities and relationships understood as in some sense erotic – but the erotic is itself a fluid concept. What is deemed erotic varies across cultures, historical eras and social contexts; what one person finds erotic another might find distasteful, morally unacceptable or simply boring; the enactment of one person's erotic desires can entail coercive acts towards others (who experience those acts as anything but erotic). What is erotic, and hence sexual, depends on what is defined as such, by whom, in specific social contexts – hence the very definition of the sexual is a social act.

For biological determinists matters are much simpler: sexuality is that which is concerned with the reproduction of the species, or the maximization of each individual's genetic legacy: sexuality is thus both definable and explicable in terms of a reproductive imperative. When we resist this reductionist account, once we accept that the complexities of human sexual lives involve far more than the acts, organs and motivations involved in reproduction, we are left with a much more slippery and indeterminate concept of sexuality. It is for this reason that social constructionism is often thought of as a morally and politically relativist stance: if it is all a matter of cultural definition, then no one sexuality is better or worse than any other. It is also thought of as relativist in the sense of lacking any anchorage to material reality: if sexual desires and identities are not determined by biology, they appear to be entirely arbitrary, unstable effects of the cultural application of meaning. Hence social constructionism is said to be 'unable to theorize the issue of determination' (Epstein, 1992: 259).

While these problems are evident in some forms of social construction-ism, they can be avoided. Rejecting biological determinism does not imply replacing it with a simplistic form of social determinism, but nor does it entail doing away with the idea of determination altogether. Despite the mutability and variability of human sexual desires and practices, this variety is not, in practice, limitless (Weeks, 1981); there is order here, but a social rather than a natural order. The forms of sexuality existing in any given society at any one time are products of a particular history and culture, particular institutionalized and habitual ways of doing sex. Viewing sexu-ality as fully social means consistently relating it to gender and recognizing that it is constructed at a number of intersecting levels.

At the level of social structure, sexuality is socially constructed through the institutionalization of heterosexuality bolstered by law, the state and social convention. The institution of heterosexuality is inherently gendered, it rests upon the assumed normality of specific forms of social and sexual relations between women and men. Sexuality is also socially constructed at the level of meaning, through its constitution as the object of discourse and through the specific discourses on the sexual in circulation at any historical moment; these discourses serve to define what is sexual, to differentiate the 'perverse' from the 'normal' and, importantly, to delimit appropriately masculine and feminine forms of sexuality. However, meaning is also deployed within and emergent from social interaction and hence finds its expression at yet another level – that of our everyday social practices, through which each of us negotiates and makes sense of our own sexual lives. Here, too, sexuality is constantly in the process of being constructed and reconstructed, enacted and re-enacted, within specific social contexts and relationships. Sexuality is thus socially constructed by what embodied individuals actually *do*. Finally, sexuality is socially constructed at the level of subjectivity, through complex social and cultural processes by which we acquire sexual and gendered desires and identities.

Central to the social ordering of sexuality is its interrelationship with gender. It is this which has been the main focus of the work reproduced here. As I understand and use the terms 'gender' and 'sexuality', they are analytically distinct but empirically interrelated. I am well aware, however, that these concepts are contested (see Chapter 9; see also Jackson, 1998a). Sexuality is not only a protean term, but has also sometimes been extended to cover what I mean by gender – the social division between women and men and the cultural construction of femininity and masculinity – especially in accounts influenced by psychoanalysis (see, for example Mitchell, 1982). In everyday usage there is considerable ambiguity surrounding the words 'sex' and 'sexual', which slip and slide between gendered and erotic meanings. In the English language the word 'sex' can denote either the distinction between male and female (as 'two sexes') or to sex as an erotic activity (to have sex). Similarly, 'sexual' can refer to the different activities or attributes of 'the two sexes' as in such phrases as 'the sexual division of labour', or it can refer to the erotic sphere of life, for example to 'sexual fantasies'. Moreover the term 'sex' can be used – more commonly in French, but sometimes in English – to refer to sexual organs which are simultaneously erogenous zones and the body parts which distinguish male from female.

This linguistic confusion is not a mere accident, but tells us something about the male dominated and heterosexually ordered culture in which we live. It is commonly assumed that being born with a particular set of genitals (sex organs) defines one as of a particular 'sex' (female or male), which means that one will normally become properly feminine or masculine (the appropriate gender) and will desire and engage in erotic activity with 'the opposite sex', with someone possessing a different set of sex organs from one's own. This circular and deterministic reasoning has served to legitimize both women's subordination and heterosexuality's privileged, normative status. Hence it is politically, as well as theoretically, important to challenge this way of thinking, to break the patriarchal chain which binds sex, gender and sexuality together as if they were inseparable and unchangeable.

The term 'gender' has been used by feminists since the early 1970s in order to emphasize that differences between women and men are socially and culturally constructed rather than given by nature. Like many feminists writing at that time, I initially followed the practice of defining gender in opposition to biological sex, and assumed that the latter denoted natural, unproblematic, pre-social differences between women and men (see Chapter 2). Increasingly, however, I became aware that treating sex as given concedes ground to essentialism, that sex differences themselves are by no means self-evident, that the ways in which we recognize and classify sex differences are themselves social. Hence, following Delphy (and to some extent anticipating Butler, 1990a), I came to see sex as the product of gender rather than the other way around in that 'the hierarchical division of humanity into two transforms an anatomical difference (which is itself devoid of social implications) into a relevant distinction for social practice' (Delphy, 1984: 144).

When I use the term 'gender' in this chapter and in my more recent work (Chapters 7–12) I am not presupposing pre-existing biological sex differences. Rather, I am treating the distinction between women and men itself, as well as the characteristics of femininity and masculinity, as socially constructed. I use the term 'gender', in preference to sex, to emphasize the social origins of the division between women and men and prefer to reserve the terms 'sex', 'sexual' and 'sexuality' for erotic activities, desires, practices and identities. This usage helps to avoid semantic ambiguity and maintain a conceptual distinction between gender relations and sexual relations. Clearly, gender and sexuality are intertwined in complex ways in our daily lives, but we cannot explore their interrelationship if we conflate the two. I will return to this issue in the final chapter, but for now I want to move on to the origins of the critique of heterosexuality – an institution which both orders specifically sexual relations and which is implicated in the perpetuation of gender hierarchy.

The social construction of (hetero)sexuality: feminism meets sociology

A central preoccupation of second wave feminism was to understand the conditions of our own existence and to link these with a wider analysis of women's subordination. Sexual relations were among the many aspects of our personal lives which came to be seen as political. In making sexuality a political issue, feminists began to conceptualize it as changeable and hence challenged the prevailing assumption that sexual desires and practices were fixed by nature. Viewing sexuality as socially constructed thus followed directly from politicizing it. Elsewhere (Jackson, 1998b) I have drawn attention to parallels between feminist thinking and C. Wright Mills' idea of the 'sociological imagination' which transforms 'personal troubles' into 'public issues' (Mills, 1970: 14–17). The exercise of a feminist imagination enabled us to see that personal troubles, such as problematic aspects of heterosexual relations, were social in origin and amenable to political change. It was this convergence between feminism and sociology which enabled me to develop feminist ideas within my academic work and bring sociological perspectives to bear on issues of sexual politics.

As Mills' formulation suggests, sociology has long been concerned with revealing the ways in which personal life is shaped by society and culture. Sociologists have also habitually questioned arrangements taken for granted as natural. In this sense it is unsurprising that social constructionist perspectives on sexuality found their first academic expression in sociology. Yet mainstream sociology in the early 1970s was not particularly receptive to new thinking on sexuality. When I expressed an interest in this area as a postgraduate, most established academics responded either with incomprehension or with ribald and sexist innuendo. At that time even gender divisions were not taken very seriously and sexuality was not generally considered a fit topic for sociological enquiry. Where sexuality was attended to at all, in such fields as the sociology of crime or the family, it was in terms of the social regulation of pre-existing, implicitly pre-social, proclivities.

More radical sociological conceptualizations of sexuality were, however, beginning to emerge especially in studies of deviance, where positivistic understandings of crime were being challenged (Epstein, 1992; Seidman, 1996b). The most prominent new perspective was labelling theory, which treated deviance not as a property of a particular act or individual but the outcome of the social application of meaning, a process of signification (Matza, 1969). Hence homosexuality, for example, could no longer be conceptualized as a pathological or immoral departure from a healthy sexual norm, but was the outcome of the labelling process. Moreover, as Mary McIntosh argued in one of the founding statements of social constructionism, the homosexual 'role' was itself social in origin and of relatively recent historical invention (McIntosh, 1968). This new work had caught my imagination, yet what I wanted to understand was not deviance but the normal everyday production of femininity and masculinity.

What most interested me was what made women (myself included) conform to normative femininity and thus collude in their own continued subordination. I had relatively little material to work with. In the field of anthropology there were some classic ethnographies and cross-cultural overviews which addressed the diversity of human sexual relations (for example, Ford and Beach, 1952; Malinowski, 1929); there was psychological work on sex differences in aptitudes, attitudes and behaviour and on 'sex role socialization' – but none of this could explain satisfactorily the ways in which my own sexuality had been constituted; finally, there was psychoanalysis, the only large body of work which explicitly addressed the constitution of sexuality. I read Freud avidly, as well as the work of other psychoanalysts, but found it literally incredible – it simply had no resonance for the ways in which I experienced my own sexuality. Moreover, like many young feminists of the time I experienced the exposé of 'the myth of the vaginal orgasm' (Koedt, 1972) as a personal revelation (and a very exciting one), which both fuelled my scepticism about Freud and which seemed to demand an explanation for the mass deception of generations of women.

Two developments in feminist and sociological thinking provided me with inspiration. The first of these was the concept of gender which initially came to my attention through the work of Ann Oakley (1972). Second, my supervisor put into my hands a copy of an article by William Simon and

John Gagnon (1969), which both provided a cogent critique of psycho-analysis and offered an alternative, sociological perspective. This approach is explained in detail in Chapter 2, but it is worth pointing up a few of its salient features here. Most importantly, Gagnon and Simon's position is thoroughly anti-essentialist. For them there is no pre-given sexuality which can be repressed; what is sexual is a matter of social definition and becoming sexual is a process of learning sexual meanings or 'scripts' and locating oneself within them. Their critique of the concept of repression, so central to psychoanalysis and to the thinking of those sexual radicals who saw capitalism as a repressive force, presaged Foucault's later critique of the 'repressive hypothesis'. So, too, did their questioning of the centrality and 'specialness' accorded to sexuality in modern society, their suggestion that rather than sex being a powerful impulse underpinning all human motivations it may be that its importance is a historical invention (Gagnon and Simon, 1974: 16). From a specifically feminist point of view, Gagnon and Simon's work also has the advantage that it foregrounds gender as central to the scripting of sexuality, the complex 'co-ordination of bodies and meanings' which sexual relations entail (1974: 9).

This is not to say that Gagnon and Simon's work was without flaws. Although they place a great deal of emphasis on gender, they tend to focus primarily on socially constructed *differences* between women and men, without sufficient emphasis on the power relations between them. They assume a relatively easy accommodation between male and female sexu-ality within heterosexual relations and have almost nothing to say about coercive sex: 'rape' is not even indexed in *Sexual Conduct* (1974). They also caused considerable irritation by dubbing lesbianism 'a conformity greater than deviance' (see Faraday, 1981) – a characterization resulting from their failure to think through the social meaning of lesbianism within a patri-archal society. Some of these shortcomings are attributable to sexist assumptions which Gagnon and Simon failed to question, but they may also be related to a central problem with their perspective itself. The concept of scripts was developed within a broadly symbolic interactionist framework – a sociological perspective which privileges human agency and meaningful social action over social structure. There is no way, within this perspective, to think about issues of power and inequality, about the privileging of male dominated heterosexuality except at the level of mean-ing and interpersonal conduct. Hence Gagnon and Simon cannot provide a fully social explanation of sexual scripts (Connell and Dowsett, 1992). Within this perspective there can be no means of explaining where scripts come from or how they might change over time, except by recourse to the idea that scripts emerge from and are modified through interaction.[2]

Nonetheless, this work was radical for its time and still provides insights worth recovering. It was not, however, a perspective which attracted legions of disciples – which in part explains its eclipsing by later forms of social constructionism. Some gay theorists took it up (Plummer, 1975; Weeks, 1981), but it had few feminist adherents. Within feminist circles, I often had to defend Gagnon and Simon's approach on two fronts: against those who thought it was nonsense to abandon the Freudian concept of repression (most of whom happily did so when Foucault made the critique of the repressive hypothesis fashionable), and those who maintained that feminist theory should be generated without reliance on male theorists. Nonetheless, I found Gagnon and Simon's perspective useful to think with. The critical edge which this theory lacked was provided by my involvement with feminism. This sometimes led to uneasy theoretical amalgams – such as superimposing the concept of patriarchy upon an analysis which it didn't quite fit (see Chapter 3) – but it helped to convince me of the theoretical and political importance of social constructionism.

In the early 1970s, the word essentialism had not yet entered my vocabulary, but what I was working with was an anti-essentialist position. It is worth restating here, as I have done elsewhere (Jackson and Scott, 1996) just why essentialist perspectives on sexuality are antithetical to my feminist sociological project.[3] In the first place, it rests on something unknowable, a hypothesized 'natural' sexuality somehow uncontaminated by cultural influences. As a result, it cannot adequately explain cultural and historical variations in human sexuality – differential repression is too crude a concept to capture the complexities of such variations. Furthermore, it conceptualizes the social regulation of sexuality as a negative force and hence does not allow for a productive and constitutive social shaping of sexuality. It cannot account for differences in masculine and feminine sexuality except in terms of 'natural' differences or differential repression. Either women and men are innately different and nothing can change this, or women's sexuality is seen as more repressed than that of men. This latter view takes current definitions of male sexuality as the bench-mark of unrepressed sexuality, in other words what sexuality should be like. Few feminists would find the political consequences of this acceptable. The concept of repression may be appealing in that it can carry a sense of the damage and danger women have experienced in the sexual arena, but this idea is better expressed as oppression rather than repression. Whereas the concept of repression suggests the holding back of some underlying force, oppression focuses attention on social relations of power and domination. Finally, and crucially in the context of my current work, the essentialist paradigm presupposes an equation between 'normal' sexuality and heterosexuality, assuming that deviations from the norm require explanation while the normativity of heterosexuality goes unquestioned.

Heterosexuality and its discontents: early feminist interventions

It is my contention that querying heterosexuality should be made central to both the theory and politics of sexuality, and that feminism has made such radical questioning possible. Yet, in the early years of 'second wave' feminism, this critique remained implicit rather than explicit. My academic interest in sexuality was fuelled by innumerable discussions with friends and in consciousness raising groups about our discontent and disillusionment with heterosexual intimacy. Although we were critical of almost every aspect of sexual relations between women and men, heterosexuality itself was rarely named and identified as the object of analysis. Indeed, we often talked simply of sexuality when we meant heterosexuality – and this is evident in my early work. With hindsight it seems strange that I could not then see what I was doing, particularly since debates on lesbianism were happening all around me and the conceptual tools with which to challenge the normality of heterosexuality were already available.

We were the generation which reached the newly lowered age of majority at the close of the 1960s, for whom the sexual revolution promised much but delivered far less. The ideas in circulation within the Left and among various counter-cultural movements of the time promoted 'free love', condemned marriage as a bourgeois institution which reduced people to possessions and, in principle at least, challenged the double standard of sexual morality. In practice, however, the consequences for women and men differed; in retrospect many women felt that the ideals of sexual liberation gave men greater access to women's bodies and removed our right to say 'no'. Hence some have argued that this period simply intensified the sexual exploitation of women (see, for example, Jeffreys, 1990). My own feelings about that era were, and are, more mixed. While the rhetoric of sexual liberation certainly did provide men with new ways of pressurizing women into sex (see Jackson and Scott, 1996), it also placed sexuality on the political agenda. Our experiences of this time profoundly influenced dis-cussions of sexuality within the Women's Liberation Movement. Many of us wanted to preserve what we saw as positive elements of the sexual liberation ethos – the dissociation of sex from reproduction, the emphasis on pleasure and freedom and the critique of marriage and monogamy – while attacking the coercive and predatory aspects of male sexuality. It was from this feminist engagement with the sexual revolution that an implicit critique of heterosexuality began to emerge, although the institution of heterosexuality itself did not come under sustained attack until the end of the 1970s.

From the beginning we questioned the conventions of heterosexual sexual practices. The publication of Anne Koedt's article 'The myth of the vaginal orgasm' (1972), enabled feminists in Britain and the USA to argue that equating sex with penetration constituted a male defined view of sexuality, prioritizing male orgasm while relegating acts which produce female orgasm to the status of 'foreplay'. Heterosexual feminists explored alternative sexual practices within which so-called 'sexual intercourse' became just one sexual act among many possibilities, rather than the predictable end point of any heterosexual encounter (Campbell, 1980). A second strand of feminist critique was to reconceptualize and rename penetration itself (for example as 'enclosure') in ways which did not position men as active doers of the act and women as passive recipients (see, for example, Hite, 1976). This, however, was perceived as less radical than challenging the very definition of sex, the dominant, patriarchal assumption that sex *is* heterosexual penetration. Subverting the equation between sex and penetration should have made it possible to question the 'normality' of heterosexuality itself – although Koedt, along with many other feminists of the time, did not go this far. However, exposing the mythical status of the vaginal orgasm did render lesbianism an attractive alternative. Moreover, it became possible to critique the construction of sexual knowledge, to reveal the androcentric and heterosexist assumptions underpinning sex manuals, sex education and everyday taken for granted assumptions about what counted as sex (see Chapters 4 and 5).

While these preoccupations reflected the pursuit of pleasure in our own sexual relationships, feminists were also confronting issues of sexual coercion and violence. This too emerged from personal experience as we made connections between being pressured into unwanted sexual encounters and activities, the everyday harassment we encountered on the streets and the brutal facts of rape. Rape was seen as a reflection of 'normal' sexual mores, such as the expectation that sexually active men would pursue and conquer passive women and the widespread idea that male desire, once aroused, was an unstoppable force (see Chapter 3). Even here, though, heterosexuality often remained unproblematized. For example, Susan Brownmiller's classic and encyclopaedic exposure of the ways in which rape reinforced women's subordination never once wavered from the assumption that the whole world is heterosexual (Brownmiller, 1975).

At the same time, much attention was given to marriage – the linchpin of institutionalized heterosexuality, but again heterosexuality per se remained an unanalysed given. Feminists also questioned the ideology of romantic love and the practice of monogamy and linked these with the subordination of women within marriage (see Comer, 1974). However, discussion of marriage and the domestic division of labour got side-tracked into analyses of the utility of housework to capitalism, precluding a focus on the heterosexual contract within which this labour took place. In France, where materialist feminists analysed how men benefited from their individual and collective appropriation of women's bodies and labour (Delphy, 1977; Guillaumin, 1981), those connections were later made (Wittig, 1992; see Chapter 9). This development, though, belongs to a later stage of my story when, at the end of the 1970s, lesbian feminists in Britain and the USA were also beginning to mount a wholesale assault on heterosexuality.

Lesbian feminists were, however, already a vocal current within the Women's Movement. In Britain and the USA the gay and feminist movements emerged almost simultaneously and initially the more radical elements of these two movements saw themselves as allies confronting a common enemy: the straight, patriarchal establishment. This alliance around sexual politics was to prove short-lived, and collapsed in the face of political differences between lesbians and gay men. Many lesbians, disillusioned with the male dominated agenda of gay liberation, concentrated their efforts into the Women's Movement, which facilitated the development of a specifically feminist perspective on heterosexuality. From the beginning of the 1970s some were arguing for lesbianism as a form of resistance to patriarchy, as in the New York Radicalesbians' assertion that a 'lesbian is the rage of all women condensed to the point of explosion' (quoted in Jeffreys, 1990: 290). The Radicalesbians went on to argue that as long as women put their energies into relationships with men, they held back the cause of Women's Liberation – an argument which was to become central to political lesbianism's attack on heterosexuality.

The challenge of political lesbianism

At the end of the 1970s and beginning of the 1980s, debates around political lesbianism and heterosexuality caused major political rifts within feminism in Britain, France and elsewhere. Many previously heterosexual women had become lesbians as a result of their involvement in the Women's Movement, and most of these defined themselves as political lesbians in that they saw their sexual self-definition as a choice, a mode of resistance to patriarchal control rather than the expression of an innate disposition. Following the lead of earlier groups like the Radicalesbians, these women began to develop a much more sustained and explicit critique of heterosexuality.

One of the landmark publications of this emergent critique was Adrienne Rich's article 'Compulsory heterosexuality and lesbian existence' (1980). Rich directly contested heterosexuality's privileged status as unquestioned norm, arguing that, far from being natural, it was imposed upon women. This coercive imposition was achieved by the erasure of lesbian existence from history and culture and by a range of social practices which constrained women into personal subordination to men. Rather than emphasizing differences between lesbians and heterosexual women, Rich argued that all forms of sociability and solidarity among women were part of a lesbian continuum – and this proved to be the most controversial aspect of her argument among other lesbians. Some felt that the idea of a lesbian continuum de-eroticized lesbianism; others thought that it concealed the specificity of both lesbian oppression and lesbian resistance (Ettorre, 1980; Snitow et al., 1984). For some radical political lesbians, Rich's critique of heterosexuality simply did not go far enough, in that it 'seems to allow heterosexual women to continue their relationships with men while feeling politically validated in sharing a lesbian continuum' (Jeffreys, 1990: 297).

From my perspective, it is a strength of Rich's analysis that she was critical of heterosexuality itself rather than heterosexual women. Some of the other analyses circulating at the time were far more discomfiting for heterosexual feminists. In Britain, heated controversy centred on a paper circulated by the Leeds Revolutionary Feminists in 1979, though tensions around political lesbianism had already reached crisis point at the final National Women's Liberation Conference the previous year. Leeds Revolutionary Feminists argued that heterosexual feminists were collaborators engaged in 'counter-revolutionary activity' which reinforced male power (see Onlywomen Press, 1981). Those who had sex with men were colluding in their own oppression and any pleasure so gained a form of masochism. For the Leeds Revolutionary Feminists, penetration is an 'extreme form of ritual humiliation', whose 'function and effect is the punishment and control of women'; every act of penetration contributes to men's power and women's subjection (1981: 6–7). Since 'no act of penetration can escape its function and symbolic power', they are highly critical of heterosexual feminists who seek to change the meaning of penetration (Leeds Revolutionary Feminists, 1981: 7).[4]

Heterosexual feminists responded with a mixture of outrage and guilty defensiveness. Some simply asserted that they liked fucking with men and that was that. Others indulged in reciprocal name-calling: revolutionary feminists were damned as prudes and kill-joys. More measured responses warned of the dangers of political vanguardism, treating other women as the enemy and excluding the majority of women from the right to call themselves feminists. For the historical record it should be noted that there was no simple divide here between lesbians and heterosexual women. Some lesbians, especially those who defined themselves as socialist feminists, remained aloof from this debate. Nor was there a split between radical feminists and others: indeed, many radical feminists, including self-defined political lesbians, opposed the revolutionary feminist stance. In Britain, for example, the radical feminist magazine *Trouble & Strife* explicitly distanced itself from the revolutionary feminists: 'While we criticise the institution of heterosexuality, we do not think that only lesbians can be feminist or that all feminists should be lesbians' (Trouble & Strife Collective, 1983: 3). The distinction between the institution of heterosexuality and individual women's heterosexual practices has become a central issue in more recent debates, but in the early 1980s it remained undeveloped. In a climate of mutual hostility it proved difficult to engage in any truly constructive interchange of ideas.

Andrea Dworkin's commentary on heterosexual practice, *Intercourse*, was published a few years after the political lesbianism controversy had died down. Dworkin was less condemnatory of heterosexual feminists than revolutionary feminists had been and was rather kinder to those who sought to reconceptualize and reform the practice of penetrative sex:

> These visions of a humane sensuality based in equality are in the aspirations of women ... they are deep humane dreams that repudiate the rapist as the final arbiter of reality. They are an underground resistance to both inferiority and brutality, visions that sustain life and further endurance. (Dworkin, 1987: 152)

Dworkin did, however, offer a sustained polemic against heterosexual penetration, cataloguing the multitude of ways in which men humiliate, objectify and possess women through sex. Nonetheless, she clearly sees all these facets of intercourse as products of patriarchal social relations rather than being intrinsic to the act itself. She speculates that intercourse might not always and inevitably be 'experienced under conditions of force, fear or inequality' that it might have 'a potential for human expression not yet recognized or realized' and might therefore be able to survive the end of male power (1987: 169–70). Although she sees little hope of changing heterosexual intercourse here and now, Dworkin's analysis does suggest a potential for transforming the practice of sex with men.

By the time *Intercourse* was published, however, the arena of conflict moved on – to the battles on pornography and sado-masochism which became known as the sex wars. In this context, Dworkin's contribution was read as yet another anti-sex, anti-pleasure tract. Moreover, the sex wars were fought out primarily among lesbians, leaving most heterosexual feminists on the sidelines. At the same time, other developments were occurring in feminist and social theory which gave rise to new perspectives on sexuality and new sources of disagreements among feminists.

Divergent developments

In the early years of the modern feminist movement, we at least had a common point of departure: that the current ordering of heterosexual relations was detrimental to women and implicated in our subordination. From this starting point, feminist theory has taken diverse directions and the divisions among us have subsequently deepened and hardened. Adherents of particular positions have pursued their own theoretical and political agendas with little constructive dialogue across the 'sex wars' battle lines. Most feminists continue to endorse the view that sexuality is socially constructed, but there is no consensus on exactly what we mean by social construction, nor on how it should be analysed, nor on what it is about sexuality as currently constituted that needs to be challenged.

Elsewhere I have identified three main strands of analysis within feminist thinking on sexuality (Jackson, 1996a, 1996b). None of these is necessarily limited to any one theoretical or political position but each has, in practice, become associated with a particular variant of feminism. What is distinctive about these tendencies is the object of their analysis: in other words, precisely what they see as being socially constructed. Each foregrounds a specific aspect of sexuality – the centrality of male domination, the variability and plasticity of sexuality and the construction of our individual desires.

These forms of theory partially map on to the different levels at which sexuality is socially constructed which I identified above – the levels of social structure, culturally constituted meaning and subjectivity. What has less often been consistently theorized is the everyday practice of hetero-sexuality, although empirical work in this area has been steadily accumu-lating, some of which is conceptually highly sophisticated and is now beginning to figure in debates on heterosexuality (see especially Holland et al., 1998). In my view, all of these aspects of heterosexuality need to be addressed if we are to arrive at an understanding of it as fully social. Historically, however, and especially since the 1980s, particular theorists have tended to focus on specific facets of sexuality to the exclusion of others.

Power and the erotic

The first tendency I have identified, which sees sexuality as a site of male power, had its roots in feminist political activism, in efforts to challenge men's sexual appropriation and abuse of women. This has brought us analyses of sexual violence and pornography and, more generally, of the ways in which sexuality had been defined and constructed from a masculine perspective. The social construction of sexuality is here seen as patriarchal, as serving the interests of men, as coercing women into compulsory heterosexuality (Rich, 1980). It is therefore linked to a structural analysis of patriarchy (for example, MacKinnon, 1982). Moreover, the erotic itself is understood as culturally constituted, so that currently prevailing definitions of eroticism are themselves the product of gendered patterns of domination and submission intrinsic to patriarchal societies and written into their cultural representations (Cameron and Frazer, 1987; Jeffreys, 1990; Kappe-ler, 1986). This form of analysis is closely (but not exclusively) associated with radical feminism and, in Britain, also with revolutionary feminism.

Although those concerned with patriarchal power have not always explicitly queried heterosexuality, they have consistently focused on its problematic and negative manifestations. From writings on sexual violence – where male sexual power is starkly evident – to research on young women's sexual relationships, this work has sensitized us to the complexity and ubiquity of power relations within heterosexuality. Such accounts, especially when framed from a radical feminist stance, are often misread as essentialist, as implying that men are naturally sexually violent and predatory and that women are innately loving and egalitarian (see, for example, Weedon, 1987). It is curious that a perspective dedicated to challenging and changing both male and female sexuality, and to radically transforming our ideas about what is erotic, should be seen as biologically determinist. The emphasis on coercive aspects of sexuality and on the interconnections between sexuality and women's oppression also led to charges of anti-sex prudery.

Opposition to specific sexual practices should not be equated with an anti-erotic stance. It is the case, however, that radical feminists have problematized the erotic and have refused to affirm desire and pleasure as self-evidently good. By the early 1980s, a strong, self-styled 'pro-pleasure' current among feminists began vigorously to contest what they saw as the radical feminist orthodoxy. There were two key moments which marked the beginnings of a well-articulated libertarian feminism and the opening skirmishes of the Sex Wars. Both originated in the USA but the cause was taken up elsewhere. The first of these critical events was the publication of the 'sex issue' of the feminist journal *Heresies* in 1981, which covered, in explicit detail, forms of sexual practice which many feminists found repugnant, including sado-masochism and butch–femme role playing in lesbian relationships.[5] In the following year, the Scholar and the Feminist Conference held at Barnard College in New York took as its theme the politics of sexuality and later led to the publication of an influential collection of papers entitled *Pleasure and Danger* (Vance, 1984). The tension between these two facets of sexuality was the central issue within both the conference and the collection. While Carole Vance, in her introduction to the book, insisted that no-one involved intended to undermine the critique of sexual danger or to deny the impact of sexual violence on women's lives, the assumption underlying most contributions was that feminists had placed too much emphasis upon the dangers of sex for women at the expense of its pleasures – and that it was the latter which required further exploration. The overall tone of *Pleasure and Danger*, like the sex issue of *Heresies*, was libertarian.

This move might be seen as an attempt to recover the impulse towards sexual freedom and the assertion of women's right to sexual pleasure which had figured strongly in early feminist critiques of (hetero)sexuality. Indeed, this was explicitly raised as an issue by Alice Echols (1984). This new libertarianism, however, departed radically from the older feminist quest for mutuality and equality in sexual relations in that it rehabilitated power. Power was seen as a source of erotic tension which should not be denied (Hollibaugh, 1984), and the condemnation of lesbian sado-masochism was seen as mere puritanical intolerance (Califia, 1981). The 'pro-pleasure' lobby also defended pornography, fearing that any attempt to restrict its availability was likely to affect the erotic writings of lesbians, gay men and others who departed from conventional heterosexual practice. The way to challenge the sexism prevalent in heterosexual pornography, according to the libertarians, was to create an erotica of our own (see, for example, McIntosh, 1992).

Libertarians refused to be shamed either by conventional morality or by other feminists. Those who advanced such views were mostly lesbians, and often those who had maintained allegiances with gay men. This alliance became bound up with the politics of AIDS and the need to eroticize safer sex (and what counted as 'safe' in this context was sex which carried minimal risk of HIV transmission), which gave a renewed edge to those opposed to anti-pornography campaigners. Libertarian theorists shifted the emphasis from gender oppression to sexual oppression. They sought to re-eroticize lesbian sex in opposition to what was damned as 'vanilla' sex and to promote sexual diversity as a form of resistance to the heterosexual norm. The defence of pornography and sado-masochism thus occurred primarily in relation to lesbian and gay sex – it was not generally suggested that such practices were acceptable in a heterosexual context. Indeed, it was often argued that playing with power did not have the same connotations of 'real' domination and submission when it was not part of the institutionalized hierarchy of heterosexuality (Califia, 1981).

In practice, however, libertarians are barely critical of heterosexuality or gender hierarchy at all. One of the most influential arguments for the maintenance of a distinction between gender oppression and sexual oppression is Gayle Rubin's 'Thinking sex' (1984). She posits a sexual hierarchy in which the most oppressed are defined by their distance from monogamous heterosexuality. Attention is directed to the 'outlaw' status of various 'sexual minorities', each judged as equally worthy of protection from oppression and opprobrium. Rubin apparently does not see that there is a world of difference between a street prostitute and a millionaire pornographer, or between a man who has sex with a child and that child. What is missing from Rubin's analysis (and libertarian theory in general) is a critique of heterosexuality. In defending sexual 'pluralism' it is often forgotten that feminist theories of sexuality began by questioning the relations of dominance and submission inscribed in conventional heterosexual practice, in suggesting that such relations were neither natural nor inevitable but resulted from the hierarchical ordering of gender. Many of the 'sexualities' currently being defended or promoted reproduce these hierarchies, whether in the form of sado-masochism or 'cross-generational relations' – Rubin's euphemism for paedophilia. There is no questioning of where such desires come from: 'the analysis begins from existing desires and thereby takes them to be "natural", immutable and ultimately valid' (Cameron and Frazer, 1987: 173). Hence such arguments are at root essentialist, as some erstwhile defenders of libertarianism have begun to admit (see Seidman, 1992).

For those opposed to libertarianism, the critique of heterosexuality continued to play an important role in anchoring critiques of sexual activities, such as butch–femme role playing and sado-masochism, which replicate patterns of dominance and subordination. This is most explicit in the work of Sheila Jeffreys (1990), for whom all practices which eroticize power and difference, whatever the gender of those engaging in them, are 'heterosexual'. This position has in turn been condemned as 'heterosexualizing' lesbian (and gay male) sex (Wilton, 1996), as failing to appreciate that lesbian sex can never conform to a heterosexual norm. Whatever one's position on the significance of particular lesbian sexual practices, it seems clear to me that a serious social constructionist position must accept that there is no total escape from the heterosexual framing of desire within a social order where heterosexuality is so privileged.

We all learn to be sexual within a society in which 'real sex' is defined as a quintessentially heterosexual act, vaginal intercourse, and in which sexual activity is thought of in terms of an active subject and passive object. However critical we are of this heterosexist norm, and however we define our sexualities, we may find the cultural opposition between active/dominant and passive/subordinate sexuality intruding into our sexual lives. Our creativity in developing alternative forms of eroticism is necessarily limited by the social conditions which have shaped our desires. If this is accepted, there is no reason for attaching personal shame or blame to every desire that departs from some notion of ideological purity, but there is no reason either to engage in uncritical celebration of all that is pleasurable. We need to think further about the possibility of engaging with the positive aspects of pleasure while remaining critical of current sexual desires and practices. Furthermore, taking account of power within sexual relations raises questions about how we trace the connections between the structural bases of patriarchal power inscribed within institutionalized heterosexuality, and the ways in which power is exercised and resisted at the level of personal sexual relations (Ramazanoglu and Holland, 1993).

Historical change and contemporary diversity

Underlying the sex wars debates are differing understandings of sexual diversity and the relationship between sexuality and power. The premise that human sexuality is historically and culturally variable is fundamental to all forms of social constructionism and is common to most feminist perspectives – although there are differences here in the extent to which sexual desires themselves are seen as fully malleable (see Vance, 1989). The need to challenge commonsense assumptions about the fixity and universality of human sexuality has provided the impetus for historical work on sexuality from a range of approaches.[6] Feminists have, for example, investigated the changing significance of romantic and erotic attachments between women, revealing both the historical construction of the category lesbian and the difficulties entailed in interpreting the emotional and sexual lives of previous generations (Faderman, 1982; Jeffreys, 1985; Liddington, 1999; Smith-Rosenberg, 1975). However, debates on lesbianism – as well as on other areas such as prostitution and sexology – reveal that history itself is contested terrain, with current theoretical positions informing interpretations of the past.[7]

If there has been any one perspective which has set the agenda for historical work on sexuality it has been that of Michel Foucault. The publication of the first volume of his *History of Sexuality* (1981) had an immense impact on academic thinking in this area. In particular, his critique of the 'repressive hypothesis' challenged the prevailing view of the Victorian age as one of repression, suggesting instead that this was a time when sexuality came into being as an object of discourse, of a 'will to truth'. In this sense sexuality is a historical construct rather than a fact of nature; it is produced by particular deployments of power rather than being a pre-given human proclivity subject to the force of repression (see Foucault, 1981: 105). While some of these ideas echo Gagnon and Simon's earlier work, it was Foucault's writings, situated within what was then becoming identified as poststructuralism, which provoked widespread intellectual questioning of the concept of repression.

Foucault's appeal to feminists lies in his radical anti-essentialism and his view of power as constitutive of sexuality, rather than merely repressive. His work also resonated with some existing feminist contestations of the 'truth' of sex as it was manifested in both scientific and popular sexology.[8] Feminists have, however, found fault with Foucault's acute gender-blindness and the difficulty of linking his conception of socially diffuse power to structural analyses of inequality (see, for example, Ramazanoglu, 1993). Most feminists working within a Foucauldian framework have sought to bring gender back in, to explore constructions of female sexuality as an object of regulatory discourses and practices (see, for example, Smart, 1992). Often, however, such historical analyses are too obsessed with disjunctions, in particular with the Victorian 'discursive explosion', at the expense of continuities. Hence the persistence and restructuring of patriarchal domination under changing historical conditions tends to be played down or ignored, as do the material social relations and practices underlying the ordering of our sexual lives.

Sexuality is also subject to synchronic variability, and here too Foucault has been drawn upon, particularly in the analysis of the constitution and surveillance of 'perverse' sexualities. While any critique of heterosexuality should attend to its institutionalization as a hegemonic norm, there are other issues which should be addressed here, particularly the intersections of gender and sexuality with class, ethnicity and other social divisions. The discourses around sexuality circulating within modern Western culture have been framed from a predominantly white and middle-class, as well as male and heterosexual, perspective, and bear the marks of our imperialist history. Moreover, we each live our sexuality from different locations within social structures. Although some attention has been given to these issues, particularly to the racism embedded in Western sexual discourses and practices, theorists drawing on Foucault generally have little to say about material inequalities and instead tend to focus on sexual diversity per se, on 'sexualities'. With this pluralization of sexuality the lack of attention to structural bases of power can become acutely problematic, especially when coupled the with denial of importance of gender – as in Gayle Rubin's (1984) work. There is then no way of establishing regularities underpinning diverse 'sexualities', of relating them to dominant modes of heterosexual practice or of locating them within power hierarchies.

Libertarian arguments use Foucault selectively, emphasizing that aspect of his work which sees 'bodies and pleasures' as the point of resistance to power, while losing sight of the constitutive effects of power as creating desire (see Foucault, 1981: 156–7). The danger lies in treating bodies and pleasures as unproblematic. As Nancy Fraser has commented, it is difficult to see 'what resistance to the deployment of sexuality … in the name of bodies and pleasures would be like', given that 'the disciplinary deployment of sexuality has, according to Foucault, produced its own panoply of bodily pleasures' and that 'disciplinary power has thoroughly marked the only bodies that we potential protesters have' (1989: 63). Hence diverse forms of sexuality are taken as given, already there to be outlawed, bringing us back to the repressive hypothesis which Foucault so effectively critiqued. The false equation of the transgressive with the progressive is in fact framed from within the very discourse of repression it seeks to subvert: one which gives undue privilege to sexuality either as the route to personal fulfilment and social liberation or as leading to individual degradation and social disintegration.

While I am wary of some applications of Foucault's analysis, I find it interesting in sensitizing us to the multiplicity of often contradictory ways in which sexuality has been constructed and regulated. The idea that our sense of what is sexual, including our desires and practices, is discursively constituted is potentially productive. However, Foucauldian analysis is unable to deal with the regularity and pervasiveness of patriarchal power, with the ways in which what counts as sexual has been constructed in terms of gender hierarchy. Foucault (1980) sees the concept of discourse as antithetical to ideology, but I would argue that we should view discourses as ideological in their effects – in that discursive constructions of sexuality have produced very particular 'truths' defining hierarchically ordered heterosexual relations as natural and inevitable. Discourses do not, therefore, float free from the structural inequalities characterizing the societies in which they are produced.

The problem of subjectivity

This still leaves us with the problem of the relationship between our individual desires and the discourses circulating within society, of how sexuality is socially constructed at the level of our individual subjectivities. Some feminists have applied Foucault to the problem of subjectivity by analysing how we locate or position ourselves within discourses (Hollway, 1984a; Weedon, 1987), or have suggested that Foucault's later work on technologies of self might be productive (McNay, 1992).[9] In neither case, however, has this led to any consistent theorization of the processes by which we become gendered, sexual subjects. Indeed, when it comes to this question, Foucault is frequently abandoned in favour of psychoanalysis. Wendy Hollway (1984a), for example, has attempted the most systematic application of Foucault to the issue of how we make sense of sexual desires and relationships, yet elsewhere she resorts to psychoanalysis in order to explain how such desires come into being (Hollway, 1989, 1993). Indeed, much of poststructuralist and postmodernist thinking is premised on the assumption that it is possible to draw simultaneously on both Foucault and

Lacan, despite Foucault's contention that psychoanalysis is just another discursive formation producing its own disciplinary regime of truth.

Psychoanalysis has established a virtual monopoly on theorizing the construction of sexuality at the level of subjectivity, despite the numerous cogent critiques of it. Many feminists agree that psychoanalysis is ahistorical, that it rests on essentialist foundations. While the Lacanian version suggests that sexed, desiring subjects are constituted through their entry into language and culture, this refers not to a historically specific language and culture but to the very process of becoming a 'speaking subject'. Moreover, psychoanalysis depends upon interpreting infantile emotions through a filter of adult assumptions and then makes incredible conceptual leaps from presumed infantile frustrations and gratifications to adult sexual desires and practices. Importantly, psychoanalysis makes no distinction between gender and sexuality: the two are conflated and ultimately reduced to the gender of our 'object choice'. 'One either identifies with a sex or desires it, but only these two relations are possible' (Butler, 1990b: 333). Hence, while psychoanalysis calls the normality of heterosexuality into question by insisting that it is not innate, it reinstates it as a norm through this linkage between gender and desire.

Although it is hardly a promising perspective for feminism, psychoanalysis retains its tenacious hold and constitutes a mode of reasoning which is very difficult to contest. Psychoanalytic propositions about the workings of the human psyche are frequently presented as self-evident 'truths', even by those who are elsewhere highly sceptical of all truth claims. In fact, most theorists working with psychoanalysis have no experience as analysts themselves and apparently little interest in its evidential foundations. As a mode of thinking it functions rather like a religion: we are invited to 'have faith' because we cannot 'know' the workings of our own unconscious (just as we cannot know a mythical god's purpose). The faith of believers is unshakeable and susceptible neither to disproof nor rational argument. They have at their disposal a variety of strategies for deflecting the objections of sceptics: we are either too stupid to see the Great Truth it offers us, or we are 'resisting' because of our unwillingness to consider what might be lurking, repressed, in our own unconscious minds. I have come to the conclusion that what divides believers from non-believers is whether this faith has any resonance for us personally, whether it makes sense in terms of our own experiences and desires. For me, it does not. While psychoanalytic theory, especially its feminist versions, has moved on a great deal since my early critiques of it (see Chapters 2 and 6), I remain among the unconverted.

Of course there are many different versions of psychoanalysis, just as there are many denominations and sects within any major religion. There have also been numerous attempts by feminists to rework psychoanalysis, to rid it of its unpalatable elements. Somehow the idea persists that psychoanalysis is the only way of accounting for the varying forms which our sexual and gendered desires and identities take, so that even those critical of it habitually genuflect in its direction or themselves contribute to the process of reworking it. A recent example is Judith Butler's 'Foucauldian redescription' of psychoanalysis, which divests it of notions of fixed psychic or symbolic structures and predetermined developmental processes. In seeking to understand the impact of the heterosexualizing imperative on our subjectivity, her 'return to psychoanalysis' is 'guided by the question of how regulatory norms form a "sexed" subject in terms which establish the indistinguishability of psychic and bodily formation' (1993: 22). Recasting her earlier elaboration of gender as bodily performance (Butler, 1990a),[10] she argues that gendered embodiment is neither a matter of an 'inside' psychic truth nor of surface appearance, but of the 'play between psyche and appearance'. What can be exteriorized, performed is limited by the 'opacity' of the unconscious and can 'only be understood by what is barred from the signifier and from the domain of corporeal legibility' (1993: 234). Here we have the familiar idea that the unknowable and (literally) unspeakable contents of the unconscious shape conscious thought and bodily action in mysterious ways.

Butler never considers whether there might be any alternative to psychoanalysis. She is not alone in this. Indeed, one of the main reasons for the influence of psychoanalytic thought may well be the apparent lack of other means of analysing the construction of embodied gendered and sexual subjectivity. It is not that there are no other viable frameworks, but that they remain fragmentary and underdeveloped. Most of us have long since abandoned conventional models of socialization, indeed the concept of socialization itself, as far too simplistic and mechanistic to reveal much about subjectivity at all. Gagnon and Simon's (1974) work on sexual scripts, although flawed by its lack of attention to structural inequalities, could still prove productive if used critically, as could Foucauldian perspectives, but neither has been applied to the problem in any consistent way. While we are engaging in ever more sophisticated modes of theorizing about gender, sexuality and subjectivity, we still have no satisfactory way of approaching the very basic question of how desiring, gendered heterosexual subjects come into being – or how and why some escape the bonds of compulsory heterosexuality. Looking back over the nearly three decades since I began inquiring into the social construction of female (hetero)sexuality, remarkably little progress has been made. For those who are sceptical of psychoanalysis the lack of a convincing theory of subjectivity is a major gap in feminist and sociological theory.

Rather than endlessly reworking psychoanalysis, it would be preferable, in my view, to strike out in new directions – there are already some foundations on which to build. It seems to me that it is worth preserving some of the earlier insights of phenomenological and interactionist sociologies, with their emphasis on the social self, the negotiation of meaning and the social practices whereby the gendered sexual world is produced as an everyday accomplishment. Moreover, the most fruitful lines of inquiry here might well be those which converge with issues raised by poststructuralists and postmodernists, especially their interrogation of the idea of an essential, fixed, rational subject and of the notion of authentic experience unmediated by language and culture. However, we also need to be alert to the limitations common to all these traditions of thought, in particular their tendency to theorize social structures out of existence.

It is essential that any perspective on subjectivity recognizes that the gendered and sexual categories we come to inhabit and enact – as men or women, as heterosexual or homosexual – are historical products with deep roots in the social and economic order. This is not to deny diversity among us, for we each are each positioned differently within any given society and culture – and those positionings are often multiple and not always static. While the social and cultural order in which and through which we live our gendered, sexual lives pre-dates us and is thus, in a sense, external to us, this does not mean that there is no room for active agency. The complexity of social life permits considerable everyday choice and negotiation. The recognition of agency is crucially important if we are to admit of the possibility of resistance to hegemonic forms of gender and heterosexuality, as well as the ways in which we might be actively complicit in their perpetuation. Agency is also central to understanding our individual sexualities, in that we each reflexively constitute for ourselves a sense of what it means to be straight or gay, feminine or masculine, we make active sense of what it feels like to desire another, to fall in love or to 'have sex'.

The idea of a reflexive, social self is sometimes resisted on the grounds that it presupposes a pre-social, or pre-discursive 'I' which does the work of reflexivity.[11] However, if we take this idea back to its origins in the work of George Herbert Mead (1934), it does not assume an essential, inner, pre-social 'I', but an 'I' which is only ever the fleeting mobilization of a socially constituted self. Moreover, this self is not a fixed structure but is always 'in process' by virtue of its constant reflexivity. One way in which this reflexive self-construction has been analysed recently, in my own work and that of others, is through the idea of narratives of self, an idea which has roots in both the sociological tradition of interactionism and in more recent discourse analysis (Jackson, 1998b; Plummer, 1995; Whisman, 1996). Such a perspective allows us to think of subjectivity as a product of individual, socially located biographies – but not in the same sense as the old idea of socialization. Here, rather than the past (or childhood) determining the present (or adulthood), the present significantly shapes the past in that we are constantly reconstructing our memories, our understanding of who and what we are through the stories we tell to ourselves and others. Experience is conceptualized not as given in raw form, but as constantly worked over, interpreted, theorized through the narrative forms and devices available to us. These cultural resources are of course historically specific, enabling us to attend to the ways in which particular modes of self-construction become available at different historical moments. Moreover, here the gendered, sexual self is never a finished product, but constantly being remade.

The social self must also be conceptualized as an embodied self in interaction with others. Sexuality is often theorized as if it were disembodied or, alternatively, as if bodies meet in sex quite outside any social or interpersonal context (see Jackson and Scott, 1998). Yet sex is a paradigmatically embodied activity, involving physical acts and sensations as well as desire and pleasure (or displeasure). Sex with a partner(s) entails bodily interaction, in given social contexts, to which each participant brings their specific, personal history – and even solo sex frequently involves fantasies of others in imagined social settings. Our bodies do not exist separately from us as subjects, subjectivity *is* embodied. The dualism between mind and body which has marked our culture does make it difficult to conceptualize their indissolubility, but I believe we can begin to think through this problem without recourse to psychoanalytic notions of the unconscious.

Even for those unwilling to abandon the psychoanalytic project, there must surely be space for conscious reflexive thought and action between Butler's unconscious depths and surface appearance. Moreover, not everything not fully conscious is necessarily 'unconscious' in the psychoanalytic sense. Much of the performance of gendered and sexual being is, in Gesa Lindemann's words, 'realized in absent-minded fashion' (1997: 79). But this absent-mindedness is social, the product of bodily dispositions which are acquired and have become habitual through a whole history of managing our bodies in social space (see, for example, Bartky, 1990; Young, 1990). The performance of gender which Butler describes, not to mention the complex process of recognizing embodied others as intelligibly gendered, assumes a process by which we somehow learn to enact and decode such performances. No such process is addressed by psychoanalytic thinking: indeed, the materiality of gender as it is continually acted out and acted upon in the social world is absent from psychoanalysis.

When we consider the specifics of everyday sexuality, it is not simply a matter of desire and identity, but of managing bodily practices and making sense of sexual situations. That this entails active learning (indeed, frantic searching out of 'knowledge') ought to be evident to anyone who has lived through adolescence in modern Western society. This learning is active in the sense that what is learnt is continually being theorized, interpreted, made sense of. It is embodied, too, in that what we learn comes from our sexual encounters as well as from the 'facts' we learn. The process also, of course, depends on the cultural resources to hand and, crucially, on our gender as well as on our location within specific, often class and ethnically differentiated, communities and localities. Any knowledge we acquire is culturally constructed and socially ordered; it entails learning, for example, how sex is conventionally defined, how categories such as gay or straight are deployed, how the reputation of a 'slag' is earned. These materially grounded processes must be acknowledged if we are to arrive at a more sociologically informed understanding of the construction of our sexual selves.

In theorizing sexuality we need a means of understanding how we become gendered and how we become sexual without conflating gender and sexuality, without assuming that particular forms of desire are automatically consequent upon acquiring feminine or masculine gender, and without reducing the complexity of desire to the gender of its object. Furthermore, we require an analysis of how this process is related to discourses on sexuality circulating within our culture and how these in turn are related to structural inequalities, particularly gender inequality. We should also be able to tie these strands together in such a way as to recognize the force of cultural and ideological constructions of sexuality and the constraints of social structure, but in a way which does not deny human agency and therefore the possibility of challenging and resisting dominant constructions of sexuality. I doubt that it is possible to produce *a* theory of gendered and sexual subjectivity, but we can begin to try to conceptualize it in ways which do make sense in terms of everyday sexual desires and practices. This demands that we cease to theorize at an entirely abstract level and pay attention to what is known about material, embodied men and women going about the business of living their sexualities.

Everyday heterosexuality

Whereas recent queer theorizing tends to focus on sexual transgression, on the subversion of the heterosexual norm and possibilities for destabilizing the heterosexual/homosexual binary, many feminists have focused instead upon the ways in which the normative constraints of male dominated heterosexuality are sustained. Much of this work is empirical and can be seen as a continuation of the earlier feminist concern with charting heterosexuality's discontents. Now, however, heterosexuality itself is no longer a hidden, taken for granted term, but has come into view as an institution and practice requiring critical examination. Such research has revealed that, despite women's aspirations towards greater equality in relationships with men, heterosexual sex remains male-defined. Indeed, it has been suggested by one group of researchers that heterosexuality is not merely masculinity and femininity in opposition, it *is* masculinity; young women and men are both regulated by and complicit in sustaining this male dominated and institutionalized heterosexuality (Holland et al., 1998).[12]

Everyday heterosexuality is not simply about sex, but is perpetuated by the regulation of marriage and family life, divisions of waged and domestic labour, patterns of economic support and dependency and the routine everyday expectations and practices through which heterosexual couple-dom persists as the normative ideal, a 'natural' way of life (see, for example, Van Every, 1996). A sociologically informed feminist understanding of heterosexuality requires that we do not over-privilege (erotic) sexuality. Part of the problem we have in thinking about sex derives from the weight we make it carry, the way we view it as qualitatively different from other aspects of social life. This is one of the few points on which I am in agreement with Gayle Rubin (1984). If we are to understand sexuality in context, neither giving it causal priority nor treating it in isolation, then a feminist analysis should consider its interlinkages with other aspects of women's subordination. There is now a considerable body of work on heterosexual sexual relations which begins to make such connections, which highlights the ways in which heterosexuality is ordered through the institutions and expectations of a male dominated society, which draws parallels between the division of emotional labour in managing intimate relations and divisions of physical labour, which demonstrates that understandings of love and sexuality remain highly gendered (Cancian, 1990; Duncombe and Marsden, 1993; Holland et al., 1998; Langford, 1999).

Having said this, most of the work reproduced in this volume concentrates on specifically sexual and emotional relations, and therefore contributes to only a part of this ongoing project. My concern, however, has always been with everyday (hetero)sexuality, with trying to understand the conditions of my own existence as a heterosexual woman at the end of the 20th century. The chapters fall roughly into two: the earlier ones, written in the context of the feminist debates of the 1970s and early 1980s, and more recent interventions published after 1990. The break between them is, in retrospect, revealing. It is not that I lost interest in sexuality (personally, politically or intellectually) during the 1980s, but that I found it difficult to write as a heterosexual feminist during the period when the 'sex wars' were at their height. There is, however, considerable continuity in the themes I have pursued during these two periods of writing, which reflect long-standing concerns within feminism. I hope to demonstrate in bringing this work together that recent explorations into heterosexuality would not have been possible without the foundations laid in the early years of second wave feminism.

Notes

1 For example, in the early 1990s Gayle Rubin recalled a discussion on the internet in which 'Foucault was credited as the originator of "social construction" theory' so that the key roles of earlier theorists and researchers were 'completely erased' (Rubin and Butler, 1994: 82). This is, in my experience, a common misapprehension. I began work on this chapter having just returned from a sociology conference at which, on several occasions, younger scholars confidently announced that social constructionism began with postmodernism. That young sociologists can be so ignorant of their own disciplinary heritage is perhaps understandable: there is now so much to read in the field of sexuality, so much pressure to keep up with the latest theoretical interventions and to complete and publish research that no one – particularly a young academic seeking a secure post – has time to read and reflect (Allen and Leonard, 1996).

2 Gagnon and Simon have subsequently addressed some of these issues, particularly the issue of permanence and change in sexual scripts (Gagnon and Simon, 1987; Simon, 1996).

3 This argument derives from work co-authored with Sue Scott (Jackson and Scott, 1996) and is reproduced here with her permission.

4 More recently Celia Kitzinger and Sue Wilkinson (1993) appeared to endorse this view, but in a later contribution to the debate (1994) they distanced themselves from personal attacks on heterosexual feminists.

5 Many feminist book shops refuse to stock this edition of *Heresies* on the grounds that it was anti-feminist and pornographic. At a well-known feminist book shop in London it was available only on request from 'under the counter'.

6 This concern has also given rise to anthropological work on cross-cultural variations in gender and sexuality (see, for example Caplan, 1987; Herdt, 1981; Mathieu, 1996).

7 A particularly good example of this is the range of perspectives on the 'moral purity' campaigns of the late 19th and early 20th centuries, where parallels can be drawn with modern campaigns on pornography (for competing views see DuBois and Gordon, 1984; Jeffreys, 1985; Walkowitz, 1980).

8 Some of these ideas are difficult to pin down in published sources, but they were certainly circulating among feminists of the time and informed my own querying of the construction of sexual knowledge (see Chapters 3 and 4).

9 Foucault himself was not much interested in the social construction of subjectivity, although he did consider that the subject is constructed, that particular subjects and forms of relating reflexively to the self were products of historical shifts in regimes of truth, effects of specific deployments of knowledge/power. He had nothing to say about the social construction of sexual desires. For example, as David Halperin points out, Foucault 'never took a position on such empirical questions as what causes homosexuality or whether it is constituted socially or biologically' (1995: 4). A Foucauldian purist would probably consider any theory on the construction of our individual desires an irrelevance, another attempt to arrive at the 'truth' of our sexualities.

10 In *Gender Trouble*, Butler theorizes gender as constituted and actively accomplished through performance, which by constant reiteration creates the illusion, the 'regulatory fiction', of a stable gender identity. Gender, then, 'should not be construed as a stable identity or locus of agency from which various acts follow; rather gender is an identity tenuously constituted in time, instituted in an exterior space through a *stylized repetition of acts*' (Butler, 1990a: 141; emphasis in original).

11 Judith Butler seems to disallow a reflexive self on these grounds (see 1990a: 143–4, 1993: 225–6), although I do not think that the Meadian 'I' would sit uncomfortably with her formulation.

12 This study, the Women Risk and AIDS Project is probably the most thorough and sophisticated research to have been carried out on young women's sexuality to date, based on in-depth interviews with 148 British women aged 16–21 from a variety of class and ethnic backgrounds, and followed up with similar interviews with 46 young men. The findings have been reported in over 40 publications, culminating in a book *The Male in the Head*, which draws together many of their findings and ideas (Holland et al., 1998). I return to this work in the final chapter, particularly its insights on the difficulty of negotiating pleasure within heterosexual relationships.

PART II

EARLY EXPLORATIONS

---

2   On the Social Construction of Female Sexuality

This chapter is an abridged version of my first piece of published writing, which began life in 1973 as my Master's dissertation in sociology at the University of York. It was updated and redrafted before it appeared in its finished form in 1978, as a pamphlet in the 'Explorations in Feminism' series produced by the editorial collective of the Women's Research and Resources Centre. With hindsight, I can now see that it should have been called 'the social construction of female (hetero)sexuality', and that I was guilty of treating sexuality as synonymous with heterosexuality and made only passing references to lesbianism. Although this work was motivated by a desire to understand my own sexuality, the question 'how did I get this way?' did not include questioning how I came to be heterosexual – even at the point when I updated it, when I was well aware of debates around lesbian feminism. It is also not as rigorously anti-essentialist as my later work, but did attempt a direct refutation of biological determinism. I have not included all the evidence I used in this endeavour, but the argument, while edited, remains more or less intact. This was one of the earliest statements of a social constructionist position on sexuality to be published in Britain, at a time when we were still feeling our way.

The remainder of the extract focuses on a critique of Freud and puts forward an alternative, interactionist perspective deriving from Gagnon and Simon (1974). Like many feminists at that time, I was highly suspicious of psychoanalysis. However, by the time the pamphlet appeared in print, some feminists had begun to re-evaluate Freud's work, particularly after the publication of Juliet Mitchell's Psychoanalysis and Feminism *(1975). As a result, my literal reading of Freud was controversial. As the editorial collective pointed out in their introduction, some feminists questioned 'whether Freud is really (or always) so inclined to explain . . . the differences between the sexes in terms of the unfolding of a variously modified or repressed sexual drive' and argued that 'his conception of the libido is a generalised quest for gratification rather than a purely sexual drive' (see Jackson 1978a:* i). *While my reading of Freud at that time might now seem simplistic, I still think that everything I attributed to him can be found in his work – and I was relying on the original texts, not on commentaries. Although I now think I underestimated the tension in Freud's writings between socio-cultural and biologistic understandings of sexuality, I do not think I grossly misrepresented him. I certainly appreciate that alternative readings of Freud are possible, but in these days when most scholars come to psychoanalysis through Lacanian and post-Lacanian thought, it is salutary to recall just how baldly, and unambiguously, Freud stated some of his ideas on infantile and female sexuality. Moreover, it is the more literal version of psychoanalysis, including the idea of innate sexual drives, which has become incorporating into everyday understandings of sexuality.*

It would be tempting to change and update the language used in this and my other early writings. For example, I would not now employ such concepts as 'socialization', 'roles' or 'psychosexual development' – all of which derive from a developmental paradigm which has long been discredited. Nor would I now talk so confidently and deterministically about an 'economic base'. While editing for continuity, I have left all the terminology as it was, since this gives a flavour of the conceptual tools in use at that time. Part of what I hope to demonstrate through the republication of this early work is that, despite the less sophisticated analytical frameworks then available to us, some of the ideas central to a critical analysis of sexuality were already in circulation.

Traditionally women have been defined in terms of their relationship to men and, although this relationship has an economic base, it is often seen as primarily a sexual one. The sexual and reproductive role of women has been used to rationalize – and to justify – their subordination, and this has misled some radical feminists into arguing that the subjection of women is rooted in sexuality (Firestone, 1972; Millett, 1972). Although it is inaccurate to view sexuality as the cause of female subordination, it is closely related to women's role in society and in the family. The particular version of female sexuality which exists in our own society is consistent with all the other attributes which are currently considered typical of females. Just as woman is characterized as passive, nurturant and dependant in wider social spheres, so her sexuality is expressed as passive, receptive and responsive. Rather than being the origin of femininity, female sexuality is an exemplification of it.

Sexuality cannot be treated in isolation: it cannot be understood as if it is separated from such things as cultural ideals of 'love' or the institution of marriage. Sexual behaviour is social behaviour; it is not just the consummation of some biological drive. Heterosexual sexuality involves at the very least a social relationship between two people and that relationship arises out of a larger socio-cultural context. Sociologists, however, have tended to acknowledge the sexual only as a starting point in order to analyse such areas as 'the family'. They have rarely questioned commonsense definitions of what is sexual (and what is not) within any society and sexuality has therefore remained unproblematic. The failure to ask such basic questions as 'What makes an act sexual?' has meant that all too often sexuality is seen in terms of 'drives' – a concept which has filtered from biology and psychology into the folk-knowledge of our society. A consequence of this is that sexuality is partitioned off from the rest of our lives. We tend to think of sex as something 'special' and apart – an idea that has to be suspended if we are to understand the ways in which sexuality fits into other aspects of social life.

We cannot define anything as sexual in an absolute sense, for what is 'sexual' in one society may not necessarily be sexual in another. An act is not sexual by virtue of its inherent properties, but becomes sexual by the application of socially learned meanings. Sexual behaviour is in this sense 'socially scripted' in that it is a 'part' that is learned and acted out within a social context, and different social contexts have different social scripts. In using the term 'sexuality', then, I am referring not just to genital sexual activity, but to all the attitudes, values, beliefs and behaviours which might be seen to have some sexual significance in our society. From this starting point it is possible to establish a theoretical framework through which female sexuality may be better understood.

The determinants of human sexuality: biology versus culture

The idea that there is some pure and uncontaminated 'human nature' underlies many theories about humanity, but nowhere has it been given more prominence than in the area of sexuality. By classifying the version of sexuality of our own society as 'natural', typical masculine and feminine forms of sexuality are assumed to be part of the natural order of things and not therefore open to negotiation. Sexual attitudes and behaviour are still often thought of as preordained and the historical and cultural contributions to this form of activity ignored. Sexual acts are classified as biological functions and it is naively assumed that the whole of human sexuality must be governed by something often referred to as 'instinct'.

These assumptions have been allowed to go unchallenged, despite the contradictory evidence which has accumulated. Biological factors do *not* determine the forms which sexuality takes, but merely set parameters within which other influences operate. Although women and men may differ genetically, hormonally and physiologically, it is not possible to leap to the conclusion that they therefore also differ in terms of personality or behaviour. Biology is not destiny in any absolute sense; it only comes to be so through the qualities which are assigned to members of each gender within any society.

The argument that specific forms of human behaviour, especially sexual behaviour, are 'natural' is often based on comparisons with animals, particularly other primates. As a species we do share some characteristics and fundamental needs with other mammals, but to apply evidence from animal observation directly to human behaviour is to ignore crucial differences. For human beings exist in a social environment structured through language and symbols, and this plays a much more influential role in determining how we behave than do the biological factors which we share with other animals. It is this very social environment and its crucial role that is likely to be forgotten in discussions of the sexual. For some reason the sexual is thought to be peculiarly representative of the 'animal' side of human nature:

> Committing the ethological fallacy, wherein we are warned that our hunting–gathering natures are the central themes around which modern man must organize his marriage and reproductive life or in which we are instructed to consider our common attributes with other primates, is an example of an unwillingness to live with the existential and changing nature of man at an individual and collective level. (Gagnon and Simon, 1974: 3)

The form that sexual behaviour takes in our own society cannot be taken as a universal norm. Far from being fixed and immutable, human sexuality takes widely diverse forms and changes over time. The message of anthropology is clear: there is an enormous range of possible styles of sexuality within our species. Within our own society women are assumed to be sexually passive and, in general, less sexual than men. To understand why female sexuality takes the form that it does, we need to examine cultural notions of femininity, attitudes to sexuality, and the whole interrelationship between our private lives and the structure of our society – an enormous task which is outside the scope of this chapter. To understand how female sexuality develops we need to explore the ways in which the process of sexual learning operates and how this is related to other aspects of social learning. It is on this that I will now focus attention.

The cultural shaping of the sexual: repressive or constructive?

How, then, does culture create the sexual? The process whereby an individual is socialized into particular modes of sexuality may be conceptualized in two essentially oppositional ways. We might begin by positing the existence of some form of innate sexual drive which is then moulded, modified or repressed by the operation of social forces: that is, that learning involves the curbing of instinctual urges. In terms of this model it could be argued that a particularly severe repression of libido undergone by women accounts for the form female sexuality takes. Alternatively, we might postulate a process of learning through social interaction whereby the sexual is assimilated into the individual's self-concept. According to this view, psychosexual development is not contingent upon biological determinants but on the milieu and content of social learning. The feminine mode of sexual expression would then be explained as the outcome of a particular form of learning rather than the repression of some quantifiable sexual energy.

The former premise is the basis on which Freudian theory was founded. Later work in this area, even when repudiating Freudianism, has tended to adopt the concept of the libido or at least the assumption that some basic sexual drive exists. This has tended to favour a rather over-determined view of sexuality as an innate force emanating from the individual. The alternative approach, as outlined by Gagnon and Simon, attempts to counter these tendencies (Gagnon and Simon, 1974). The latter approach has several advantages. In the first place, by disallowing the primacy of biological drives, it permits a more positive conception of the socio-cultural influences involved, providing a sense of the social construction of sexuality rather than viewing the learning process as a negative tampering with innate biological mechanisms – even supposing that it is possible to identify an inborn, unsocialized drive. Second, this approach lends itself to a more sophisticated handling of the concept of socialization. To view this as the repression of innate drives is to present the individual as the passive product of a struggle between biological and social forces. Even if the latter are declared the victors of the battle, there is a danger of replacing biological determinism with an equally rigid and oversimplified sociologistic explanation. Gagnon and Simon provide an interactionist framework within which the subject may be seen as active in her or his socialization: in the construction of the sexual self.

Finally, and perhaps most importantly, this perspective avoids the difficulties posed by the heritage of Freudian phallocentricity. It has been argued that 'the fact is that the male sex is not only considered relatively superior to the female, but it is taken as the universal human norm' (Simmel, quoted in Klein, 1946: 82). This assumption is an integral part of Freudian theory – the libido is seen as an active, masculine force. If female sexuality is assumed to be the product of a repressed libido, there is a danger of perceiving it as either a distorted version of the masculine (and therefore evaluating male sexuality as 'better') or as a functional complement to it. Most of the theorizing in this area has been done by men who have indeed conceptualized female sexuality in these terms. Gagnon and Simon's model enables us to see masculine and feminine forms of sexuality as the results of differing learning experiences rather than as the outcome of differential repression. Hence the problem of treating the feminine as merely the negation of the masculine is avoided.

Although Freud's theory may be rejected on these grounds, it cannot easily be dismissed, for his massive contribution to theories of sexuality should not be ignored. His work represents the first comprehensive theory of psychosexual development and is a most impressive attempt to come to terms with the complexities of the problem, to understand the interrelationship between biological, psychological and environmental influences and to relate sexuality to the rest of personality. Freud's theory assumes further importance by virtue of the great impact it has had upon everyday thinking about the sexual. Not only did it provide a starting point for the development of later theories, but it has helped to shape commonsense conceptions of sexuality. An examination of Freud's ideas and of the criticisms Gagnon and Simon offer will illuminate some of the problems involved in discussing the emergence and development of sexuality.

Tales of trauma and transference: Freud on femininity and sexuality

Freud traces the development of the libido, an inborn sexual energy, through various stages which condition the final form of adult sexuality. The significance of this development is not only sexual: for him the whole human personality is determined by a series of crises assailing the libido. He hopes to find the key to the 'mystery' of femininity and female sexuality in such phenomena as penis envy, the Oedipal situation, and the clitoral–vaginal transference. Of these it is the 'genital trauma' which is apparently the major influence upon the female psyche.

When a little girl of three or four years of age first sets eyes upon the male organ, Freud informs us, she is immediately overcome by an intense envy from which she will never recover. On the basis of her own experience of clitoral activity she will make a correct judgement of the sexual, or at least masturbatory, function of this organ and will 'realize' that her own is inadequate for the purpose. She will see herself as castrated. This traumatic discovery, Freud argues, is responsible for the greater degree of envy in the mental life of women and for their 'extraordinary vanity', the latter being a compensation for their anatomical 'deficiency'. Babies, too, are compensation; a male baby is particularly desired since he brings with him the 'longed-for penis' (Freud, 1925, 1931, 1933).

Yet why should the little girl covet the boy's penis in the first place? It is more likely that she will regard the male genitals as an ugly protuberance rather than as something desirable, and see her own body as whole and complete. Why should she then decide that her own organ is inferior for masturbatory purposes? It is unlikely that she will see her clitoris as a truncated penis, even if she is aware of its existence, which she need not be to engage in infantile styles of masturbation. In all likelihood she will come to the conclusion that the penis is simply a urinary organ, and in respect of this function it is true she may feel some envy. Simone de Beauvoir argues that, since children of this age are fascinated by their excretory functions, the girl may envy the boy's practical advantage in this matter. There is nothing to suggest, however, that this envy assumes the obsessive proportions Freud attributes to it. Moreover, this feeling would evaporate once the child outgrew her interest in such things (de Beauvoir, 1972). It is possible that the anatomical difference comes to be symbolic of male prestige. So perhaps in this sense the penis may become an object of envy – not for what it is, but for what it has come to represent.

Freud makes much of the ideas that, in the course of her psychic development, a girl has to change both her object choice – from her mother to her father, and her leading erotic zone – from the clitoris to the vagina. The energy absorbed in this process is supposed to lead to an arrest of psychic development, and hence to a psychic rigidity and lack of creativity. Furthermore, because the girl, lacking a penis to begin with, has no castration fears, she remains in the Oedipal situation indefinitely. In not being forced to abandon it, she fails to develop the strong superego characteristic of the male and her mental life therefore remains closer to the instinctual level: she is somehow less civilized than the male.

Her situation is the reverse of his: whereas the male's castration complex drives him away from the Oedipal situation, the girl's genital trauma prepares her for it. It is her envy of the penis that enables the girl to transfer her object choice from her mother to her father. She blames her mother for her lack of a penis and therefore feels hostility towards her. She realizes, too, that her mother shares her 'inferiority' since castration is a fate common to all women, and so she comes to devalue all that is feminine, including her mother. No explanation is given to why a child should blame her mother for this cruel fate. Nor is it by any means obvious that she will see that her mother's body is like her own. It is, after all, as unlike hers as that of her father if presence or absence of a penis is not taken to be the sole criterion by which such comparisons are made.

Penis envy, Freud argues, also prepares the way for the clitoral–vaginal transference which is crucial in the development of 'normal' femininity and mature, passive, narcissistic and masochistic sexuality. It is now known that physiologically such a transference is a myth and that orgasms are not vaginally, but clitorally centred (Masters and Johnson, 1966). Juliet Mitchell (1972) suggests that we interpret this transference as being a change in mental attitude. In this sense the idea retains some validity. Women in Western societies are expected to be sexually passive, to think of sexuality as synonymous with coitus, and to associate coitus with reproduction. Hence they must abandon the pursuit of sexual pleasure associated with the clitoris, and prepare for the passive, receptive, reproductive role consistent with vaginal penetration. If it is viewed in this way, however, this transference cannot be seen as 'constitutionally prescribed' or as determining (in the sense that Freud used the term) the final form of sexuality. Rather, the transference itself depends upon expectations concerning the form that adult female sexuality ought to take.

In making pronouncements on femininity, Freud never looked beyond the fixed concepts and categories he imposed upon his observations. His obvious prejudices, made clear in his use of language, distort his analysis. The female is a mutilated male; that which is masculine is normal and unmysterious, while things feminine are seen as aberrations, as enigmas. Underlying all this, however, are the more basic problems concerning the

nature of sexual drives, the idea of infantile sexuality and lack of appreciation of the influence of social factors on the moulding of the personality.

In formulating his theories on sexuality, Freud interprets a wide range of
infant behaviours as being inherently sexual, as prototypical of adult
sexuality, and as determining its character. Though social factors are
assumed to play some part, it is doubtful whether Freud would concede
their primacy, for he seems to regard 'inhibitions' as being as much
constitutionally determined as culturally imposed. He conceptualizes these
as 'dams ... restricting the flow ... of sexual development':

> One gets the impression from civilized children that the construction of these
> dams is the product of education, and no doubt education has much to do with it.
> But in reality this development is organically determined and fixed by heredity.
> ... Education [is] following the lines already laid down organically and ...
> impressing them somewhat more clearly and deeply. (Freud, 1905: 177–8)

So education (or socialization) plays only a secondary part in the process;
that of furthering 'nature's' ends.

Freud's use of the term 'repression' is also ambiguous. He states, for
instance, that puberty leads to an accession of libido in boys, but it is
'marked in girls by a fresh wave of repression' (1905: 220). His words seem
carefully chosen, here and elsewhere, to leave us in ignorance of the source
of this repression. Is it to be viewed as originating from within the individual
or from without, as innate or acquired, as constitutional or imposed? Since
this repression provides the impetus for the clitoral–vaginal transference
which Freud perceives as essential to the development of normal femininity, it must be assumed that he considers it to be an integral part of psychic
development. He seems, in effect, to be assuming that organic factors take
precedence over socio-cultural ones.

It is with Freud's conception of these innate sexual drives that Gagnon
and Simon take issue. They argue that he has mistakenly imposed the
language of adult sexual experience on the behaviour of children and has
imputed sexual motives to them solely on the basis of the meaning their
behaviour would have if performed by an adult actor. No act, in their terms,
is sexual in itself, but only if it is defined as such. A child's behaviour cannot
be construed as sexual since it does not, as yet, carry such meaning for the
child. If this is accepted then there is little basis for assuming that sexual
drives exist: 'Sexual behaviour is socially scripted behaviour and not the ...
expression of some primordial drive' (Simon and Gagnon, 1969: 736).

It is not until the onset of puberty in our society that these socio-sexual
scripts are learnt, for it is not until then that the subject comes to be defined
as a potential sexual actor and to accept herself or himself as such. An
emphasis on continuity with childhood is, from this perspective, misleading.
Obviously sexual learning does not happen all at once with no reference to
previous experience, but the aspect of pre-adolescent development that has
greatest relevance for sexuality is the learning of gender roles. It is the

feminine or masculine self-identity acquired through this process which provides the framework within which the learning of sexual scripts occurs. 'The crucial period of childhood has significance not because what happens is of a sexual nature, but because of the non-sexual development that will condition subsequent encounters with sexuality' (Simon and Gagnon, 1969: 741).

Gagnon and Simon are, in effect, reversing Freud's conception of the interrelationships between sexuality and gender. Whereas Freud sees the sexual as determining all other areas of personality development, they view the emergence of sexuality as contingent upon the development of other, non-sexual, aspects of gender identity. For Freud, the feminine character is created by the pattern of female sexual development, while for Gagnon and Simon female sexuality is itself built upon an earlier foundation of gender role learning. Adolescence is the crucial turning point in the development of the sexual self. The onset of this period is heralded by the physical changes of puberty, but it is not these changes in themselves which determine the development of sexuality, but the meaning which is attached to them. They serve, in effect, as signals to others, indicating that the child may be defined as a potential sexual actor and will be expected to learn the scripts which govern adult sexual behaviour. In the course of this new phase of learning the individual assimilates the sexual into her or his self-identity and comes to see herself or himself as capable of playing a sexual role. Previous to these developments, before learning the scripts of socio-sexual behaviour and casting themselves in them, an individual's behaviour cannot be said to be sexual.

> It is in the process of converting external labels into internal capacities for naming that activities become more precisely defined and linked to a structure of socio-cultural expectations and needs that define the sexual. (Simon and Gagnon, 1969: 734)

Perceptions of childhood eroticism: pleasure and the sexual

These theoretical frameworks raise two interrelated and interdependent questions concerning the process of sexual learning. First, to what extent can the development of sexuality in adolescence be seen as continuous or discontinuous with childhood experience? And second, what is the nature of those childhood experiences which might be perceived as having implications for the emergence of sexuality?

I would argue, with Gagnon and Simon, that in terms of sexual learning in our society adolescent experiences do involve a significant break with the past. It is in this period of life that the individual becomes fully aware of the sexual meanings attached to certain aspects of her or his social environment, comes to be defined as a sexual actor, and begins to build an image of herself or himself as such. It is the time when conscious sexual learning begins, when new discoveries are made and novel experiences undergone that are not always easy to relate to childhood experience.

This is not say that all this occurs totally independently of any former influences. Some continuity must exist, for in childhood the basis of the individual's self-identity, to which the sexual is assimilated, is established. Also, certain childhood experiences may, when combined with the new knowledge gained in adolescence, contribute to the individual's understanding of sexuality. There is an implicit distinction here between two categories of learning which have implications for later psycho-sexual development. The first involves the creation of a larger framework of self-identity of which gender identity is an essential component, and in terms of which sexual scripts are learnt and interpreted. The second arises out of the behaviour which, though not intrinsically sexual, is likely to be labelled as such and which might, therefore, be retrospectively interpreted as sexually relevant in the light of later experience and so provide a more direct link between childhood and adolescence. By positing the possible existence of such a link I do not wish to attribute some sort of causal precedence to this variety of childhood experiences. Their importance lies not in determining later sexual development, but in providing the adolescent with data that she or he may be able to build into her or his emerging conception of the erotic or which may provide moral categories for sexual activities.

This in no sense, then, implies an acceptance of Freud's interpretations of children's sexuality. Whether based on observations of children or psychoanalytical case studies, his conclusions are somewhat suspect. In the former case he tends to arrive at somewhat absurd conclusions, not simply because he apprehends the behaviour of young children through the vocabulary of adult sexual experience, but because, in doing so, he imputes specifically sexual motives to them. He does not simply note the affinities between infant behaviour and adult sexual acts, but regards them as being manifestations of the same primordial drive, as satisfying the same need. So, for example, he holds that the child's flushed cheek and contented sleep after being fed is analogous to the adult post-orgasmic state (Freud, 1905). That these two varieties of contentment may have something in common is no grounds for arguing, as Freud does, that one is an early expression of the other, a manifestation of infantile sexuality.

The other source of 'evidence', involving retrospective interpretation of childhood experiences, may also be distorting. As Simon and Gagnon argue:

> ... rather than the past determining the present it is possible that the present reshapes the past, as we reconstruct our autobiographies in an effort to bring them greater congruence with our present identities, roles and available vocabularies. (Simon and Gagnon, 1969: 734)

It is such a biographical reconstruction, attempting to explain the present by reference to the past, that forms the basis of the psychoanalytical method.

Freud, reasoning from the premised existence of the libido as a powerful sexual drive determining human personality, may then interpret adult behaviour in terms of inferred childhood sexual experiences. In the process the child's behaviour, responses and affections are infused with sexual meaning. It is the nature of psychoanalysis that it imposes preconceived categories on to behavioural phenomena and then purports to have explained them.

Freud, having stated (correctly) that we must not confuse the sexual with the genital, proceeds to interpret a wide range of behaviour and responses as sexual, as satisfying some drive. He argues that the child *needs* to have such sensations repeated, rather than that she or he finds them simply pleasurable and therefore enjoys their repetition. He notes the rhythmical nature of activities such as thumb sucking and regards them as proof of their sexual nature. This is a prime example of the mislabelling of childhood experiences: could it not be that the child simply finds this activity pleasurable? That sexual acts may also incorporate this characteristic may only mean that rhythmical stimuli in general are found to be pleasurable, rather than that such sensations are inherently sexual. It is, says Freud, the quality of stimuli that determines whether or not they are sexual, but apart from offering the example of rhythmical sensations he declines to elaborate further. Apparently the ineffable wisdom of psychoanalysis can uncover sexual motives underlying such apparently innocent childish activities and desires as playing on swings or wanting to be an engine driver!

By such arguments as these, Freud contrives to label as sexual almost anything a child apprehends as pleasurable. It might be argued against this that anything we perceive as sexual in children's behaviour is, for them, merely a pleasurable experience. If sexuality lies not in the quality of an act but in the meaning given to it, then a child's behaviour or responses cannot be interpreted as being sexual when the child has not yet learnt the vocabulary of motives through which sexual activity is mediated.

Adolescence: the period of sexual discovery

Adolescence is the period of life when conscious sexual learning begins. At this time children make discoveries concerning the facts of sex and reproduction, experience changes in their bodies, and begin to learn the socio-sexual scripts that govern adult sexual behaviour. These scripts are not just guidelines for sexual action, but also the means by which the individual comes to understand and comes to terms with sexuality. In effect they provide a sexual vocabulary of motives.[1]

> Elements of such scripting occur across many aspects of the sexual situation. Scripts are involved in learning the meaning of internal states, organizing the sequences of specifically sexual acts, decoding novel situations, setting the limits

on sexual responses, and linking meanings from non-sexual aspects of life to specifically sexual experience. (Gagnon and Simon, 1974: 19)

The ways in which these scripts are learnt is profoundly affected by the gender-role learning of childhood, so that girls and boys learn to be sexual in different ways. These diverging lines of development are not the results of repression or accession of libido, but of differential learning experiences built on to a firmly established sense of gender identity.

Adolescence involves, in the first instance, coming to terms with the physical changes of puberty, which signify that a girl is growing up, that she is becoming a potential sexual actor. She will interpret these experiences in the light of what she knows about her sexual role and will thus begin to develop a sexual self-identity. Although, biologically, puberty in both sexes signals reproductive maturity, this will be more immediately obvious to a girl, signifying that she can now 'have babies', whereas a boy may interpret his body's development as meaning he can now 'have sex'. A girl is likely to have learnt about sex in the context of marriage and motherhood, and its reproductive purpose will be clear. Genital taboos encountered during childhood will probably ensure that she does not engage in active explorations of her own body, and it is therefore unlikely she will have discovered the pleasurable sensations it is capable of producing. She has, however, received a thorough training in romanticism, and this may lend a more attractive aspect to the sexual, providing perhaps the only positive associations that sex, as such, has for her.

One important result of current attitudes to female sexuality is that a girl is unlikely to learn, from any source, about the nature of her own sexual response. Formal and informal sources of information convey a reproductive or male defined view of sexuality, so that a girl has little chance of understanding how to gain pleasure from her own body. The emphasis in sex education is on the act of coition and most information available to adolescents is based on the assumption (both sexist and heterosexist) that this is what sexuality is about. Girls therefore receive the impression that the vagina is the most sexually important part of their bodies and are unaware that they possess a clitoris and of the importance of this organ for their sexual pleasure.

The acquisition of biological facts comprises only a small part of adolescent sexual learning. In order to become a competent actor within socio-sexual dramas and to develop a sexual commitment, the individual needs to be able to interpret her or his own emotions in sexual terms, to recognize potentially sexual situations, and to be able to make decisions on how to act in them.

Without the proper elements of a script that defines the situation, names the actors and plots the behaviour, nothing sexual is likely to happen ... combining such elements as desire, privacy and a physically attractive person of the appropriate sex, the probability of something sexual happening will, under normal circumstances, remain exceedingly small until either one or both actors organize these behaviours into an appropriate script. (Gagnon and Simon, 1974: 19)

Before an adolescent girl can begin to participate fully in sexual scenes she must become familiar with the scripts that govern them and be able to locate her own actions within them.

Girls learn to enact sexual scripts within the milieu of their peer group, an environment which may be characterized as homo-social and heterosexual (Simon and Gagnon, 1969). So, although their sexual interest is focused on the opposite sex, it is primarily to their same-sex peers that adolescents will look for validation of their sexual attitudes and accomplishments. In such a situation, girls and boys develop markedly different sexual expectations and hence continue their psycho-sexual development along divergent paths. Among their peers, boys' sexual commitment will be confirmed through the social validation accorded to male sexual exploits. But although the sexual world is a major preoccupation of boys in their early teens, it is not until later that they become adept at the social skills necessary for the establishment and maintenance of relationships with girls. For a girl, however, this pattern is reversed, she acquires a socio-sexual commitment before developing a specifically sexual one (Gagnon and Simon, 1974). Each sex, then, has only partial knowledge of sexual scripts, and girls are best trained in precisely those areas for which boys are least well prepared. While girls are learning the language of romantic love, the boys are concerning themselves with rather more directly sexual interests. It is not until the later years of adolescence that they are able to negotiate socio-sexual relationships with each other. In the meantime, it is likely that girls' romantic interests will be focused on more distant fantasy figures – until such time as their male counterparts are able to behave in a manner that is congruent with feminine expectations.

Early in their teens girls begin to evaluate boys as sexual partners and to compete for their attention. Yet at the same time as they are trying out their skills as seductresses, and finding that they may be admired and envied for popularity with boys, they will find they receive no social support for sexual activity per se. A girl has nothing to gain and her 'reputation' to lose if she is too sexually active. The maintenance of a positive feminine self-concept depends on the successful management of romantic relationships, rather than on specifically sexual achievements. So girls carefully guard their reputations and, with the help of a sexual response tuned to romantic stimuli, endeavour to establish ongoing relationships as a precondition for sexual activity. Most girls pass into adulthood still unsure of their sexual identity and with a romantic, passive and dependent orientation towards erotic activity. They enter into adult sexual careers governed by scripts which deny them the possibility of a self-defined sexuality in a world in which the sexual is partitioned off from the rest of everyday life.

The end product: female sexuality in a changing erotic environment

It is far too simplistic to argue that women's sexuality is repressed by the demands of a patriarchal capitalist society. It is preferable to conceptualize the relationship between society and sexuality in terms of the latter being socially constructed to fit in with the current institutions, ideology and morality of that society. The advance of capitalism has created a gulf between the public sphere of production and exchange and the private sphere of the family and personal relationships. Within the latter, sexuality has become so extremely privatized and exclusively personal that it constitutes a world apart from the rest of our lives, even in their most intimate aspects. It is a subject set aside to be learnt at a particular time and in unique ways. Whether this separateness leads to a guilty, negative orientation to the sexual or to ideals of specialness and spontaneity, it results in problems of communication. Even within the privacy of the sexual dyad, sex itself is rarely discussed. Sexual activity is usually initiated by, and proceeds through, innuendo and gesture rather than open talk. Hence sexual interaction is characterized by a degree of confusion and doubt about the intentions and interpretations of the other which is not typical of more routine forms of interaction.

Such problems are heightened by the fact that men and women have learnt to be sexual in different ways, that sexual dramas are scripted for actors who have different sexual vocabularies of motive and different orientations to and expectations of sexual relationships. Feminine and masculine sexual roles are popularly believed to fit together and be complementary, but in reality the relation between them is more often one of disjunction. Each gender is, as Gagnon and Simon (1974) point out, estranged from the existential nature of the other's sexual experience. For women, all this is further complicated by the institutionalized superiority of men which is carried over into the bedroom (and not the other way around as some feminists would have us believe). As a result the most widely disseminated ideas and ideals of sexuality are masculine ones and sexual relationships are male dominated. The heterosexual marriage bed becomes a scene of confusion and deception rather than of conjugal bliss. It is hardly surprising that lesbian women appear more at home in their sexual lives than their heterosexual sisters (Whiting, 1972).

Notes

1 The term 'vocabulary of motives' derives from the work of C. Wright Mills (1940). See Chapter 3 for a further elaboration of this concept.

3   The Social Context of Rape: Sexual Scripts and Motivation

Sexual violence emerged as a central issue for feminist theory and activism in the middle of the 1970s. Feminists sought to challenge many of the myths surrounding rape – that women 'ask for it', that it is the product of irrepressible male 'drives', and so on. Instead of seeing rape as an individual act, incited by a 'provocative' woman or inspired by a man's pathological state of mind, it was reconceptualized as a social and political manifestation of male power. This article was my attempt, inspired by discussions within the Women's Movement, to analyse the conduct of rapists. Using the interactionist perspective on sexuality I had already developed (see Chapter 2), and drawing on sociological theories of deviance, I set out to challenge the idea that rape is an abnormal act. Rape, I argued, is less of an aberration than an extension of conventional (hetero)sexual relations, and of the power differentials these entail, and should thus be understood as a social, rather than a psychological, problem.

Many years after its first publication (in 1978) this piece was reprinted in a reader on rape, where it is credited with articulating 'what has become a classic feminist view' (Searles and Berger, 1995: 2). Certainly my ideas reflected the feminist thinking of the time, but they were not uncontentious. In activist circles it was common to play down the sexual element of rape in order to emphasize its violence, to argue that it should be treated primarily as an assault. I maintained then, and still think now, that the sexual dimension to rape cannot be ignored, since concentrating instead on violence and power cannot explain how and why sex comes to be used as a weapon. Moreover, we need to understand how it is that power and violence can, for men, become fused with desire. In a much later study of convicted rapists, Diana Scully (1990) revealed the pleasures of rape for men, characterizing it as a low risk, high reward activity. Any analysis of rape, then, must take account of the social construction of male sexuality.

Power did feature strongly in my argument, in that I endorsed the accepted feminist view that rape helps to maintain the subordination of women. This, however, created a considerable theoretical inconsistency. As Sylvia Walby (1990) points out, I dealt with power relations by introducing the idea of patriarchy (although in fact I did so only implicitly). As a structural concept, patriarchy (or systematic male dominance) is inadmissible within the symbolic interactionist perspective that informed my discussion of the motives for rape. She comments that my account 'succeeds in its analysis of rape precisely as it moves outside a symbolic interactionist frame of reference' (Walby, 1990: 114). This problem, of course, reflects the tension between agency and structure and the difficulty – still so hard to resolve – of conceptualizing the social construction of sexuality both at the level of social structure and as emergent from everyday social practices (see Chapter 1).

The subject of rape has provided the raw material for propaganda, jokes and pornography. It has been used as an ideological weapon in times of war, to inject an element of humour into otherwise dull lectures on law and criminology, has fed the erotic fantasies of men and inspired fear in women. Yet it is a subject which has received very little serious scrutiny and remains shrouded in myths, denied the status of a 'real' problem. The academic community has remained strangely silent about rape. Criminologists, psychologists and sociologists have ignored it or accorded it only cursory recognition of a kind which tends to reinforce rather than challenge the myths.

Rape is a complex issue. It is both a sexual act and an act of aggression; it has been viewed as a crime against the person and as a crime against property and, more recently, as a political crime (Brownmiller, 1975; Medea and Thompson, 1974). From the victim's perspective it is more than a sexual crime, more than simple physical assault: it is an attack on her mind as well as her body, an attack on her whole person, undermining her will and self-esteem.

The stranger in the dark alley: misconceptions of rapist and victim

The perpetrators of this act are not the rapists of the popular imagination, psychopaths lurking in dark alleys waiting to pounce on any likely victim and inflict their uncontrollable desires upon her. This is just one of the many widely believed myths about rape and one which has been fostered by most of the few existing studies of the subject. Psychologists have characterized the rapist as the unfortunate victim of an unsatisfactory relationship with his overbearing mother, exacerbated by a teasing, frigid wife. Sociologists have concentrated on the analysis of police statistics without allowing for the possibility that these may be little more than a record of the preconceptions of the police as to the nature of the act of rape.

Neither of these approaches confronts the problem of why rape should occur at all. While psychologists assume that the rapist is abnormal and therefore account for his behaviour in terms of individual pathology, sociologists have sidestepped the question of motivation altogether, preferring to confine themselves to factor analysis. Where they do step back from their statistics to ponder the issue of causation, they do so in terms of their folk-knowledge of rape, so that their hypotheses and conclusions are merely echoes of the rape mythology. Thus Svalastoga (1962) looks for an explanation in the sex ratio of the population, presumably on the assumption that rape is the result of unsatisfied sex-drives resulting from a relative shortage of women. Amir's (1967) concept of victim precipitation, at first sight a more sophisticated approach, is simply a reworking of the idea that raped women are often responsible for their fate. Both these authors implicitly assume that sexual desire per se provides the motive for rape and all that needs to be explained is the conditions which result in the unleashing of the male's supposedly uncontrollable urges.

Reliance on police statistics also produces the impression that rape is something which occurs primarily between strangers. But if the police believe that rape reports are more likely to be genuine where this is the case, their decisions on whether to record a case will be influenced by this preconception. In her study of the Memphis police department, Brenda Brown discovered that the police are likely to treat a rape report as unfounded if the victim and assailant knew each other and that, as a result, 73 per cent of founded rapes were committed by strangers (cited in Brownmiller, 1975). It is also probable that, for a variety of reasons, women will be more inclined to report rape if their attacker is unknown to them. If we look instead at the victims' accounts provided by Medea and Thompson (1974) we find that only 33 per cent reported being raped by someone they did not know at all.

The rapist who becomes a police statistic, although he is not representative of all rapists, is a long way from the stereotype of a sex-starved/crazed lunatic who is clearly distinguishable from 'normal' men. While Svalastoga informs us that psychological tests reveal that most rapists are normal or show only a slight deviation from the normal, Amir's (1971) more detailed analysis provides us with a comprehensive picture of them which is very similar to that of other youthful offenders whose misdeeds find their way into police records. If we accept that rape is far more widespread than the statistics show, then it is likely that the rapist is not so very different from his fellow men.[1]

The victims of rape are, in all likelihood, no more unusual than their attackers. Amir (1971) found that most of the victims in his study came from similar social backgrounds to their attackers and hence most were from the lower classes. Presumably if more middle-class rapists came to the attention of the police, more middle-class victims would be discovered. There is certainly no evidence to support the popular idea that rape victims are likely to be of dubious moral standing. This misconception is no doubt based on the belief that no 'respectable' woman would be walking alone past dark alleys when the rapist pounced. But rape occurs in a wide variety of contexts and locations and it cannot be assumed that a woman's presence in a rape setting is somehow indicative of immorality. All the evidence suggests that Mr Average rapes Ms Average.

The idea that both rapist and victim are in some way different from other members of society is based on the assumption that rape is very different from normal sexual acts, an idea that persists despite the great difficulty our laws have in distinguishing between them. There is an element of double-think here: the belief in rape as something apart from everyday expressions of sexuality exists side by side with the notion that rape is impossible, that it doesn't happen at all, that the victim is a woman who has 'changed her mind afterwards'. It is simultaneously thought of as both a heinous crime and as a normal sexual encounter mislabelled criminal. In practice, these apparently contradictory beliefs are used to distinguish the 'real rapes', involving a brutal madman and an innocent victim, from the 'fakes'. This confusion as to the nature of rape serves to disguise its affinity with normal sexual behaviour:

> There is a convenient notion of rape that places it at a vast distance from anything which may be commonly experienced.... The popular view is that, if the rapist cannot be labelled 'fiend' or 'monster' or 'maniac', then he probably isn't a rapist at all. (Toner, 1977: 47)

It is my contention that a close relationship exists between rape and more conventional modes of sexual expression. It is therefore neither an aberration nor a particularly unusual occurrence. If rape is to be understood, then it must be placed within the context of the patterns of sexual relationships typical of our society. Explanations for rape are not to be found within the individual psyche of rapist or victim but within our accepted sexual mores, for it is these which condition interaction in rape settings and which provide vocabularies of motive for the rapist.

> A sociological conception of motives ... translates the question of 'why' into a 'how' that is answerable in terms of a situation and its typical vocabularies of motives, i.e. those which conventionally accompany that type of situation and function as cues and justifications for normative actions in it. (Mills, 1940: 440)

Rather than asking why some men rape, we should ask how rape is possible within certain situations, how features of conventional sexual scenes create the potential for rape.

Sexual scripts, motives and neutralization

A framework for analysis of rape in terms of conventional sexual behaviour is provided by Gagnon and Simon's (1974) work on sexual scripts. Rejecting theories of sexuality predicated on the assumption of inbuilt sexual drives, they conceptualize it as the outcome of a complex process of learning whereby the individual develops a capacity to interpret and enact sexual scripts. These scripts serve to organize both internal states and outward behaviour, enabling us to interpret emotions and sensations as sexually meaningful, and providing us with methods of recognizing potential sexual situations and acting effectively within them (see Chapter 2).

It is these scripts which provide the motivations for sexual conduct. As Mills (1940) has argued, motives are not merely inner states of mind but cultural creations, governed by some delineated vocabulary by which individuals anticipate the outcome of their actions. Hence sexual behaviour is not an expression of inner drives but is structured by an accepted vocabulary of motives pertaining to the erotic. Sexual desire is not aroused through a simple stimulus–response mechanism but through the attribution of sexual meanings to specific stimuli, and desire alone will not produce sexual behaviour unless the actor is able to define the situation as one in which such conduct is appropriate.

The same scripts which motivate 'normal' sexual behaviour also provide a potential vocabulary of motives for the rapist. It is a mistake to assume that those who engage in acts perceived as deviant necessarily subscribe to a morality at variance with that of non-deviant members of society, or that their motives for engaging in deviant acts are qualitatively different from those that govern conformist behaviour. The moral prescriptions and proscriptions that define the limitations of acceptable conduct may well contain escape clauses, allowing behaviour that would generally be considered immoral to be seen as justifiable under certain conditions. These extenuating circumstances, or neutralizations (Sykes and Matza, 1957), are not mobilized only after the act in order to enable the offender to beg our pardon: knowledge of acceptable justifications may control conduct. By absolving himself of guilt in advance, an individual may break or bend rules of conduct.

Like the juvenile delinquents whose behaviour Sykes and Matza (1957) sought to explain, the rapist does not invent techniques of neutralization, but derives them from generally accepted cultural norms. Indeed, some of them are acceptable in the courts as pleas for defence or mitigation. When overlaid by the motives and meanings incorporated into sexual scripts, neutralization techniques become specifically applicable to rape, providing the potential rapist with a positive evaluation of his projected action. Hence the vocabularies of motive appropriate to conventional situations are extended, enabling the rapist to see his acts as acceptable.

Setting the scene for rape: actors, scripts and motives

Sexual scripts do not exist in a vacuum, but are bound up with cultural notions of femininity and masculinity. It is gender identity which provides the framework within which sexuality is learnt and through which erotic self-identity is created. Thus men and women learn to be sexual in different ways, to enact different roles in the sexual drama, to utilize different vocabularies of motive. The attributes of masculinity and femininity, learnt from the beginning of childhood and incorporated into expectations of sexual behaviour, provide the motivational and interactional basis of rape.

In the first place, conventional sexual scenes are scripted for an active male and a passive female, activity and passivity being defining characteristics of masculinity and femininity respectively. From the beginning boys learn to be independent, to seek success actively through their own efforts and abilities, while girls are encouraged to be dependent, to seek success passively through pleasing others. It is hardly surprising that when they learn of the erotic implications of relationships between them they should express their sexuality this way. The man becomes the seducer, the woman the seduced, he the hunter, she the prey. It is he who is expected to initiate sexual encounters and to determine the direction in which they develop, her part is merely to acquiesce or refuse. Aggression is part of man's activity. He is not only expected to take the lead but to establish dominance over the woman, to make her please him, and his 'masculinity' is threatened if he fails to do so. Sexual conquest becomes an acceptable way of validating masculinity, of demonstrating dominance of and superiority over women.

> Rape is in this sense a mirror-image of our ordinary sex folkways. Two basic beliefs of these folkways are the natural sexual aggressiveness of man and man's natural physical superiority over women. Put these two beliefs together, set up a competition for masculine prowess such as we have today and no-one should be surprised at the incidence of rape. (Herschberger, 1970: 15)

If sexuality were not bound up with power and aggression, rape would not be possible.[2] When these attributes of masculinity are accentuated, as in war, rape reaches epidemic proportions (see Brownmiller, 1975). Male sexual aggression is also popularly believed to be uncontrollable. Once a man's sexual response has been set in motion, he is supposed to be totally at the mercy of his desires:

> One of the most pervasive myths which feed our distorted understanding of rape is the belief in the urgent sexual potency of men. Men are believed to have a virtually uncontrollable sexual desire, which once awakened must find satisfaction regardless of the consequences. (Smart, 1976: 95)

This places the responsibility for setting limits on sexual activity in the hands of the woman. She must take care not to arouse him too much lest she fails to control the powerful forces she has unleashed. It is this belief in the urgency of male sexual drives which provides the first technique of neutralization available to the rapist: denial of responsibility. If a man attributes this to himself, perceives himself as a helpless slave to his desire, then he will be less inclined to curb himself in the face of a woman's refusal and more inclined to resort to force to attain his ends.

The male's supposedly uncontrollable sexual aggression is, moreover, backed by conceptions of female sexuality and the feminine character which conveniently rationalize away any protests a woman might make. The vocabularies of motive of conventional sexual scripts not only provide the rapist with an acceptable account of his actions in terms of his own desires, but also in terms of his perspective on his victim. Where he denies responsibility, he neutralizes the immorality of his behaviour without reference to that of his victim; where he denies injury or denies the victim, it is her actions which are being called to account.

Denial of injury rests on a common misconception of sexual relations which tends to overestimate the effects of male sexual potency and under-estimate female sexual autonomy, so that a woman's satisfaction is assumed to be dependent on male activity. It is supposed that women need some degree of persuasion before they will engage in sexual activity but that, once their inhibitions have been overcome or their sense of propriety demonstrated, they will respond. A popular belief of the male culture is that what matters in success with women is not attractiveness per se, but an ability to apply techniques of seduction, cleverness in countering a woman's objections and persistence in overcoming her resistance (Toner, 1977). This manipulation is a more subtle manifestation of power than brute force. It may not be that rape is forced seduction but that seduction is a subtler form of rape.

The masterful male and yielding female form a common motif of our popular culture. In countless books and films the male hero is portrayed overcoming the anger or indifference of a woman by means of a passionate embrace, which she at first resists and then returns with equal fervour. Sex is seen as a means of forcing a woman into loving submission. Ruth Herschberger suggests that this is a large part of the appeal of the male rape fantasy:

> When the man turns to the sensational image of rape he learns of an act which, if effected with any unwilling woman, can force her into a sexual relationship with him. She can be forced into a psychological intimacy with him ... the unwilling woman magically becomes willing, her sensory nerves respond gratefully, stubborn reflexes react obediently, and the beautiful stranger willy-nilly enters into a state of sexual intimacy with her aggressor. (Herschberger, 1970: 24)

This view of female sexuality, given added credibility by the Freudian premise of woman's masochism, leads on to the myth that all women secretly want to be raped and that the best course of action for them to take should the fantasy become reality is to 'lie back and enjoy it'. Where the rapist denies injury it is not inconceivable that he thinks that he is doing his victim a favour: rapists have been known to ask to see their victim again.

These ideas also, of course, cast doubt on the credibility of the victim. In part this is a result of a perceived ambivalence towards sex on the part of women. They will say 'no' but apparently mean 'yes' since they ultimately consent, or rather relent. But this may not represent real ambivalence. Female passivity often results in women participating in sexual acts against their will. They are supposed to control the pace at which the encounter proceeds, but they are supposed to do so gently. Being conditioned to please, to bolster up a man's ego, to refrain from hurting him, a woman's gentle protestations are no match for a determined male with distorted ideas of his own sexuality and sexual capabilities. In some instances women may be too confused or embarrassed to know how to react. Either way the man will see her resistance as a pretence and hence reinforce his beliefs in the efficacy of his seduction techniques and his conviction that women will consent if only he tries hard enough.

A rapist may deny that his victim is a victim at all. But even if he does not delude himself as to the extent of her participation in the act he might see her as a *legitimate* victim (Weiss and Borges, 1973).[3] For denial of the victim to operate as a motive for rape, the victim must be seen as being in some way responsible for her fate. The principle that governs this is that, while rape is wrong, some women deserve to be raped. The victim is seen as a 'cock-teaser', the cruel woman who leads men on only to reject them. She has acted provocatively and can hardly expect any other response, she 'had it coming'. The provocation may be slight or non-existent from the point of view of the victim. It is enough, insofar as accounting for the rapist's motives is concerned, that he is capable of construing her actions in this way. It is possible for a man to see his prey as a legitimate victim even where no sexual invitation is perceived, where, for instance, a woman is too aloof and refuses to respond to sexual overtures. Medea and Thompson (1974) report an incident at a rape conference where a man expressed this view, saying that women who are raped are those who are 'too good to talk to'. They comment:

> ... women are damned both ways – they seem to be looking for it or they are too good for it, they are touchable or they are untouchable. Either way they are candidates for rape. (Medea and Thompson, 1974: 5)

Denial of the victim may also incorporate a notion of revenge. Here rape is explicitly used as a weapon, a method of punishing a woman. When it is said of the victim that she 'had it coming', it may mean that she is perceived as having provoked rape as an act of aggression rather than as a sexual act. In this case rape becomes a stark expression of male domination. It has been argued that it has this effect, whether intended or not:

> Rape operates as a social control mechanism to keep women in their 'place' or put them there. The fear of rape, common to most women, socially controls them as it limits their ability to move about freely. As such, it establishes and maintains the woman in a position of subordination. (Weiss and Borges, 1973: 94)

This rationale for rape gains additional significance in situations of conflict or war. Here women become doubly legitimate victims by virtue of being members of some despised race, class or nation as well as being female. Rape may be used as a weapon not only against women, but against the social group of which they are members. Eldridge Cleaver's comments on his career as a rapist are illustrative:

Rape was an insurrectionary act. It delighted me that I was defying and trampling on the white man's law, upon his system of values, and that I was defiling his women – and this point, I believe, was the most satisfying to me because I was very resentful over the historical fact of how the white man had used black women. I felt I was getting revenge. (Cleaver, 1970: 26)

This statement reveals a great deal about the attitude of the rapist in this type of situation and about rape in general. Cleaver's vengeance is directed towards white *men*, but it is through white women that it is realized. He is simply establishing a right of access to their bodies as he has already done with black women – whom he used as practice targets until be considered himself 'smooth' enough to 'cross the tracks'. His concern with the usage of black women by white men is not with the humiliation, degradation and pain suffered by those women, but for the deprivation of sexual rights suffered by black men. When he repents, he does so because of his own dehumanization through rape, not that of his victims – black or white.

This tendency to discount the feelings of the victim is by no means a personal quirk of Cleaver's. It is quite commonplace in everyday theorizing about rape and is often expressed in justifications of it. These justifications arise out of our sexual scripts and are easily mobilized before the event as techniques of neutralization such that any sexual encounter involving the exercise of male domination may culminate in rape.

Barter and theft

The possibility of rape is heightened by the incorporation into our sexual scripts of non-sexual motives. Sexuality for men is a means of validating their masculinity as well as being a source of pleasure. For women it is also a means to other ends, in particular a way of earning the love, support and protection of a man. In this game, where each player has different expectations and desires different outcomes, the woman's sexuality assumes the status of a commodity. It is not simply that she is regarded as a sexual object to be acted upon, but that she objectifies her own sexuality in utilizing it as an object of barter. She attempts to extract the highest price possible, marriage, while the man is hoping for a bargain. The objectification of female sexuality which is implied in this form of exchange exposes women to the risk of rape. If something may be bought and sold, it can also be stolen: what can be given can also be taken by force.

Sexual barter creates further ambiguities in the enactment of sexual scripts for it creates the possibility of differential evaluation of the commodity to be exchanged, for there is no fixed price. This problem is even more evident now that women are no longer expected to be as chaste as they once were. Where once 'good' women only traded sex in exchange for marriage, they are now often prepared to settle for a lower price (McCall, 1966). Rape may occur where the man has paid the amount he thinks is appropriate while the woman defines the situation with reference to a different system of values. She may then easily find herself short-changed.

Competing definitions of the situation are a constant source of misinterpretation and misunderstanding in the unfolding of the sexual drama. Where the woman is the passive partner, when selling herself depends on being attractive but not too eager, her methods of communicating desire must be subtle. The man has to rely on successfully decoding the gestural and verbal cues which she provides and it is therefore possible for him to perceive a sexual invitation where none was intended. It is also possible that the woman might not realize that he has defined a situation in sexual terms when she has not. This ambiguity may provide a pretext for the mobilization of the appropriate techniques of neutralization. If the man does not reassess his initial definition of the situation and proceeds to interpret all that transpires within its terms, the likely outcome is rape.

> The stereotypic notions of male and female roles and their relationship to conceptions of masculine and feminine sexuality, coupled with a situation which is fraught with ambiguous expectations, provide the ingredients for systematically socialized actors who can participate in the drama of rape. (Weiss and Borges, 1973: 86)

Undercurrents: negativity and hostility

The motivations for rape have so far been considered in mainly sexual terms. But rape is not simply a sexual act, it is also an act of aggression and hostility:

> It is a vain delusion that rape is the expression of uncontrollable desire or some kind of compulsive response to overwhelming attraction.... The act is one of murderous aggression, spawned in self-loathing and enacted upon the hated other. (Greer, 1970: 251)

Rape frequently involves many forms of humiliation apart from the straightforward sexual act. The degree of violence employed may be far more extreme than is necessary to force the woman into submission, and she may also be further degraded. Victims are often subjected to such treatment as repeated intercourse, forced fellatio, objects being thrust into the vagina or rectum, and being excreted upon (Amir, 1971).

This, like rape itself, is not a manifestation of personal pathology, but of the undercurrent of hostility that runs through our sexual scripts. The divergent goals and expectations held by men and women with regard to sexual relationships, the elements of exploitation that are thus brought into them, the ambivalence and ambiguity surrounding them, are bound to create tensions. Add to this the overall inferior status of women and the derisive attitude of many men towards them, and hostility becomes an ever-present threat.

There is, moreover, a great deal of guilt written into sexual scripts. Learning about sex in our society involves learning about guilt, indeed children learn taboos associated with sexuality before they are made aware of the scripts within which they operate (Gagnon and Simon, 1974). The association between sex and dirtiness is still with us despite the so-called 'sexual revolution' and our supposedly 'permissive' society. Children still learn about sex through dirty jokes and whispered clandestine secrets and find the taboo nature of sexuality confirmed by the evasive or negative attitudes of adults towards it. It would be surprising if some of this did not stay with them through adulthood.

If a man regards sex as a necessity, sees himself as being at the mercy of his powerful sexual drives while at the same time viewing the act as distasteful, he may displace his guilt on to the object of his desire, woman:

> The man regards her as a receptacle into which he has emptied his sperm, a kind of human spittoon, and turns from her in disgust. As long as man is at odds with his own sexuality and as long as he keeps woman as a solely sexual creature, he will hate her, at least some of the time. (Greer, 1970: 254)

There is, in the minds of many men, a strong association between women, sex and filth; many still see sexuality as part of our 'animal' nature in contradistinction to our higher human or humane nature. And this animal-ity has been ascribed to women. This has been a constant theme in theology and latterly in psychology. The witch-hunters of the 16th century operated on the assumption that women were more corruptible than men as a result of their insatiable lust, upon which Satan capitalized (Szasz, 1973). Freud picked up the same theme when he argued that women were closer to the instinctual, less fully human than men because of their inability to develop a strong super-ego (Freud, 1933). This tradition is carried on today and finds its expression in our sexual argot and the non-sexual meanings which it has acquired. As Kate Millett argues:

> ... the four-letter word derives from a puritanical tradition which is vigorously anti-sexual, seeing the act as dirty etc. This in turn derives from a conviction that the female sex is therefore both dirty and inferior to the intellectual and rational and therefore 'masculine' higher nature of humanity. (Millett, 1970: 355)

It is interesting that so many words which originally applied to sexual acts and to female sexual organs have now become terms of abuse.

Thus woman-as-sexual object is paradoxically thought of as asexual and as totally sexual. Denied sexual self-determination she is nonetheless held responsible for the debasement of mankind through her sexuality. If men regard women as somehow less than human, believing the while in their own superiority, and are trapped in the assumption of the irresistibility of their sexual urges, it is only to be expected that an explosive alliance between sex and violence should exist within our culture and find its outlet in rape:

... our highly repressive and puritan tradition has almost hopelessly confused sexuality with sadism, cruelty and that which is in general inhumane and anti-social. (Millett, 1970: 356)

Even if this degree of hostility towards women were unusual, some degree of negativity is necessary to explain the ease with which the typical motives are avowed by the rapist or ascribed to him, since these involve either implicating the victim or discounting her. These attitudes underpin motives for rape, are a more constant, less immediate contributory factor than techniques of neutralization, providing the background for their mobilization.[4]

Motives, action and interaction

The battery of motivations in the rapist's armoury are continuously available to him. Once he has mobilized one or other or a combination of them, neutralizing his guilt in advance, he is then morally free to act. There is no deterministic link between motives and action; neutralization simply transforms a constant possibility into a specific probability. Having found himself in a state of drift, on a form of 'moral holiday' where he feels rape is justifiable, the rapist must summon the will to act and be able to act. Situational and interactional features of the setting intervene between motivation and action and condition the eventual outcome. The sequence of events need not occur in this order. The rapist may want to act, have selected his victim and planned the action before he employs the techniques of neutralization which render him morally capable of rape. Rape is not always a spontaneous act: there is evidence to suggest that it is often planned.[5] In the case where the rapist lays his plans and motivates himself in advance, interaction between rapist and victim has little significance as a contributory factor to rape. In other cases, however, situations may occur where interaction between participants will itself bring techniques of neutralization into play and may provide the opportunity to translate motives into action. Where the rapist, being motivated in advance, is in a state of drift, interaction between him and a potential victim may increase or decrease the probability of rape occurring.

Explanations of motivation are, then, necessary but not sufficient to account for rape. The eventual outcome of a potential rape will depend on how the actors define that situation and the interaction which arises out of their definitions. Here again sexual scripts come into play, for these not only provide possible motives for rape but shape the process of sexual negotiation. No situation is sexual in itself; whether it becomes so depends on interpretations of it. Gagnon and Simon argue that unless or until both actors in a situation mobilize appropriate sexual scripts, 'the probability of something sexual happening will, under normal circumstances, remain exceedingly small' (1974: 19).

Circumstances may not, however, remain normal and, since there are no hard and fast rules for determining whether or not a situation may be defined as sexual, it is possible that one actor may perceive that sexual scripts are applicable while the other does not. It is possible that, insofar as men evaluate women almost exclusively in terms of their potential as sexual actors, they are capable of applying sexual scripts and becoming sexually motivated in a far wider range of situations than are women. Hence the interactional context, in which motives for rape arise and which mediates between motives and action, is governed by the same scripts in which those motives themselves originate, those which govern conventional sexual behaviour.

Conclusion: a note on rape and sexual politics

Rape is more than an attack on a specific victim. The sexual divisions of our society create a situation where rape is a constant threat to all women. In the course of their psycho-sexual development, men and women learn the typical vocabularies of motive of rapist and victim respectively. In enacting sexual scripts they enter into prescribed forms of interaction from which rape may emerge. The risk of being raped is one every woman takes, not only when she walks along dark streets at night, but every time she negotiates a socio-sexual relationship, or indeed any time she participates in interaction with men. Sexual behaviour is social behaviour: though it may appear to be a private matter, something uniquely personal, each sexual relationship is structured by the cultural values of the society in which it takes place:

> Coitus can scarcely be said to take place in a vacuum; although of itself it appears a biological and physical activity, it is set so deeply within the larger context of human affairs that it serves as a charged microcosm of the variety of attitudes and values to which culture subscribes. Among other things it may serve as a model of sexual politics on an individual or personal plane. (Millett, 1972: 23)

Sexual relationships are built around sexual inequalities, are scripted for actors whose roles have been predefined as subordinate and superordinate, and hence involve the exercise of power which may be manifested in the sexual act itself, as well as in other aspects of the relationship.

Rape, then, is simply an extreme manifestation of our culturally accepted patterns of male–female relationships. It is, in effect, an unofficial buttress of the status quo. It may be argued that it not only demonstrates male dominance but serves to preserve it:

> A world without rapists would be a world in which women moved freely without fear of men. That some men rape provides a sufficient threat to keep all women in a state of intimidation, forever conscious of the knowledge that the biological tool must be held in awe for it may turn to weapon with a swiftness borne of harmful

intent. Myrmidons to the cause of male dominance ... rapists have performed their duty well, so well in fact that the true meaning of their acts has largely gone unnoticed. Rather than society's aberrants or 'spoilers of purity', men who commit rape have served in effect as front-line masculine shock troops, terrorist guerillas in the longest sustained battle the world has ever known. (Brownmiller, 1975: 209)

Notes

1 Bias in police statistics has been well documented. It is possible that this is likely to be even more evident in the case of rape, since it is a notoriously under-reported crime. Estimates of report rates vary, but it is likely that only 9–20 per cent of rapes are reported, and there is no reason to assume that non-reports are a random selection of all rapes. Underreportage may be very high in the middle classes (see Kirkpatrick and Kanin, 1957), which might exaggerate the over-representation of working-class criminals already present in official statistics. It is certainly likely that the victim's decision to report the crime will be governed by the likelihood of her being believed, and that as a result reported rapes are those which come closest to fitting in with the dominant rape mythology.

2 This is borne out by the most famous example of a society where rape is unknown – the Mountain Arapesh of New Guinea. Not only do the Arapesh conceive of sex as dangerous, even between consenting partners, but the whole notion of sexual aggression is alien to them. Either sex may initiate sexual acts and the emphasis is on mutual preparedness and ease. Any form of compulsion, even within marriage, would be abhorrent to them. There is then, no element in their sexual scripts which could create the possibility of rape (Mead, 1935).

3 Weiss and Borges comment that members of low-status groups are frequently cast in the role of legitimate victim. Possibly the mere fact of his victim being female and therefore of no account is enough to motivate some rapists.

4   In this sense the undercurrents of hostility and negativity may be analogous to 'the condemnation of the condemners' cited by Sykes and Matza as a technique of neutralization in their original paper (Sykes and Matza, 1957), but later reshaped by Matza and seen as an attitude underlying the subculture of delinquency, rather than a specific technique of neutralization (Matza, 1964). If the possible condemners of the rapist are women in general, condemnation of them is a constant feature of the male (rapist) subculture.

5 Amir's data suggest that 71 per cent of rapes are planned, but this may possibly be inaccurate since it is based on official statistics (Amir, 1967). *Editorial note*: Scully's more recent study of convicted rapists also found that many rapes, especially gang rapes, involved some degree of planning (Scully, 1990).

4   How to Make Babies: Sexism in Sex Education

This chapter and the next draw on research conducted between 1973 and 1975 in schools and youth clubs in East Kent, entailing interviews with 24 girls aged 13–17. The study explored how girls in their teens made sense of their sexuality and constructed a sense of themselves as sexually feminine. This piece, focusing on sexual knowledge, could be read as a slice of history, a glimpse of the appalling state of sex education in the early 1970s. Some of the quotations from sex-education books in circulation at the time (all of which were taken from the library of the teacher training college in which I then worked) now seem ridiculously outdated. There are now far better resources available to those teachers who choose to use them, yet school sex education remains patchy. In some schools concern about HIV transmission and safer sex has led teachers to attend to the present actualities of young people's sexual lives, but in others sex education still does little more than impart the basic 'facts' of biological reproduction. For the most part sex education still defines sex in reproductive terms. Moreover, sex education continues to be publicly controversial and the issues being debated remain much the same: the boundaries of parental and school responsibility, the moral messages which should or should not be imparted, what it is appropriate for young people to know about and when they should learn it. Government legislation and guidelines issued to teachers in the UK ensure that even the best sex education is hedged around by concerns about parents' rights and the 'moral welfare' of school pupils (see Thomson, 1994). Girls can now glean far more sexual information from such informal sources as magazines than was the case in the 1970s – yet the availability of such information has itself been contentious (see Chapter 10).

Much has changed since the 1970s, but much has remained the same. The process of learning about sex and sexuality, even today, involves piecing together information from a variety of sources and young people do not necessarily find it easy to find out the things they most want to know. The jigsaw puzzle analogy I used here remains apt (see Scott et al., 1998). More recent research with young people suggests that they still see school sex education as inadequate and largely irrelevant to their immediate sexual lives; their complaints echo those made by the girls I interviewed over two decades ago (see Holland et al., 1998; Thomson and Scott, 1991).

My discussion of sexual knowledge was informed by my interest in

*childhood as a social institution and reflected the thinking underpinning my
first book,* Childhood and Sexuality *(1982a). My other analytical concern in
writing this piece was the social construction and regulation of sexual
knowledge. Were I considering the same issue today, I would no doubt draw
on a Foucauldian framework. This, however, was not then available to me
and I relied instead on those perspectives which did question the status of
knowledge, particularly those deriving from phenomenological sociology.
The conceptualization of ideology within this chapter is one I now see as
crude; while I have argued for the need to retain some notion of the
ideological framing and effects of discourse (see Chapters 1 and 8), I would
now neither assume some 'truth' to which ideology stands opposed, nor
would I posit some authentic female sexuality denied expression by the
workings of ideology. Nonetheless, the central argument presented here
remains as valid today as it was when it was first published (1978): that
sexual knowledge is a social product and that it is constructed in terms of a
male defined, reproductively focused heterosexual imperative.*

Of all school 'subjects', sex education is perhaps the most obviously sexist.
Here the differences between the sexes are made the focus of the knowledge to be imparted so that assumptions about gender, which elsewhere in
the curriculum are submerged and implicit, are brought to the surface and
made explicit. Sexism is evident both in the 'facts' that are taught and in the
moral attitudes conveyed with them, in the emphasis on reproductive
biology and in the value placed on marriage and the family. This bias
limits the relevance of sex education for all adolescents and, in particular,
excludes information related to female sexuality which might help girls to
discover and develop their sexual potential.

The sources of this sexism cannot be understood merely by listing the
types of misinformation, misrepresentation and misunderstanding through
which it is manifested. The question of content, of what is included and
what is omitted or distorted, should not be divorced from the context in
which it is taught, for context and content are interrelated. The sexist bias of
school education needs to be analysed within a broader perspective, taking
in cultural attitudes to sexuality and children, the ways in which these are
incorporated into such sex education programmes as exist and the constraints on the discussion of sexuality in the school.

This chapter is concerned mainly with girls' sex education, with the
information they are given, its usefulness to them and their appraisal of it.
The discussion of these questions, however, is set against the background of
more general problems concerning sex education.

Sex education as a social problem

Sex education is a highly contentious issue around which a great deal of
public debate takes place and as such may be seen as a social problem, that

is: 'a condition in society that is defined by members of the society as a problem about which something ought to be done' (Becker, 1966: 2). The problem, so defined, is the degree of sexual knowledge possessed by young people and the means by which they acquire it, but, when it comes to questions of whether too much or too little information is available and the ways in which it is disseminated, there is little consensus. A study of newspaper coverage of the subject in Scotland revealed four major areas of controversy: whether sex education increased or decreased problems associated with 'promiscuity', whether it should be the responsibility of the family or the school, at what age children ought to receive it and whether it should be confined to biological facts or include some 'moral guidance' (Gill et al., 1974). That public debate is organized around these questions reveals a great deal about the place of sexuality in contemporary society, not least the anxiety which it provokes where children and young people are concerned. It also suggests another sense in which sex education may be considered to be a social problem – that it is socially created.

The need for sex education is created by a society in which sexual activity is highly privatized and where children are considered to need protecting from the realities of adult life such that their presumed 'innocence' is equated with sexual ignorance. In consequence, children do not learn about sex as a routine part of growing up in the way that they learn other 'facts of life' relevant to their adult roles. In our pre-industrial past, privacy was neither possible nor desired and children became aware of sexuality through observing, listening to and interacting with others (see Jackson, 1982a). But it is not simply the existence of private bedrooms and reasonably soundproof walls that keep sex hidden from children, for the withholding of information is often deliberate. Sexual knowledge is deemed inappropriate for them and possibly damaging to them, as needing to be imparted with caution when a child is considered 'ready' to receive it.[1]

This lack of direct sexual learning in childhood does not, of course, mean that children do not possess any sexually relevant knowledge. Adult responses to children's behaviour and questions teach something of the moral meanings of sexuality and the social taboos which surround it. More important, perhaps, is the learning of gender-appropriate patterns of behaviour which will later acquire erotic significance. Girls, for example, learn to project themselves as physically attractive and to act in accordance with conventions of feminine modesty long before they are aware of the implications of such behaviour.

Children thus have access to a few pieces of the jigsaw puzzle, but most have been kept from them so that they have no way of knowing that they belong to the same puzzle or how they fit together until the missing portion is supplied. As children approach adolescence the adult world is forced to recognize them as potential sexual actors, assumes that sooner or later they will find the rest of the puzzle to fit it together and worries about how they will do so and what they will do with this new knowledge. Sex education, then, becomes a problem of how best to impart to the adolescent information that was systematically denied her as a child.

So here the notion of sexuality as a special area of life meets the conception of the child as a special category of person. Between childhood and adulthood the peculiar interstitial status of adolescence has been created, where the individual is assumed to require sexual knowledge in preparation for the future but is not yet considered mature enough to engage in sexual activity. It is the uneasiness that this ambiguity produces in the minds of parents and educators which makes sex education so problematic.

Why sex education in schools?

Since the need for deliberate sex education is created by the institution of childhood it is perhaps fitting that it should take place in an institution for children. Yet schools are patently ill-equipped to deal with the subject; it does not fit in with conventional educational objectives and no-one is trained to teach it. School-based sex education is usually seen as a regrettable necessity, born of the uncomfortable knowledge that sexuality is very much a part of the social life of adolescents and the realization that they are not acquiring sexual information efficiently in any other context. The family is commonly regarded as the appropriate place for the learning of sexual facts and moral attitudes, but since so many parents abdicate responsibility educational authorities tend to see it as incumbent on themselves to fill the gap.

To a large extent adolescent girls concur with this definition of the role of sex education. Although most of those I talked to were critical of the content of what they had received, they were unanimous in considering sex education in schools 'a good idea'. Where they justified this opinion it was not with reference to their own experience of it, since for most of them the school had played little part in their sexual learning, but in terms of the lack of availability of information elsewhere, especially from parents:

> I think it's very stupid if there isn't sex education in schools – I think it's essential because some parents just can't talk to their children and they're not going to tell them, and if they're not told in school then they'll find out, you know, through trial and error.

> I think it's a good idea really, because I think some parents, they're a bit embarrassed to tell their children.

Few of the girls had learnt anything either from parents or school but had just 'picked it up' from a variety of sources. Nearly all admitted difficulty in understanding and piecing together information gleaned in this way and would have liked sex education to have been given earlier. A similar picture emerges from Schofield's findings. In interviewing adolescents he found that only 12 per cent of boys and 18 per cent of girls learnt about conception from teachers, but in re-interviewing the same subjects as young adults discovered that 63 per cent of the men and 50 per cent of the women would have preferred to learn from this source (Schofield, 1965, 1973).

So it seems that, from their separate perspectives, both educators and pupils agree that some form of sex education is desirable under present circumstances, but only the former have a say in discussions of how and when it will take place and what is to be included. There is, however, no clear policy on the subject. Several government reports have referred to the need for sex education and local authorities have issued guidelines, but neither gives a clear indication of what the purposes of sex education are or how the content of it is to be defined. Most of these official documents refer in rather vague terms to educating young people for marriage and parent-hood or making them aware of the feelings of the opposite sex along with such moralistic statements as:

> Sexual intercourse should never be seen as a transient pleasure but as a joyful consummation of close friendship, love and understanding which in marriage have time to grow and deepen. (Quoted in Harris, 1974: 70)

It is clear from this and similar statements that educators see sex education as preparing adolescents for the future rather than helping them to come to terms with their own sexuality in the present. Its aim would seem to be to dissuade young people from expressing their sexuality in keeping with the middle-class ethic of deferred gratification.

American sex education in the 1950s has been described as being:

> ... focused on the necessity and unfortunate aspects of sexuality, treating it as a dangerous force requiring careful control. The concept of sex education classes was that the teacher was imparting safety precautions such as those used in handling highly explosive materials. (Gagnon and Simon, 1974: 113)

These attitudes are reported as features of the past, but there is little evidence of them having been eroded in Britain. An indication of the persistence of this emphasis on the dangers of sexual activity is given by the responses of 500 headteachers who filled in questionnaires about sex education. Eighty-five per cent of secondary school heads claimed that their pupils were given information on VD, but only 10 per cent of schools gave information on contraception and the majority thought that this should not be included in sex education. This would seem to represent a distinct focus on the 'unfortunate' aspects of sexuality, with the threat of disease being used as a dire warning against engaging in sexual activity.[2] Sex education is often seen as a way of preventing illegitimacy, but given the lack of contraceptive advice it seems that the means of achieving this aim is simply the preaching of abstinence. Moreover, those assumed to be most vulnerable to this problem (the 'deprived') are precisely those for whom education as a whole has failed and who are hardly likely to be receptive to moral injunctions from teachers.

This approach to sex education offers little help to young people and for girls the avoidance of the issue of contraception may be disastrous. There is some evidence, however, that a few teachers are prepared to widen the concept of sex education, and recent literature on the subject stresses the need to relate it to adolescents' own feelings and experiences. But such good intentions are likely to be lost sight of in the face of constraints imposed by the school.

Sexual knowledge and educational knowledge

Restrictions on the form and content of school sex education in part derive from the difficulties of incorporating it into the curriculum and dealing with it in terms of conventional definitions of educational knowledge, and methods of imparting it. Teaching typically involves the presentation of 'packages' of knowledge to pupils, in the form of academic 'subjects', as a series of objective 'facts' external to both teachers and learners. School knowledge is, moreover, differentiated from everyday knowledge in that school subjects are taken to 'represent the way in which the world is normally known in an "expert" as opposed to a "commonsense" mode of knowing' (Keddie, 1971: 156). Thus, even when the topic under discussion is related to pupils' everyday experiences, they are encouraged to 'transcend' this subjective experience and accept redefinitions of it from an 'objective' perspective:

> It would appear that willingness to take over the teacher's definition of what is to constitute the problem and what is to count as knowledge may require pupils to regard as irrelevant or inappropriate what they might see as problems in the context of everyday meaning. (Keddie, 1971: 151)

This concept of school knowledge creates difficulties when the subject to be taught is sex education. One major rationale for teaching it at all appears to be that sexuality is part of the present or future everyday lives of the pupils. Presenting it within the school, however, makes the linking of facts and experience problematic, for to create such a link teachers would need to abandon the conventions of educational knowledge which they normally seek to uphold. This would imply a commitment to accept, or at least to give greater credence to, pupils' definitions of what is problematic and to work through, rather than against, subjective experience. It would, of course, also undermine the teacher's status as a purveyor of 'expert' knowledge, since in the realm of personal relationships s/he is no more likely to possess expertise than any other member of the adult community. Nor will the quality of rapport necessary for such open discussion easily be established when at other times it is discouraged.[3]

This problem is further complicated by certain of our everyday notions about sexuality, in particular ideas regarding sexual privacy, the innocence of children and sex as a powerful drive. Our sexual experiences not only take place in private settings but are also rarely talked about outside them, are not made topics for public conversation and are therefore not available for discussion in the formal school context. For example, a teacher might use selected items of personal experience arising from a summer spent in France to illustrate a point in a French or geography class, but is unlikely to utilize personal sexual experience acquired at the same time to raise questions about cultural variations in sexual mores and practices. Here the more general reluctance to discuss sexual matters is compounded by the nature of adult–child and teacher–pupil relationships. The debarring of children from sexual discourse creates problems in initiating them into it, especially within the authority structure of the school, where both teachers and pupils are vulnerable to sanction. Add to this the popular conception of sex as a powerful urge that needs to be curbed and the fear that adolescents might go 'too far' and it is not surprising that teachers play safe, that sex education does not, in practice, involve a restructuring of school knowledge. Instead it is reduced to imparting 'facts' within a 'de-eroticized instructional repertoire' (Gagnon and Simon, 1974: 112).

Further limitations of the scope of sex education arise from the ways in which it is located within the school curriculum. Two alternatives exist: either to teach it within a pre-existing school subject, such as biology, religious education, physical education or social studies, or to set it apart as a special event outside the normal school routine. If the first option is taken it will increase the likelihood of content being dictated by the 'objectivist view of knowledge', where 'it is assumed that zones of knowledge are objects which can be considered to have meaning other than in the minds of the individuals in which they are constituted' (Esland, 1971: 75).

In schools such zones of knowledge, the various 'subjects', are considered to have definite boundaries determining the limits of what is relevant within them, and these criteria of relevance will affect what is taught as sex education. If it is subsumed under biology (the most frequent choice), it will be limited to the anatomy and physiology of sexual differentiation, conception and birth. If relegated to the relative backwaters of RE, PE or social studies it is likely to be dealt with in terms of morality, health or family structure. Nowhere is it likely to be related to the experience of the recipients.

The 'special event' tactic may avoid the limits imposed by subject boundaries, but is apt to create its own difficulties. The very fact that it is taught outside the routine curriculum emphasizes the slightly risqué nature of the enterprise. It is likely to precipitate much speculation, joking and giggling among the pupils regarding the forthcoming entertainment, it having been defined in advance by the school as something unusual and rather clandestine. This is heightened by the common ritual of sending letters to parents asking their permission to subject their children to sex education, a practice resulting from the school authorities' anxiety regarding the presentation of sexual knowledge where it cannot be justified as a necessary aspect of 'subject' knowledge.[4]

The same fear of causing offense is likely to ensure that the occasion does not live up to pupils' expectations, that the information they receive will be very limited. The most conservative of sexual attitudes are usually taken into consideration in deciding on the form that such sex education is to take. It often means yet again that it is reduced to the common denominator of reproductive biology, perhaps accompanied by some moralizing on the virtues of marriage and the risk of disease to those who indulge outside marriage. It is interesting to note that the most commonly used outside speakers in Harris's (1974) sample of schools were doctors and officials from the Public Health Department!

These constraints may also be partly responsible for the extremely erratic nature of school sex education. The picture built up by Harris from the replies to his questionnaires indicates a rather haphazard approach, with responsibility for the subject being left with individual teachers (mostly biology and RE teachers), apart from occasional visits from the above mentioned 'experts' (Harris, 1974). My own research also indicates the lack of planned, coherent sex education programmes. I found, for example, that girls attending the same school reported very different experiences. One girl commented positively on the open discussion on sexual matters conducted by a teacher who, she said, was willing to discuss 'literally anything'; yet two girls then in the fifth form of the same secondary modern school (which the other had just left) complained that they had only had a film explaining the mechanics of conception. The headmaster of a grammar school in which I conducted some interviews told me that he left the subject to the discretion of individual teachers (which, to do him justice, he recognized was not the best solution). In yet other schools only those who took some form of biology to 'O' level or CSE received any sexual information from the school. None of the girls had experience of anything like a consistent, continuous sex education programme. For most it had been passed over quickly in a biology lesson or through one or two films.

It is not surprising, then, that the school proves to be an inadequate source of sexual information and that most learning takes place in conversations with friends. 'The continued advantage of peer groups as sources of sex education is that they can do what very few schools can even begin to do – relate sexual learning to sexual experience' (Gagnon and Simon, 1974: 117). For girls, however, this method of learning is limited by the lack of certain vital information regarding their own sexual response. School sex education is inadequate for both sexes, but is particularly misleading regarding female sexuality and is therefore less potentially meaningful for girls. The factual information given in schools is open to reinterpretation in the male peer group as in some sense related to male sexual experience. Girls, on the other hand, are usually given not simply no information about their own sexuality, but *wrong* information which, when reshaped in informal settings, is likely to lead them to false conclusions. This misinformation results from the way in which the content of sex education is defined and the sexist bias implicit or explicit in it, plus the lack of reliable alternative sources of information for most girls.

Sexist bias in the content of school sex education

I have argued that an over-cautious approach to the teaching of sex education often leads to it consisting of little more than an outline of reproductive biology. In effect the two are considered synonymous, with any additional information being regarded as an optional extra. This definition of what sex education *is* means that what adolescents are deemed to need to know are the facts of conception and reproduction, and this premise is rarely challenged. But is most of this information that vital? It is obviously important to be aware of the fact that coition is likely to lead to pregnancy unless adequate precautions are taken, but the way in which the biological facts are presented is often misleading even on this simple level; it tends to include information that is superfluous to the immediate needs of children and adolescents and to exclude information that might be more useful. The more usual explanations present sexual intercourse as a small part of a larger sequence of biological events in which much greater emphasis is placed on the functioning of the internal processes – the meeting of egg and sperm and implantation of the fertilized egg – than on what is actually subjectively experienced by the individual during this act.

> The most typical imagery is that of the noble sperm heroically swimming upstream to fulfil its destiny by meeting and fertilizing the egg. The sexual act is described in ways that either misrepresent or totally obscure the sources of pleasure and meaning in sex. (Gagnon and Simon, 1974: 112)

This type of imagery hardly relates to the sexual feelings and experiences of adolescents and, moreover, presents female sexual and reproductive functioning as an entirely passive experience. The egg can never be heroic – it just waits around for the sperm. (Even babies, apparently, sometimes just 'come out' of their own volition, again obscuring the strength of women's bodies which are often seen merely as receptacles for the man's penis and the growing baby.) The processes of fertilization, foetal development and birth all have their fascination, but what young people would seem to be more interested in is coming to terms with their sexuality, and reproductive biology offers little help with this.

> Few of the problems young people have with managing their own sexuality ... derive directly from a lack of knowledge of the biological processes involved. The

fact that whole societies have survived in ignorance of the technical biological facts ... suggests a different order of priorities in defining the content of sex education. (Gagnon and Simon, 1974: 112)

As long as sex education is defined as it is, its content is unlikely to change radically. As conventionally taught it has little to do with *sexuality* but is confined purely to *sex*. This distinction is not merely a play on words, for sexuality involves a great deal more than biological sex, it is concerned with feelings, experiences, values and, above all, relationships.

Not only is sexuality usually reduced to biological sex, but to facts related only to reproductive sex. In the first place, this can be misleading. One of the few handbooks for teachers on the subject includes lesson plans for use with children aged 10 to 12 offering the following information: 'The penis, as you know, is for getting rid of liquid waste, but it has another use when a man is married: it is used for fertilizing eggs' (Dawkins, 1967: 47). Quite how this is supposed to relate to the pubescent boy on the verge of the discovery of his orgasm, the book does not say, but it does hint that there might be something more to it. 'Sexual intercourse is a very special way in which husbands and wives show their love for one another' (Dawkins, 1967: 48). This act, however, is described as an entirely mechanical operation, followed by a description of fertilization which makes it clear that this is its real purpose.

A second and more lasting consequence of this approach is the lack of information girls can glean about their own sexual response. Since 'sex' is equated with intercourse (even adult sex manuals call anything else 'foreplay'), boys cannot help but correctly identify the penis as their chief sexual organ; but the clitoris rarely receives a mention and is usually absent from diagrams of 'sexual' organs in educational books and films, since what they are really illustrating are reproductive organs. The textbook quoted above tells girls that they should know the correct terms for such organs as the ovaries, the uterus, the vagina and so on, but fails to mention the clitoris here or in the sections of the book where sex education for older children is dealt with. In the latter context the author follows the liberal line on masturbation, saying that 'masturbation should always be discussed with boys' and justifying this by reference to avoiding 'guilt' over a 'natural' process. But masturbation 'is far less common in girls and need not be discussed'. Girls are, however, entitled to be told, although only if they ask, that it will do them no harm (Dawkins, 1967: 71).

This is a common pattern in more liberal forms of sex education. Male masturbation, since it can be explained in terms of biological imperatives, as the result of a build-up of excess sperm, is thought worthy of mention, female masturbation is not. Male orgasm, too, is usually covered since it is necessary for conception, the female orgasm is not. Thus the female sexual organ, orgasm and masturbation are all defined as irrelevant.

The tendency to equate sex education with reproductive biology thus leads automatically to a form of sexism whereby information regarding the female sexual response is omitted. Ironically this form of sex education is considered more relevant to girls in keeping with the definition of them as future wives and mothers. Among Schofield's sample, 86 per cent of the girls but only 47 per cent of the boys had received some form of sex education in school (Schofield, 1965). Yet girls, unlike boys, often remain in ignorance of the means of deriving pleasure from their own bodies, for they are offered only knowledge concerning their reproductive rather than erotic potential.

One reason why sexual pleasure and the means of producing it are ruled out of sex education is that educators are fighting a rearguard action against those right-wing extremists who fear that youth is being corrupted by exposure to sexual information. But young people discover for themselves that sex is supposed to be pleasurable, and the reproductive focus of sex education may mislead girls into assuming that full intercourse is the ultimate source of such pleasure. This could conceivably lead them to taste the forbidden fruit where more accurate knowledge might be more of a deterrent. Perhaps nature, in endowing women with separate sexual and reproductive organs, has provided us with a means of contraception. If one of the reasons for giving sex education to girls is to prevent unwanted pregnancies, should it not be seen as relevant to inform them of their own sexual potential and that full sexual pleasure is not dependent on engaging in the act of coitus?

The traditional emphasis on reproduction is not only sexist but hetero-sexist, perpetuating the assumption that homosexual relationships are in some way unnatural. Homosexuality is, not surprisingly, rarely discussed, and if it is, it is likely to be dismissed as a sickness or as a passing phase of sexual development. For example, the guidelines on sex education provided by Newcastle education authorities, far more liberal and comprehensive than most, include in their list of topics which should be discussed 'sexual perversion' (Harris, 1974). This attitude will not help any young people experiencing feelings of attraction to their own sex, nor will it make them any less negative in their attitudes towards homosexual and lesbian members of society. If sex were portrayed instead as a pleasurable activity, as a way of relating to people rather than a means of reproducing, homosexuality as well as female sexuality could be viewed more positively.

The reproductive bias tends also to perpetuate the idea that males are inherently more sexual than females, that women and girls are sexually passive. This occurs not only through the 'noble sperm' imagery and the exclusion from discussion of female orgasm and masturbation, but also through the language used to described sexual acts. Coitus is usually described as 'penetration' or the 'insertion' of the penis into the vagina. As with the egg and sperm the female body is portrayed as passive and the male as active.

Even if sex education confines itself to 'the facts' it tends to be sexist in the way such facts are selected and presented. Attempts to go beyond this, to discuss sexual feelings and relationships, may often compound rather than resolve the problem. If teachers seek guidance on how to approach such topics they may well turn to books intended for the purpose. Most of those offering help to teachers, however, tend to overemphasize the differences between the sexes and incorporate many unfounded sexist assumptions. For example, one such 'expert' stresses the need for boys to understand female sexuality in the following terms:

> It is not always easy for a man ... to understand her (often unconscious) desire for pregnancy as a result of intercourse when to him the physical relief of tension is the more important aspect. (Schill, 1971)

Another, arguing for beginning sex education before puberty, says:

> ... it is especially important for boys to know the further implications of the woman's role in sex and how it is linked with homemaking and motherhood and her whole emotional life before their own sex drive becomes too persistent. (Lennhoff, 1971)

The latter author recommends, as a book to be made available to adolescents, Barnes' *He and She*, which has the following gem of wisdom to offer: 'until she is married and deeply roused by all that marriage means, the desire for sexual intercourse is not very strong in a girl' (Barnes, 1958: 155).

It would be possible to provide an almost endless string of similar quotes pontificating on the differences between the sexes and stressing the greater urgency of male sexual desire. If teachers rely on such literature in their attempts to explore the area of sexual feelings they are likely to add to the misconceptions drawn from reproductive biology. If, as is often the case, such feelings are discussed primarily in relation to marriage, the problem will be further compounded by inhibiting any discussion of alternative means of sexual expression. The content of sex education will then be firmly related to the traditional feminine role.

Girls' experience of sex education

I have argued that school sex education is both sexist and heterosexist, bears little relation to girls' sexual feelings and experiences and offers them little help in managing their sexuality. But what do girls themselves think of the sex education they have received? Here are a selection of comments made by those I interviewed:

> We had a lesson showing you how you get pregnant and how a baby's born – that was all. Only films where you see, you know, sort of a picture of a matchstick man here and a matchstick woman there.

> It was always something talked about after marriage, there was never any doubt

about that. You get married, then you have sex, then you have a baby, and that was how it was done.

I think it's wrong to stop it when they did stop it. We had it in the third year, we had films and all sorts of things about it and they stopped it then and I think the teachers were a bit embarrassed to go on into the upper school. I knew most of it, because it was in the third year which would make us, what, 13, and so I knew already.

We haven't had any apart from straight biology. I think they should start with a lot of the emotional sex as well as the straight physical.

Not very helpful.

A bit off-putting.

Boring.

It is clear that these girls were far from satisfied. Many of these comments were echoed throughout the interviews, showing a degree of consensus about the failings of sex education. Most girls had experience of the standard sex-as-reproduction approach; only one mentioned information regarding contraception and only one reported discussion of attitudes and feelings.

The most frequent criticism was that sex education had been given too late. Most had received it in the third or fourth forms and since it consisted mainly of reproductive biology it told them little that they did not already know. Most had learnt 'the facts of life' between the ages of 9 and 12 and some much earlier. They felt, on the whole, that sex education should occur in junior school or in the first year of secondary school. Another frequent complaint was that too much emphasis was placed on biology, that it was rather clinical and did not seem to relate to their feelings. None of them received any advice from either parents or teachers which could help them link facts with emotions and experiences and they felt that friends and older sisters were more helpful.

Despite the varied sources from which the girls had found out about sex, all had initially learnt of it in terms of reproduction, as where babies come from. This in itself seemed to be related to an initial negative response to this knowledge, sex being seen as something rather unpleasant but necessary, as a means to an end. If teaching sex education in schools is meant to reduce the traumas caused by insufficient information about sex or erroneous ideas about it, this should be kept in mind. The reproductive focus is itself calculated to make children think of sexual activity as rather odd and perhaps unwholesome. One girl, who linked her feelings directly to having learnt in this way, described her reactions as follows: 'I was a bit confused, I couldn't quite fathom it. It seemed a bit, well, peculiar, a dreadful thing to do.'

There were, however, few complaints about not receiving enough information. Like the educators, these girls, for the most part, saw sex education as a finite body of knowledge consisting of the awareness of the link between sex and reproduction. They would have welcomed more information on contraception (to help them break this link) and a more sensitive handling of the subject which related more to their own feelings, but they did not think there was much else to know. The usual response to my questions as to whether they thought they knew enough about sexuality can be summed up by one girl's response: 'I know enough not to fall pregnant'.

On the whole they expected sex, as intercourse, to be a pleasurable, unproblematic experience, as simply 'doing what comes naturally'.

The knowledge gap

The most frequently discussed area of ignorance among adolescents, and the only one identified by my subjects, is contraception. Most of the girls had some knowledge of methods of contraception, although I could not be sure that they knew where to obtain them or how to use them. But contraception is a subject on which there is considerable public debate and all girls, whatever their specific knowledge, were aware that it existed. If they did not know a great deal of detail about the subject they at least knew that they did not know, and awareness of ignorance does at least create the possibility of rectifying it.

Total ignorance, lack of awareness that one is ignorant, is more difficult to remedy, since those in such a position cannot ask for help. On the subject of female sexual response and orgasm, ignorance was almost total. The reason why girls did not comment on this gap in their sex education was that they were unaware that such knowledge existed and therefore could not know that they had been deprived of it.[5] Only two girls knew of the existence of the clitoris and had experience of orgasm and both these were in some sense exceptional. The first had been involved in a relationship with an older man who had explained (and obviously demonstrated) the function of the clitoris. The other was interested in feminism, read *Spare Rib* and found out from there. Another knew that the clitoris was 'the part of the body that turns you on' but did not know where or what it was. (She had gone to considerable trouble to find out, consulting a teacher, a dictionary and some books but with no success.) All the others, when asked which part of a woman's body was most important for her sexual pleasure either said they did not know or, more often, that it was the vagina. Certainly most had been deceived into expecting maximum pleasure from intercourse alone. (This was as true for those who admitted sexual experience as for those who did not.)

More surprising was the ignorance of the existence of the female orgasm. Apart from the first two girls cited above and one other who claimed to experience orgasm during intercourse, all were confused about the existence of a female orgasm. They had heard the word, or some colloquial equivalent, but only as it applied to men. Some had direct experience of male orgasm and ejaculation but had no idea that women had orgasms. Again, this seems to be a consequence of learning about sex as reproduction, of which male orgasm is a part, so that orgasm and ejaculation were thought to be synonymous. A similar pattern emerged regarding masturbation. More girls were aware that this was possible for women, though none admitted trying it. Most, however, thought it was purely a male activity and were surprised and, in some cases, horrified that I should ask them about it. One girl, who admitted masturbating her boyfriend to orgasm, did not know that women were capable of orgasm and, when I asked her about masturbation, said with considerable force: 'I wouldn't touch myself down there'.

It is not easy for girls to identify and remedy this gap in their knowledge, nor will they automatically develop a more positive attitude to their own sexuality solely by acquiring theoretical knowledge. But once they become aware of their deprivation in this respect, they quickly identify it with the one area of life in which they feel that considerable injustice exists in relations between the sexes: the double standard.

Conclusion

The existence of such a sense of injustice suggests the possibility of a wider awareness of sexual inequality among adolescent girls than is usually realized. If sex education could be modified to encompass a broader approach to sexuality, it could be used as a basis for a wider discussion of sex roles which might help girls to develop their potential in both sexual and non-sexual spheres of life and encourage them to step outside the restrictions of conventional femininity. But such an approach is unlikely to be developed at present, for it would involve far more than simply eradicating the more obvious forms of sexism in sex education. The constraints within the educational system cannot easily be overcome and will continue to define the limits of sex education, keeping it within the boundaries of reproduction, marriage and the family.

Notes

1 This is not simply a question of attitudes to sexuality and to children, for these are part of a wider ideology of the family that arose in conjunction with the historical process of change accompanying the rise and development of industrial capitalism.

2 *Editorial note*: this has become an issue in the context of AIDS, with sexual abstinence programmes being widely promoted as central to sex education in the USA – although this development was not mirrored in the UK (see Thomson, 1994).

3 The degree to which such problems exist will vary within and between schools according to the educational objectives pursued by the school as a whole and by individual teachers. In particular, they may well be lessened by moves towards a more 'integrated curriculum' with relatively weak 'classification' and 'framing' of educational knowledge (see Bernstein, 1971).
4 *Editorial note*: in the UK the right of parents to withdraw their children from all aspects of sex education other than those relating to reproductive biology was reinstated in 1993. This included teaching on HIV and AIDS, which was withdrawn from the National Curriculum, of which it had been a part since 1988. Guidelines issued following the 1993 Education Act instructed teachers of sex education to inform parents about 'precocious' questions or anything else which made them suspect that a pupil was at 'moral risk' (see Thomson, 1994).
5 I am not suggesting here that sexuality should be reduced to questions of organs and orgasms, merely that this is an important aspect of self-knowledge which girls seem to lack.

5   Femininity, Masculinity and Sexuality

This short polemical chapter originated as a paper presented at the Women's Research and Resources Centre Summer School which took place in Bradford in 1979. It was later published in a collection of papers from this and another feminist conference. Like the previous chapter it draws on my research with young, teenaged women and addresses the social organization of sexual knowledge. It also reflects my continued preoccupation with the denial of women's sexual autonomy and the maintenance of the myth of the vaginal orgasm. I have reproduced it here since it marks a move in the direction of a more explicit critique of heterosexuality, insofar as it addresses the ways in which heterosexuality presupposes a femininity and masculinity defined in opposition to each other. Moreover, I was beginning to think about heterosexuality in more materialist terms, with the commodification of women's sexuality being linked to their economic dependence on men.

As with the previous chapter, the conceptual language derives from the time in which it was written, with the emphasis on ideology rather than discourse. We are now more accustomed to talking about 'difference' than the term I use here, 'differentness' – although I think that the latter has something to recommend it. We would now expect this issue to be discussed in the language of deconstruction, with the emphasis on questioning binaries. Finally, no-one would now rely on notions of 'stereotyping', aware as we are of the ways in which all categories are products of discourse and necessarily constituted in relation to each other. Yet, precisely because it is a product of its time, and of ideas then being debated among feminists, it is worth revisiting. It should be remembered that, even before we imported the conceptual vocabulary of 'French Theory', feminists were already discussing gender categories as necessarily constituted in relation to each other and sexual knowledge as socially constructed.[1]

Having said this, one reason why I could get no further with these ideas at the time was the lack of a conceptual framework which might have enabled me to think more rigorously about the ways in which femininity and masculinity were constructed in relation to heterosexuality. Moreover, I was still finding it difficult to escape from the residual essentialism entailed in thinking of women's sexuality as capable of being liberated from the bonds of patriarchal ideology. In these respects some real theoretical advances have been made since this was written.

My intention in this chapter is to look at some ideological aspects of femininity and masculinity as manifested in the sexual sphere. I will concentrate on two areas: first, the organization and distribution of sexual knowledge and, second, ideas about the 'differentness' of women and men. I am not so much concerned with the process whereby men and women come to express their sexuality in different ways, as with the ideologies surrounding these differences. I will, however, say a little about the ways in which these ideologies affect our sexual learning, especially the part they play in gaining women's approval of male domination. In order to bring these ideas into sharper focus I will make use of rather extreme, polarized notions of femininity and masculinity which are, perhaps, already outdated.

The organization of sexual knowledge

I have come to believe that the organization and distribution of sexual knowledge is of crucial importance to our sexuality. There are two reasons for this: first, it serves to define sexuality in masculine terms and has denied women and girls access to vital information concerning their sexuality. Second, it disguises ideology as fact. All knowledge is socially constructed, produced within a given society under particular historical conditions and it reflects the interests and priorities of dominant groups within that society (in this context, men). But knowledge tends to appear as objective 'fact' – hence statements which are really about what ought to be come disguised as what *is*.

Now what sex *is* in conventional terms, is heterosexual intercourse. Equating sex with one particular type of sexual act means that any other form of sexual activity is automatically defined as a perversion, as second best, or as leading up to the 'real thing'. These labels then assume the appearance of factual descriptions rather than reflections of values or preferences. In these supposedly 'enlightened' times, women's sexual functioning is given some recognition and some concessions are made to it. But take a look at the average sex manual and you will find that everything intended to turn us on is called 'foreplay'. The 'real thing' is still copulation, even if we are now expected to have orgasms and are entitled to get on top once in a while, and to have a little clitoral stimulation thrown in as an optional extra.

All the evidence confirms what we know from our own experience and that of our sisters: that many women find sexual intercourse emotionally or psychologically satisfying, but few of us find it totally physically satisfying. Part of the reason we enjoy it, if and when we do, is because men do – a kind of vicarious pleasure. While not denying that enjoyment of turning on your partner is part of what sexual relationships are all about, we need to question the way in which sexual intercourse is seen as the end point, the final and culminating act in any sexual encounter.

Sexuality is defined in these masculine terms partly because it is defined in reproductive terms. This is how we learn about it: as the 'facts of life'. In learning this way, the average boy cannot help but notice that the penis is his chief sexual organ, whereas amid all the information about penises and vaginas, eggs and sperm, or in the more vague versions of 'where babies come from', it is unlikely that girls will even hear the clitoris mentioned, let alone learn of its function. What passes as sex education is, in fact, education about reproduction rather than sex and rarely about sexuality in its broader sense (see Chapter 4). Most of us learn, either at the same time as we are assimilating these facts about reproduction or later, that sex is supposed to be pleasurable. Since sex has been predefined for us as coitus, it is assumed that the ultimate in pleasure must derive from this act. How many of us during adolescence enjoyed petting, expected the 'real thing' to be even better and were disappointed when it was not?

Of course, it may be just coincidence that the emphasis on reproduction leads us to view as the 'real thing' something that is more pleasurable for men than for women – but I doubt it. If men happened to have separate sexual and reproductive organs, I'm sure we would all know about it. The present structuring of sexual knowledge is, after all, the product of a male dominated society. Often in the past this has been legitimated by equating women's sexual desire with a sort of reproductive urge, and it is no coincidence that the link between this form of sexual activity and reproduction is part of a system that denies us control over our own bodies. Another aspect of the way in which sexual knowledge is organized is the language used to depict the 'sexual act'. Terms such as penetration or the insertion of the penis into the vagina give the impression of male activity and female passivity. Hence 'factual' descriptions contain within them ideological assumptions.

When interviewing teenage girls as part of my research I was struck by the way in which they discussed sexual encounters in terms of what was done to them. They talked of themselves as passive objects (except insofar as they referred to what they 'let' boys do) and I recalled that I and my friends had once done the same. It is sometimes suggested that this way of talking about sexuality has little to do with the way people really think and act, that it is 'just a manner of speaking'. But language is not merely a tool we use to express ourselves, it also shapes the way we think, which in turn affects our actions.

The ideology of male dominance, then, is expressed in the organization of sexual knowledge through the selection of a particular set of 'facts' which constitute what is taken to be sexual knowledge, and by the language through which these 'facts' are made available. What emerges from this could be summed up by the following equation: sex = coitus = something men do to women. This definition of what sex is illustrates the extent to which coercion is an inbuilt element of current sexual arrangements.

This definition of sex conditions what we learn about sexuality, and how we learn it. Most of us first encounter sexual knowledge in a male defined, reproductively-focused form. This has two consequences, one relatively short-term and one longer-term or even permanent. First, learning of sex as a means to an end may in part explain why so many of the girls I talked to reacted negatively to their first awareness of the sexual, expressing shock and revulsion – feelings that might be heightened if they were also being given the impression that this was something that would be done to them. Somehow most girls eventually overcome these negative attitudes. This change, however, by no means implies a move towards self-defined sexuality, but rather an accommodation to conventional sexuality involving the assumption that sexual intercourse is the key to erotic pleasure. This leads on to the second consequence of learning about sexuality in this way: that it makes it difficult for girls and women to gain access to information about their own sexuality. Almost all of the girls I interviewed were totally ignorant of the existence of the clitoris and the nature of the female orgasm – most did not even know it was possible for women to have orgasms (see Chapter 4).

Although knowledge of our own sexuality is important if we are to control our own bodies and be self-determining in our sexual relationships, knowledge alone is not enough. The women whose experiences are recorded in *The Hite Report* were, on the whole, well informed about female sexuality and knew how to gain pleasure from their own bodies. Most, however, found it difficult to put such knowledge into practice in their relationships with men (Hite, 1976). Even given knowledge of our own sexuality, we do not enter heterosexual relationships on equal terms with our partners. Men's definitions of what sex entails are the conventional and accepted ones, so if we attempt to restructure the sequence of events in a sexual encounter, to give precedence to acts other than sexual intercourse, we are challenging not just ideas of how sex ought to be, but how it is. This makes us vulnerable to a variety of derogatory labels; we may be called perverted, frigid, or be categorized as cock-teasers. If we have come to accept (for whatever reason) that we ought to be deferential towards men, that we should minister to their fragile egos, then our difficulties are compounded.

Traditional ideas about the 'differentness' of men and women come into play here. This also plays a large part in our sexual learning: along with the facts we learn that men 'need' sex more, that they are more easily aroused and less in control of themselves than women are, and that they are more easily satisfied. However much women know that these ideas are myths, they still seem to affect the ability of many of us to make demands on male sexual partners. The idea of differentness also acts as a barrier to those women who remain in ignorance of the 'mechanics' of female sexuality, preventing them from asking what is wrong and working towards discovering their sexual potential. The idea that women's orgasm is more 'diffuse' than that of men is still around. It would not be surprising if many women do not know whether or not they experience orgasm since what we are supposed to feel is often explained in romantic rather than physical terms. If sex turns out not to be as great as we expected, we can always fall back on the idea that it is not the same for us, that we've always 'known' that men enjoy it more – without thinking that if it was organized differently we might enjoy it too.

Maybe we should also try to challenge the whole notion of goal-oriented, orgasm-as-end-point sexuality – but it is not easy to persuade the average man that love-making doesn't have to involve genitals and orgasms.

The ideology of differentness

Ideas about the differentness of women and men are not only incorporated into what counts as sexual knowledge, but form part of a more explicit ideology. In the sexual sphere this ideology provides a major means of justifying sexual apartheid: the 'vive la différence' lobby, the notion that sexual attraction itself depends on women and men behaving as two separate species. The ways in which boundaries are drawn between feminine and masculine attributes serve to illustrate both the fact of women's subordination and the manner in which it is legitimated.

One aspect of this ideology is the parallel that may be drawn between stereotypes of women and stereotypes of children (which are oppressive to both). Stereotypes tend to polarize into dichotomies: masculine/feminine, adult/childlike. What is adult is often equated with what is masculine, and that which is childlike with that which is feminine. An example of this is provided by a study of American clinicians' assessment of indicators of mental health (Broverman et al., 1970). Their depiction of the 'normal healthy adult' proved to be almost identical with that of the 'normal healthy man' while the characteristics of the 'normal healthy woman' were virtually the opposite. Women, in order to be characterized as 'healthy', should be dependent, emotional, vulnerable, childlike creatures.

If normal, adult humanness is by definition male, then, given our cultural tendency to think in opposites, the female of the species is not quite normal, not quite adult, and not quite human. Conceptions of maturity are gender bound: there is a contradiction between the requirements of maturity per se and those of mature womanhood. The attainment of the latter would seem to be dependent upon retaining certain childlike attributes in order to progress from being a girl child to become a feminine child-woman. This is an obvious ideological reflection of women's material dependence in the form of a psychological dependence which we are supposed to share with that archetypal dependent: the child. Just as children are deemed to be in need of adult protection, so are we – where adult = male.

This may well be the basis for the commonplace observation that girls mature earlier than boys. Possibly girls have less to mature into, that maturity for them is little more than a superficial gloss on existing childlike attributes. This seems to be the implication of the upper-class myth of the finishing school, wherein the gawky schoolgirl is transformed almost over-night into a sophisticated 'young lady' by virtue of a few lessons in dress and deportment. This superficial gloss on childishness has much to do with sexuality or, more specifically, with what passes as sexual attractiveness. Signs that a girl is 'growing up' tend to be bound up with her interest in, and ability to attract, the opposite sex: not for her such characteristics as independence and self-determination which indicate 'normal' (male) maturity. In presenting herself as sexually desirable, a girl may well find that certain childlike attributes such as 'cuteness' are useful in gaining attention and approval. Of course, only young women can play this game successfully.

Other aspects of the feminine/masculine dichotomy are also bound up with notions of sexual attractiveness. I have said that the 'vive la différence' idea rests on the assumption that heterosexual attraction depends on these oppositions. More specifically, it is believed that what makes women attractive is their differentness, their mysteriousness. This may be important in gaining women's support for the feminine ideal. If, for many women, both economic survival and a positive self-image depend on nailing your man, then this notion of femininity becomes an ideal to be aimed for, thus encouraging women to collude in maintaining images of womanhood which are part of their oppression.

Those men who eulogize femininity, its differentness and mystery, imply that women are somehow both less than human and more than human. This too may serve to legitimate male dominance. If in most spheres of life one is considered less than human, it helps if one male (or, if you are successful, many) is prepared to put you on a pedestal and worship you as more than human. Shulamith Firestone (1972), in discussing love, argued that men have to put the woman they love on a pedestal in order to place her above the despised common herd of womankind. If this is the case, the idea of women as more than human may serve both to reinforce and legitimate male opinion of us as less than human. Many anti-feminist women assert that, although we may seem to be treated as inferior, really we have men just where we want them – provided, of course, that we are skilled in the use of 'feminine wiles'.

Part of the allure of femininity is sexual unattainability, which depends on women projecting themselves as attractive but not available. Here there may again be a connection between women and children. Both are seen as requiring protection from the sexual. Both, of course, are vulnerable to sexual coercion, but it is not this, but sex itself, which is seen as potentially damaging to them, as somehow degrading and defiling them. In maturing to adulthood, men are expected to become sexually active, women to become sexually attractive. To be too active would destroy the allure and mystery of femininity and the childlike 'innocence' which is paradoxically a part of it. But while children are not supposed to be sexual, women are expected to express their sexuality only within certain boundaries. We are not supposed to own our sexuality: it is something detached from us with which we can bargain with men. Here there is another reflection of the material conditions of our lives: our sexuality is the only commodity with which we may bargain for economic, social and emotional security. The relationship between women and their sexuality is expressed very well by Lorenne Clark and Debra Lewis in this passage from *Rape: The Price of Coercive Sexuality*:

> Prior to marriage, a woman's sexuality is a commodity to be held in trust for its rightful owner. Making 'free' use of one's own sexuality is like making 'free' use of someone else's money. One can act autonomously only with things that belong to oneself. Things held in trust for others are surrounded with special duties which place the trustee under strict obligations for the care and maintenance of the assets in question.... Women are not regarded as being entitled to use their sexuality according to their own desires because their sexuality is not theirs for the use of such purposes. Their duty is to preserve it in the best possible condition for the ultimate use and disposition of its rightful owner. (1977: 122)

Femininity involves a detachment from our own sexuality, conveying the impression that it is something precious which we might offer to some man who is willing to pay the appropriate price. This was another common theme emerging from my interviews with teenage girls. Not only did they tend to describe sexual acts in terms of what was done to them, but also referred to sex itself as something they 'gave' in exchange for something else. The girl who expressed this trustee relationship most strongly said, when describing her relationships with boys: 'They can have some of this (indicating her breasts) but not that down here – that's for the man I marry.' It was she who responded so indignantly to my question about masturbation (see Chapter 4): 'I wouldn't touch myself down there!' No one, it seems, had the right to do so except her future husband.

This degree of conformity is, no doubt, extreme, but the end point of the feminine–masculine dichotomy is our alienation and detachment from our own sexuality.

Note

1 *Editorial note*: one aspect of this, also discussed in Chapter 1, is the feminist challenge to conventional definitions of what sex *is*. I was recently confidently assured by one of my postgraduate students that feminists never challenged conventional definitions of what sex is until the arrival of queer theory on the scene. Hence it is worth underlining just how central this was to feminist thought in the 1970s .

6   The Desire for Freud: Psychoanalysis and Feminism

Like the previous chapter, this is also a polemical piece originating as a conference paper. It was subsequently published in the first issue of the radical feminist magazine Trouble & Strife *(1983). By this time, the 'cultural turn' in feminist and social theory was well under way and, as part of this trend, psychoanalysis was becoming increasingly influential. It was, of course, a new version of psychoanalysis, that influenced by the work of Jacques Lacan. Like many feminists, I became aware of this work through secondhand sources. When I wrote this, I was only just beginning to grapple with Lacan's own writings and finding them exceedingly difficult. However, it was not Lacan's own work which particularly interested me, but the uses to which feminists were putting it. I was prompted to write this critique because I was sceptical of this rehabilitation of psychoanalysis, and because I felt that the complexity of the theories being woven around it silenced criticism.*

I concentrated on a few early feminist appropriations of Lacan precisely because many of these had been written in order to explain new psychoanalytic thinking to other feminists and to convert them to the faith. There are some obvious omissions, however. While I had encountered Gallop's (1982) work, I was at the time unaware of the collection of Lacan's writings edited by Juliet Mitchell and Jacqueline Rose – and published in the same year. Had I read their very useful introductions, my account of Lacan might have been improved. Nonetheless, my overview, while very basic, does serve as a simple introduction to Lacan's ideas and their impact on feminism – and I would still stand by my critique, even if I might now couch it in more sophisticated terms.

It is no longer possible for those of us who reject psychoanalysis to ignore it. It has gained too strong a hold to be easily dismissed. In the early days of the Women's Liberation movement, Freud's theories were rejected, but new 'readings' of his work have gained many adherents among feminists today. I remain sceptical and I want to show that, despite the great claims made for it, the new brand of psychoanalysis has nothing to offer feminists. The new interpretation is written in such complex, difficult language that the rest of us are barred from entering the debate. Thus those who promote the 'new readings' escape criticism. I have tried to explain their ideas clearly and simply in order to reveal the unproven and unprovable assumptions on which psychoanalysis rests, to expose explanations that rely more on faith than fact. I draw mainly on Juliet Mitchell's *Psychoanalysis and Feminism* published in 1975, and on the work of Rosalind Coward and her associates (Coward, 1978; Coward and Ellis, 1977; Coward et al., 1976).[1]

The 'new readings' are said to be 'anti-essentialist', that is, to make no assumptions about biological differences between the sexes or biologically based sexual drives. This is important since an essentialist approach effectively denies the possibility of change. However, I argue that the 'new readings' *are* essentialist, just as were the 'old readings' of Freud. These ideas are of no help at all in understanding and resisting our oppression today; the 'new' and the 'old' readings are equally reactionary. It is always important for feminists to understand ideas that seek to 'explain' female subordination as 'natural' or as unchanging and unchangeable.

Deferring to Freud

In debates around sexuality, psychoanalysis is often treated as if it were the only possible way of explaining things. The failure of traditional academic disciplines and established bodies of theory to produce an adequate theory of sexuality is taken as sufficient justification for the reliance on psycho-analytic explanations. Even those who are critical of psychoanalysis and opposed to its being used as an explanation for the persistence of patriarchy frequently display considerable deference towards it. There is a tendency to assume that any aspect of women's experience, especially sexual experi-ence, that is not immediately explicable by any other means must come within the realm of psychoanalysis, that psychoanalysis provides a key for decoding mysteries which would otherwise remain unfathomable.

An example of this deference is provided by Michèle Barrett (1980). Having made some telling criticisms of psychoanalysis, she falls back on it as soon as she encounters an aspect of women's subjective experience which she believes not to coincide with objective fact. Discussing Masters and Johnson's insistence that all female orgasms are clitorally centred, she says that this: '... did not tally with many women's lived experience of inter-course'. She goes on: 'It is at this point that Freud's account may be useful, precisely in demarcating the psychic processes that underlie the pleasure of this experience' (Barrett, 1980: 66). Even supposing she is right in saying that what women feel does not match with the known facts – which I would dispute – why should she suggest, even tentatively, that Freudianism can explain it? In particular, why is this the only possible explanation she considers? I would agree with her that we need 'an understanding of sexuality in terms of meanings, definitions, the discourse of pleasure in relation to our knowledge of the technical processes involved in sexual activity' (1980: 66) – but this is precisely what psychoanalysis does not provide.

The original feminist gut-reaction against Freud was, I believe, justified. I do not accept that we 'read' his work incorrectly or misunderstood and misrepresented him. It is sheer arrogance to suggest, as Juliet Mitchell does, that we could only come to this negative conclusion on the basis of secondhand, popularized versions of Freud, or because we only read the bits on femininity without understanding their place in psychoanalytic theory, or simply because we thought penis envy was a silly idea (see Mitchell, 1975: xv–xvi).

We are now told that new 'readings' of Freud, specifically those deriving from the work of Jacques Lacan, have purged his work of all the elements which feminists found unsavoury, magically disposing of all its sexist elements – these were in any case products of our misinterpretations. The 'new readings' say that we are not born feminine or masculine but are constructed as 'sexed subjects' through our acquisition of language. Language structures both consciousness and the unconscious. It is also at this 'moment' of our 'entry into language and culture' (as they put it) that 'desire' is constituted, that is, that we become sexual. Nor need we worry about penis envy any more because it's all symbolic and has nothing to do with that organ being intrinsically 'better' than anything women are endowed with. To quote Rosalind Coward, who comes closer than most to expressing these ideas in plain English:

> [A]ll reference to the anatomical superiority of the penis is removed. The phallus is the symbolic representation of the penis, not the actual organ. This is because of its role in the symbolic, the pre-existent linguistic and cultural order. (Coward, 1978: 46)

The role of this symbolic phallus is crucial for that all-important entry into language and culture. In Lacanian theory it is the 'privileged signifier' around which all 'difference' – which is taken to be the basis of language and culture – is organized. In structuralist linguistics, the filter through which Lacan reads Freud, the meaning of a word or symbol (the signifier) is not sustained by its relationship to the concept it represents (the signified), but only in relation to other words, other signifiers. That is, a word means something not merely because we know what object it refers to, but because it marks a difference from other objects. We only know what a word means by knowing what it doesn't mean. Thus language is a system of differences in that it differentiates objects, concepts and ideas from each other.

The meaning of the penis/phallus therefore has nothing to do with the physical difference between the sexes as such, but with the cultural significance which the phallus is given as the mark of *the* difference which governs entry into language and our construction as sexed subjects, that is, the difference between the sexes is fundamental to our becoming language-using social beings. In short, psychoanalysis is seen as phallocentric only because it is analysing a phallocentric, patriarchal culture. So we can forgive Freud his occasional misogynist lapses since basically, it is claimed, he was right.

I remain unconvinced. One problem concerns the status of this reading of Freud. Lacan is seen as offering the 'correct' reading of Freud, the key to what Freud's writings really mean. Writers on psychoanalysis treat Freud and Lacan as if they were saying the same thing. Lacan's own position appears to be that Freud anticipated the insights of structural linguistics.

> Freud could not take into account this notion which postdates him, but I would claim that Freud's discovery stands out precisely because, although it sets out from a domain in which one would not expect to recognize its reign, it could not fail to anticipate its formulas. Conversely, it is Freud's discovery that gives to the signifier/signified division the full extent of its implications: namely, that the signifier has an active function in determining certain effects in which the signifiable appears as submitting to its mark. (Lacan, *Écrits*, quoted in Coward and Ellis, 1977: 95–6)

Lacan's obscure writings are thus taken as revealing what Freud really meant and, therefore, anyone who 'reads' Freud literally has got it all wrong.

It seems to me, however, that Freud said what he meant and meant what he said. That is to say, I hold the unfashionable view that the literal reading of Freud is the correct one and that the insights claimed for Freud by the Lacanians are often little more than wishful thinking. What Freud was concerned with was children's responses to their discovery of physical differences between the sexes. Briefly, he argues that a boy, seeing that girls lack a penis, thinks they have been castrated and fears that this will happen to him as punishment for desiring his mother and his rivalry with his father. This leads him to resolve his oedipal complex (his desire for his mother and hatred of his father) by giving up his desire for his mother. A girl, on the other hand, seeing the penis, is overcome with envy, feels she is castrated, blames her mother for this condition and therefore turns away from her mother towards her father.

The tension between biological and cultural determination of human sexuality evident in Freud's writings is more often resolved in favour of the biological than his recent apologists seem willing to admit. There are, however, more fundamental problems which are not attributable to the misogynist bias of Freud but which are intrinsic to psychoanalysis, its status as 'knowledge', its assumptions, its methodology. It is these problems which I wish to address.

The first line of defence: discrediting the opposition

The difficulty of these modern psychoanalytic writings is widely acknowledged. The style is tortuous, the vocabulary esoteric and the concepts slippery. The unwillingness or inability of the proponents of psychoanalysis to translate their ideas into terms which the uninitiated can comprehend has been rightly damned as elitist. It makes these writers relatively immune from criticism from outsiders and this, I think, accounts for much of the deference towards psychoanalysis. How can we presume to criticize something we don't understand? Those working within this framework can smugly reassure themselves that if the rest of us have doubts it is only because of our ignorance. Juliet Mitchell's work, being less directly influenced by Lacan than many of the other writers of this genre, is more comprehensible.[2] She makes up for this by constantly implying that if we reject Freud it is because we are too stupid to see the Great Truths that he has uncovered. The whole tone of *Psychoanalysis and Feminism* (1975) is arrogant and condescending.

Faced with either incomprehensibility or condescension, our confidence is undermined and we are denied the possibility of assessing what, if anything, psychoanalysis has to offer. I admit to being as confused as anyone else when it comes to unravelling the complexities of this brand of theory. I am aware that I am laying myself open to the charge that I am misrepresenting it, aware that I may have missed some vital points or misunderstood essential steps in the argument. But I have yet to read anything that persuades me that my doubts about psychoanalysis and its relevance to feminism are unfounded and I know that others share these doubts. I believe that we must resist being cowed into silence by elitist mystifications.

This is all the more important since what psychoanalysis purports to offer us is an explanation of our 'lived experience' as women. We need, therefore, to challenge the strategies which prevent us from testing it against that experience. These are not all reducible to the inarticulateness of its supporters for they have a second line of defence.

The second line of defence: the mysteries of the unconscious

Any criticism of psychoanalysis we might offer, on the basis of any data or experience, is subject to the instant rebuttal: 'ah, but in the unconscious ...'. Juliet Mitchell repeatedly asserts the need for us to understand the nature of the unconscious, for without such understanding Freud makes no sense. She constantly chastises his critics for claiming to dispute specific points when, in reality, they are rejecting the whole idea of the unconscious. She makes such a rejection sound like a neurosis. I am willing to admit, quite openly, that I suffer from this sickness. I cannot be convinced, by Mitchell or anyone else, that we are dealing with a body of irrefutable fact concerning the unconscious. I submit that we are merely being asked to have faith – whatever she says to the contrary.

I am not denying the existence of any psychic processes beyond our consciousness. What I do contest is that the non-conscious mind is knowable in the systematic fashion claimed by psychoanalysis and that everyone's unconscious is subject to similar processes and contains similar repressed wishes or drives. By definition it is not knowable by the conscious mind: it is claimed that it can only be made available through analysis, through the piecing together of dreams, slips of speech and so on. Analysis is a highly intuitive process. The results of such intuition can hardly be taken as objective fact. Analysts' conclusions on the construction of gender and sexuality cannot but be affected by patriarchal culture and frames of reference drawn from it. Moreover, the method of psychoanalysis is to work back from the present to the past. It is self-evident that, as Mitchell says, each of us has a past which exists in our present. But the danger is that in reconstructing the past we mould it to fit the present. This is made worse by the fact that psychoanalysis rests on a closed system of circular reasoning. Everything is interpreted so that it fits in with the dogma already laid down by Freud. Yet we are expected to accept on faith all the theorizing that rests upon these presuppositions about the unconscious. Much of this theorizing, in any case, seems to be based on pure speculation with no reference even to the dubious evidence of analysis.

It is these 'discoveries' about the nature of the unconscious which are supposed to provide the radical thrust to psychoanalysis. It is held to be the means by which 'the process of the construction of the subject in relation to social relations becomes available to scientific analysis' (Coward and Ellis, 1977: 94). Not only am I unconvinced as to the 'scientific' status of this enterprise, but I fail to see why you need to believe in the unconscious to see that our 'subjectivity', our sense of ourselves, is built up through a particular language and culture, in relation to specific social relations.

It is further claimed that Lacanian psychoanalysis in particular makes a radical break with 'the notion of the "wholeness" of identity and consciousness' (Coward and Ellis, 1977: 121). The argument appears to be that, without these preconceptions as to the nature of the unconscious, we cannot account for the complexities and contradictions of our subjectivity. While it may be true that many social scientific formulations are guilty of assuming 'a unified subject of self consciousness' (Coward and Ellis, 1977: 121), there are no grounds for asserting that this is an automatic consequence of failure to accept the psychoanalytic theory of the unconscious. Of course we are complex, contradictory and inconsistent beings; we are, after all, products of complex, contradictory and inconsistent experience. We do not need any assumptions about the unconscious to account for the lack of a unified 'self'.

Just as these general conclusions on the effect of culture on our 'subjectivity' and the nature of the 'subjectivity' so constructed could be arrived at without any preconceptions as to the nature of the unconscious, so could many of the more specific conclusions yielded by psychoanalytic theories. For example, Toril Moi, in an article on sexual jealousy, after meandering through the usual Freudian arguments that jealous women are normally depressive, concludes:

> Feelings of loss and wounded self-esteem are conducive to depression. In order to be respected and esteemed, women in patriarchal society must demonstrate that

they can catch and keep a man. To lose one's lover/husband is interpreted as a blow to the woman's worth as a human being. It is easy to understand why depression should be a widespread reaction in women who discover they have a rival. (Moi, 1982: 61)

This seems a reasonable, commonsense explanation. But why did she have to jump through Freudian hoops demonstrating that female jealousy is somehow 'pre-oedipal' in order to arrive at a conclusion that most of us could have reached without the benefit of the 'insights' of psychoanalysis!

When psychoanalytic accounts yield reasonable conclusions it is in spite of, rather than because of, their assumptions about the unconscious. But these assumptions can lead to very dubious arguments, especially those based on the notion of repression – the idea that certain drives or needs are denied expression and therefore repressed. It is this which undermines the claims of many of these writers that they are dealing with the cultural construction of subjectivity, for it assumes the existence of drives which exist *outside* culture – which are presumably innate, products of biology rather than culture, and which reside in the unconscious.

An example of the sort of explanation I find dubious is this, from Mitchell (1975). She maintains that our 'amnesia' about infantile sexuality is the result of repressing wishes which our culture does not allow to be fulfilled. Along with other psychoanalysts, Mitchell seems to assume that this amnesia validates the claims made about repression and the unconscious. I am sceptical of this for two reasons. First, it presupposes that these infantile experiences are essentially, in themselves, sexual, independent of any such meaning being applied to them (except by psychoanalysts). This assertion that certain experiences are inherently sexual seems to have no foundation beyond the fact that Freud said so. I would argue that nothing is sexual unless it is subjectively defined as such; a point I will return to later. Second, most of us remember little or nothing about our earliest years. Are we to believe that all of this was repressed, that everything that happened in that phase of life comes under the heading of that which our culture does not permit? There is a perfectly simple explanation for the loss of these early memories, one which does not require any assumptions about repression or the unconscious: that we lacked the language with which to represent these experiences to ourselves.

Language, the phallus and the production of sexed subjects

The process of acquiring language has become central to psychoanalysis. It is through this process that we become social beings, that we enter culture and culture enters us, constructing us as 'sexed subjects'. This I do not see as particularly contentious and I am quite prepared to accept that language structures experience. Language is not merely a tool with which we express ideas. It shapes how we think, indeed what it is possible to think about and therefore orders the way we make sense of our experience. Psychoanalysis is far from being the only perspective within which this point is made. What is more problematic is the idea of the oedipal situation and the role of the phallus as 'primary signifier'. The notion of penis envy as such is still very much there in Mitchell's work, albeit an envy of what the penis represents rather than of the physical organ. Coward and associates place the emphasis much more on the importance of recognizing this difference as *the* difference, so that the phallus becomes the crucial symbol around which entry into language and culture is ordered. It is only after the mirror phase (in which the child differentiates itself from its environment, accomplishes a separation between self and other)[3] and the castration complex, 'that the subject can find a signifying place in language where it can represent itself adequately to the structure that already includes it.' In this process the phallus 'governs this positionality by which the subject can represent itself in language' (Coward et al., 1982: 287).

What this apparently means is that the child cannot place herself in the world specifically as a sexed subject without having taken note of this crucial difference and cannot, therefore, become a fully social, language-using human being. While male children make a positive entry into the symbolic since they 'find themselves in a relation of possession of the "symbolic function"' (Coward et. al., 1982: 287), girls enter in a negative relation, one of lacking, of not possessing the phallus, the mark of difference.

One aspect of this formulation which I find confusing is the exact relation between the constitution of the sexed subject and the learning of language, a confusion heightened by the obscure terminology they use. Coward and Ellis (1977) assert that becoming a fully language-using subject is dependent on the castration complex. It is claimed that in order to 'use' language the subject must take up 'a position in regards to meaning'. This 'positionality' is 'achieved through ... the mirror phase and the castration complex' (Coward and Ellis, 1977: 105). So it seems that language can be learned but not used prior to the oedipus complex. Presumably this means that a child cannot speak (or at least not speak properly) until s/he has been constructed as a sexed subject. If this meant merely that learning language involves being aware that one's position in the world was as a boy or a girl, then this would not be too problematic. It seems to be the case that girls do enter into culture in a negative relation, being defined in relation to the male, as not-male. What is problematic is the notion that the child cannot enter culture as a sexed subject and cannot speak until she has negotiated the castration complex: that is, has positioned herself in language and culture in terms of lacking the phallus. These processes are seen as absolutely necessary in order to enter into (patriarchal) culture.

While these explanations of our construction as sexed subjects rest on the symbolic function of the phallus rather than on envy of the penis itself, it nonetheless seems to assume an awareness of, a representation of, this real physical difference. Now it seems to me that it is quite possible for a girl to remain unaware of the existence of penises until well after she is fluent in language and has identified and placed herself as a little girl. Are we to assume that it all somehow happens 'in the head' without a child having a basis for it in experience? Surely, even the unconscious mind (as it is postulated within psychoanalytic theory) must reflect real tangible experience and not merely an abstract system of symbols? Symbols or language may order our experience, but they do not create it out of thin air. Are we to believe that children magically 'know' the phallus without ever having seen or heard of the penis?

Little girls who do not know of these physical differences and therefore cannot represent them to themselves, are not stunted asocial beings nor are they guaranteed to be unfeminine, nor do they inevitably 'fall ill' (as those who do not negotiate the proper stages of development must, according to psychoanalysis). Many other well-documented processes are occurring which allow a girl to place herself as a sexed subject – and language, of course *is* crucial to this. Psychoanalysis, however, appears to claim that all other data are false or irrelevant. More conventional studies have revealed that the processes contributing to the construction of gender and sexuality are many, varied and complex and I see no reason to discount these findings, to dismiss them as superficial and inconsequential. At least they refer to real children; psychoanalytic explanations, on the other hand, seem to rest on a theoretical construct called 'the child'.

Psychoanalysis is also very bad news for anyone attempting to rear children so that they do not grow up to be walking feminine or masculine stereotypes. We know it is difficult, but the formulations of psychoanalysis suggest that it is impossible, that the critical processes involved are way beyond our control. So we may as well encourage girls to be vulnerable, narcissistic and masochistic because that is how they will end up anyway.

Within psychoanalysis the category 'woman' is taken to be virtually universal, applying to all (patriarchal) societies. Now obviously people are constructed as 'sexed subjects' in all cultures but I doubt this happens in exactly the same way in all contexts. Mitchell maintains that while there may be variations in 'the expression of femininity', this does not fundamentally alter what it is to be a woman, the basic functioning of women's psyches. Patriarchal societies may be subject to variation but since the significance of the phallus remains constant, so does female (and male) psychology. It is not at all clear how Mitchell distinguishes between expressions of femininity and the fundamentals of feminine psychology. It looks like a form of words to avoid taking seriously any anthropological evidence which might otherwise contradict psychoanalysis. The assumption that evidence drawn from psychoanalysing women in Western societies can be applied to all other cultures is in any case clearly untenable.

The problem with phallocentrism, then, is not so much that it is possibly sexist but that it precludes any understanding of the complexity and variation of women's experiences under patriarchy and of the full range of processes that contribute to the construction of gender and sexuality. But psychoanalysis is so closed in upon itself, its adherents so immersed in its methods and assumptions, that they cannot conceive of any alternatives and the only means of avoiding phallocentrism they can envisage is a retreat into a belief that femininity is some innate essence distorted by patriarchy.

The problem of sexuality

There are major problems with psychoanalytic ideas about sexuality itself. Just as Mitchell insists that we must accept the existence of the unconscious so we must take as indisputable fact Freud's 'discovery' of infantile sexuality. Other psychoanalytic analyses concentrate on the constitution of 'desire' when we enter into language and culture but still retain some notion of drives which exist before this time. It is claimed that this is not an essentialist position, since a drive is not the same thing as an instinct in that it has no 'object', that is, it is not oriented towards any particular outlet, any specific category of person. Sexuality is not seen as something we are born with but is constructed in particular ways through our entry into patriarchal culture. Yet it still seems to be assumed that certain infantile experiences are intrinsically, essentially sexual. What is apparently being argued is that while sexuality is socially constructed, the drives we are born with are sexual in themselves.

Not only is this contradictory, but the whole notion of sexual 'drives' is rather dubious. A drive is an inborn urge towards physical gratification. While the satisfaction of hunger, for example, can be seen in this way (since it is necessary for physical survival), other forms of sensual pleasure do not so easily fit this model. Obviously infants do experience sensual pleasure but this does not mean that this experience involves either the gratification of a drive or that it is specifically sexual. To think of sexuality in terms of drives is to see it as something we are impelled towards by inner urges beyond our control and beyond the reach of social forces. To see any form of sensual pleasure as sexual in itself is to view sexuality as a natural biological endowment rather than something which is learnt. Both these assumptions are essentialist. Both imply that sexuality is unchanging and unchangeable.

In order to escape the consequence of essentialism, sexuality must be seen as something which is socially defined rather than as something which exists independently of our subjective definitions of it. In other words, nothing, no act, no sensation, is sexual in itself. What is sexual depends on culturally defined and socially learnt meanings. An infant gaining pleasure from her own body cannot be said to be behaving sexually even if she is doing something that an adult would define as sexual. She has not yet learnt language and therefore cannot yet categorize her world and her experiences and does not yet have access to the concepts which would endow certain pleasures with sexual, erotic meaning. It is nonsense, therefore, to talk of 'infantile sexuality'. Similar problems arise concerning the nature of the 'desire' supposedly constituted at the 'oedipal moment', when children become oriented towards the appropriate heterosexual 'object'. In what sense can a child be said to have desire when the concept of desire and, indeed, all knowledge through which she could make sense of her experience as sexual, is not available to her? We cannot ignore the fact that most children in our society are kept ignorant of those aspects of life which adults label sexual. Once again I would argue that such a child cannot be experiencing sexual desire in the sense that an adult would, since she cannot make sense of her feelings in those terms. And here, too, those proposing psychoanalytic explanations tend to contradict themselves. Many of them, like Ros Coward, maintain that language structures and orders our experience. So how can a child who cannot name desire be said to experience it?

Maybe this would only be problematic if it was being argued that desire exists at this stage at a conscious level, whereas most of these writers appear to be saying that it is constituted in the unconscious. But if this is the case, then the notion of the unconscious is simply being used as a conceptual dumping ground to explain away things which do not fit in elsewhere. We are left again with a residual essentialism – that even if something is not, cannot, be defined subjectively as sexual, it is nonetheless, in itself, sexual. We are also left not knowing what 'desire' is supposed to mean. In some contexts they clearly are referring to sexual desire, since their account of the social construction of sexuality consists of processes by which desire is constituted. At other times, however, they seem to be talking about something more nebulous: a desire to be completed by and to complete someone else, some sort of yearning after a 'wholeness' disrupted by the linguistic capacity to categorize and differentiate experience. I suspect the term 'desire' is favoured precisely because it is so ambiguous.

There are further difficulties with this slippery concept. It seems to me that the processes whereby we are conditioned towards genital, reproductive sexuality are far more continuous throughout childhood and adolescence than the psychoanalytic account allows for. I cannot accept that it all depends on what happens at the 'oedipal moment', which in any case seems to be more of an abstract, mythical 'moment' than a real event in time. Most of our learning experiences define sex for us in genital reproductive terms. Moreover, a full account of the social construction of sexuality needs to explain more than merely why most of us become heterosexual. If what we define as sexual involves selecting from a very broad sensual potential, then there are many possible forms of eroticism consistent with heterosexuality. Does heterosexuality have to involve passive femininity and active masculinity? Does it have to be genitally and reproductively focused, involving the goal of orgasm as end point? Psychoanalytic explanations of 'desire' imply that all this is essential to heterosexuality, that heterosexuality is fixed and unchangeable. Nor can the existence of desire itself explain all facets of our sexuality. Both women and men may engage in acts conventionally defined as sexual without desire being their primary motive.

A central difficulty here lies in the conflation of gender and sexuality, a criticism Barrett (1980) makes of other perspectives but not of psychoanalysis – where it is most prevalent. Indeed, in psychoanalytic accounts the term 'sexuality' is often taken as synonymous with gender or at least as subsuming it. I, like Barrett, would argue that while gender and (erotic) sexuality are obviously linked, we should not confuse them and should investigate these links rather than prejudging them. In psychoanalytic theory, however, both gender and sexuality appear to be constituted simultaneously at the oedipal moment. It is with the formation of desire, in taking the appropriate object, that we become sexed subjects. This, in any case, gives far too much determining force to sexuality in forming our psychic life, and implies that it has some intrinsic power to do so.

It is this confusion of gender and sexuality, and the reduction of sexuality to desire and its object, which I think accounts for the failure of psychoanalysis to confront the issue of lesbianism and homosexuality noted recently by Elizabeth Wilson (1981). For if our desire is directed towards an object disallowed by our culture, how can we be fully sexed subjects? If gender and sexuality are one and the same, what gender has a lesbian or homosexual? The only way of resolving these questions within the psychoanalytic framework would seem to lead us back to the realms of limp-wristed men and Amazonian women.

Feminism and psychoanalysis: why the attraction?

I have argued that psychoanalysis, built on a dubious methodology, on unfounded assumptions about the unconscious and containing within it a residual essentialism, does not offer us a very fruitful means of analysing sexuality. As an explanation for the persistence of patriarchy and of its effects on our consciousness it is an extremely depressing doctrine, for it offers us little chance of changing the situation. We are trapped in a vicious circle. Why is the phallus the privileged signifier? Because we live in a patriarchal culture. Why is our culture patriarchal? Because the phallus is the privileged signifier. Linking this to the notion of relations of reproduction as Coward and associates do (1976) does not help much. This is itself a difficult concept that can mean many things and, in this case, it seems to mean little more than biological reproduction; or, as Coward and Ellis would have it, it is through the castration complex that 'the reproduction of the species is ensured' (1977: 112). If it is the reproduction of the species rather than of specific social relations which are ensured by all this, then there is nothing we can do about it.

Why, then, should psychoanalysis appeal to feminists? Various factors have been suggested, for example by Wilson (1981) and Sayers (1979). The most important of these is that psychoanalysis offers an analysis of patriarchy as a structure in its own right and rests on a universalism that stresses the commonality of women's oppression. This being the case, it would be expected to appeal to radical feminists. But it is Marxist feminists who have adopted it. While Wilson sees in this a potential retreat from Marxism, I disagree. There are very good reasons for its appeal to Marxist feminists in that it helps them to deal with theoretical difficulties which radical feminists do not have to face.

Psychoanalysis has been appropriated by Marxists generally to account for aspects of lived experience to which conventional Marxist categories are inapplicable. But it has a more specific appeal to Marxist feminists in its ability to create a space for theorizing gender relations and sexuality in their own right without challenging pre-existing Marxist concepts and categories. By placing this theorization in the realm of the ideological, the problems of trying to relate women's subordination to specific modes of production are avoided. In doing so, however, some of the failings inherent in attempts to place women's oppression at the economic level as somehow contributing to the maintenance of capitalist economy are repeated. Such explanations tend to take the sexual division of labour as given and therefore rest on an implicit biological reductionism. This, of course, is also true of a theory which regards specific psychic processes as necessary to the reproduction of the species.

The appropriation of psychoanalysis also serves to perpetuate another common omission in Marxist thought: the unwillingness to confront the issue of male power, the preference for considering women's oppression solely in terms of structures (whether economic or symbolic) at the expense of analysing the ways in which real men exercise and benefit by their power over women. Radical feminists have never doubted that patriarchy is worthy of consideration in its own right, have never been afraid of confronting the day-to-day realities of male dominance and are not trapped within the confines of any existing body of theory. For them psychoanalysis can have little appeal.

Notes

1 *Editorial note*: in the original article I noted that these were early feminist reworkings of Freud and referred readers to more recent developments such as Jane Gallop's *Feminism and Psychoanalysis: The Daughter's Seduction* (1982) and articles in the journal *m/f*.

2 *Editorial note*: this comment refers to Mitchell's *Psychoanalysis and Feminism* (1975). In her later work, particularly in the introduction to the collection of Lacan's writings that she co-edited with Jacqueline Rose (Mitchell and Rose, 1982), she became more of a Lacanian. Even here, however, there is a distinct difference in tone between Mitchell's introduction, which deals with different psychoanalytic interpretations of Freud, and Rose's, which more directly addresses Lacan's contribution. Mitchell, on my reading, is the less Lacanian of the two.

3 *Editorial note*: what I failed to make clear here (though it makes little difference

to my argument) is that the sense of a distinct self which comes into being with the mirror stage is an 'imaginary capture' in which the child identifies with an image of itself, imagines itself (it is, as yet ungendered) into being as an 'ideal-I'. This process, in Lacan's words, 'situates the agency of the ego ... in a fictional direction' (1977: 2).

PART III

RECENT INTERVENTIONS

---

7   Even Sociologists Fall In Love: An Exploration In The Sociology Of Emotions

This chapter, originally published as an article in Sociology *in 1993, marked my return to the field of sexuality – although it meant re-entering it at a rather oblique angle. Yet I had always seen emotions, including love, as part of sexuality and there are strong points of continuity here with my earlier work. In seeking a means of theorizing love as a socially constructed emotion, I was looking, as always, for explanations which resonated with my own experience and which were consonant with the findings of empirical research.*

  What remains carefully concealed in most mainstream research is the personal experience and political investment which lie behind a theorist's or researcher's intellectual endeavours. Although in this article I urged sociologists to draw on rather than neglect their own experience, what I did not feel able to say, in the pages of a mainstream academic journal, was that the initial idea for the article derived from a recent experience of 'falling in love'. The title was inspired by a friend's teasing: 'What, you mean even sociologists fall in love? Aren't you too busy analysing relationships to feel such things?' Writing the article was a product of my capacity both to feel and to theorize – and suggests that 'feelings' are themselves understood through our everyday theorizing. Moreover, my continued awareness that the personal is always political encouraged me to think that my emotions were not mine alone, but were products of the culture I inhabit.

  This is the first occasion on which I explicitly invoked the concept of discourse as central to my analysis, but also the beginning of my interest in narratives of self. When I wrote this, the idea of narratives seemed to be 'in the air' among feminists and in much cultural and social theory, and had some congruence with the interactionist perspectives I had drawn on in the past – particularly with the idea of 'scripts'. A key insight was provided by Michelle Rosaldo's anthropological work, specifically her idea that emotions are 'social practices organized by stories that we both enact and tell' (1984:

143). As I suggested in Chapter 1, it may be fruitful to think about subjectivity in general, and specifically our sexual selves, as a process of narrative construction.

Here, in addressing 'love' as a social and gendered phenomenon, I began to think myself back into a feminist critique of heterosexuality, which became more explicit as I developed these ideas further (see Chapter 8).

Love, like other emotions, has received little attention from sociologists although there have been a few recent publications, written from diverse perspectives, which indicate a new interest in this area (Bertilsson, 1986; Brunt, 1988; Cancian, 1990; Douglas and Atwell, 1988; Luhmann, 1986). Given that sociologists are wont to theorize on any and every aspect of everyday life, are generally interested in demonstrating that all relationships and institutions are social, why has 'love' escaped serious scrutiny?

It may be that love is seen as too personal, too individual to be subjected to sociological analysis. As Sarsby says:

> The very idea that social forces, rather than one's uniquely personal needs and desires, might have shaped the form of one's love seems like an infringement of personal liberty, an intrusion into that mysterious, private world, the irrational splendour of one's finer feelings. (1983: 1)

Sociologists have, however, been questioning the boundaries between public and private, social and personal for some time. There has been no reluctance to theorize other, equally personal, areas of life. Sexuality, in particular, has been a fashionable area of theoretical debate for nearly 20 years, yet love, which we might expect to be treated as an aspect of the sexual, is rarely mentioned. Within these debates feminist work on love, such as that of de Beauvoir (1972) and Firestone (1972), has largely been ignored. It is tempting to conclude that much of this theorizing has taken place within masculinist discourses which maintain a separation between love and sex and within which the former is seen as a peculiarly feminine concern, of little import for serious critical analysis. Even within feminist theory, however, the critiques of love developed early in the second wave of feminism have not been elaborated further. Romance as a popular cultural form has received far more attention than love itself (see, for example Christian-Smith, 1991; Fowler, 1991; Griffin, 1982; McRobbie, 1982, 1991; Modleski, 1984; Radway, 1987; Taylor, 1989b).

Far from being just a personal, private phenomenon, love is very much a part of our public culture. We are surrounded by representations of love in what is deemed 'great' art and literature as well as in soap opera, popular music, fiction and advertising. The pervasiveness of love as a representational theme is related to its institutionalization in marriage and family life. Feminists and non-feminists alike have recognized the centrality of the concept of 'love' to familial ideology, to the maintenance of heterosexual monogamy and patriarchal marriage. Love may also serve to bind us to the existing social order in a more subtle and more general way. The point which Heath (1982) has made about the 'sexual fix' could be just as applicable to love: that we are continually enjoined to seek fulfilment in personal relationships and to treat these as unrelated to, outside, the social. Hence we strive to improve our personal lives rather than the structures which constrain and limit them.

Any speculation on the sociological importance of love rests upon the assumption that ideologies in some way connect with individual subjectivity. The idea of romantic love would have little effect if it did not have some resonance for individuals, did not make sense in terms of our felt emotional states and personal relationships. The capacity to 'fall in love' thus itself requires explanation.

Love cannot be treated as if it has an existence independent of the social and cultural context within which it is experienced. The idea that emotions are somehow pre-social, and therefore outside the sociologist's field of vision, is beginning to be challenged. It has been suggested that feeling is subject to individual and social management and that 'in managing feeling we contribute to the creation of it' (Hochschild, 1983: 18), that our sense of what emotions are is culturally specific (Lutz, 1986; Rosaldo, 1984), and that 'there are complex linguistic and other social preconditions for the ... existence of human emotions' (Jagger, 1989: 151).

Following those who maintain that emotions are socially and culturally constructed, I want to argue for an approach to 'love' which regards the emotion itself as just as much cultural as the conventions which surround it, but which still takes seriously the subjective experience of love. I will begin by looking critically at some existing sociological and feminist perspectives on love. I will then go on to explore the possibilities for building on the insights of these analyses while avoiding the essentialist conceptualizations of emotion which often informed them. While not pretending to have developed a wholly adequate theorization, I suggest some lines of enquiry which I think it worthwhile to pursue. After all, even sociologists fall in love and perhaps we should recognize and make use of this in exploring theoretical possibilities.

Sociological perspectives on love

One aspect of love which has received some attention from social theorists is the link between romantic love and marriage. The idea that the former is a necessary condition for the latter has frequently been identified, by anthropologists and historians as well as sociologists, as a peculiarity of modern Western societies. Generally this is explained in terms of a decline in obligations towards kin beyond the conjugal unit and the rise of capitalist individual freedoms (Goode, 1959; Luhmann, 1986; Shorter, 1976; Stone, 1977). As Bertilsson puts it, summarizing Luhmann, 'the economic market finds a correspondence in the market of free emotions' (1986: 28). What

Luhmann states explicitly is often implied by others – that there is a functional fit between romantic love and modern society. It provides a means of communication and self-realization in a complex, impersonal and anonymous world. Weber (1948) ties love to modernity slightly differently, as simultaneously a product of and a reaction to rationalization. For Weber love is a way of seeking personal salvation in this world (as opposed to other-worldly salvation), but it is also an assertion of the irrational in opposition to the rational, although the threat this potentially poses is neutralized by the domestication of love.

The extent to which all this is modern has been challenged. In Europe free choice of marriage partners long pre-dates both industrialization and the rise of capitalism (Macfarlane, 1978, 1987; Sarsby, 1983). Macfarlane (1987) endorses the orthodox view that marriage for love is related to a lack of extended kinship obligations and to market oriented individualistic values but, in keeping with his general historical thesis (1978), argues that these conditions were present, at least in England, long before the rise of capitalism. Sarsby (1983), on the other hand, argues that the long history of free choice in marriage does not necessarily mean that love has remained unchanged throughout this history.

If love has changed historically then it cannot be a pre-given constant feature of human life (Luhmann, 1986; Sarsby, 1983). Yet, paradoxically, arguments concerning the historical and cultural variability of romantic love are frequently underpinned by essentialist, or even downright biologistic, assumptions. Macfarlane, for example, while claiming that romantic love is a culturally specific phenomenon, says:

> Something about the kinship system in parts of Europe, and the way it is interlocked with politics, economics and religion, gave the biological drives a great deal of freedom. Indeed the economy and society seemed positively to stimulate the natural emotions. (1987: 142)

Here it appears that 'falling in love' is a natural emotion which happens to people when social controls upon it are lifted, that love is suppressed where it is dysfunctional and allowed to flourish where it is functional. Goode's cross-cultural analysis similarly regards love as a 'universal psychological potential, which is controlled by a range of ... structural patterns' (Goode, 1974: 156). His basic thesis is that, left to their own devices, young people everywhere would fall in love. In some societies they are prevented from doing so, while in others social control takes the more subtle form of ensuring that the young fall in love with appropriate partners. Like those who focus on social change, Goode accounts for this variation in terms of the importance of marriage relative to other kinship ties.

The essentialism underpinning these analyses involves taking the concept of 'love' as unproblematic, proceeding as if we all know what it is and can recognize it whenever and wherever it occurs, even in societies very different from our own.[1] The fact that free choice of marriage partners has existed in other cultures or in our own society in the past should not lead us to claim some universality for the experience of romantic love.

A further, and crucial, issue here is that of gender. It has often been claimed that romantic love results from an equalization of relationships between men and women (Shorter, 1976), or is only truly attainable where material equality between partners prevails (Engels, 1891). Weber is unusual among pre-feminist theorists in raising the possibility that love might not be experienced in the same way by women and men and that it might involve the subjugation of women. This, of course, was central to the critique of heterosexual love developed by de Beauvoir (1972) and later elaborated by others in the early years of 'second wave' feminism (Comer, 1974; Firestone, 1972). These analyses opened up the possibility of theoretical debates on love, but the way in which they were framed subsequently silenced further explorations. Once the oppressive nature of love for women had been exposed, to try to explore it further seemed at best banal and at worst ideologically unsound.

Feminist critiques of love

It starts when you sink into his arms and ends with your arms in his sink.

This slogan sums up the central tenet of feminist critiques of love. Love was seen as an ideology which legitimated women's oppression and which trapped them into exploitative heterosexual relationships. Some accorded it even greater effectivity than this. Firestone, for example, asserted that 'love, perhaps even more than childbearing, is the pivot of women's oppression today' (1972: 121).[2]

What was so dangerous about love was women's tendency to become totally immersed in it. For de Beauvoir, women's self-abnegation through love not only reinforced their subordination but resulted from a subjectivity constituted through that subordination.

There is no other way out for her but to lose herself, body and soul, in him who is represented to her as absolute, as the essential.... She chooses to desire her enslavement so ardently that it will seem to her the expression of her liberty ... she will humble herself to nothingness before him. Love becomes for her a religion. (de Beauvoir, 1972: 653)

Being so obsessed with love was seen as diverting energies from other possible achievements. Moreover, making one person the centre of one's emotional universe was taken as symptomatic of emotional impoverishment elsewhere, the exclusivity of love meant quantifying and confining our emotions. As Lee Comer expressed it:

... monogamy has come to be the definition of love, a yardstick by which we measure the rest of our emotions. 'Real' love is only that which is exclusively focused on one person of the opposite sex – all else is labelled 'liking'. Like so much butter, romantic love must be spread thickly on one slice of bread; to spread it over several is to spread it 'thinly'. (1974: 219)

Love was also seen as making women vulnerable, not just to exploitation, but to being hurt by men. As de Beauvoir said, 'the word love has by no means the same meaning for both sexes' (1972: 652), a view endorsed by Firestone (1972). Although these two theorists differed in their analyses of the meaning of love for men and women, they agreed that women invest far more in love and that they give far more affection to men than they receive in return.[3] This was not seen as part of women's nature, rooted in some essential way in the feminine psyche, but as a product of the material conditions of women's lives. Love was linked to women's search for a positive identity, a sense of themselves as valued, in a society which undervalues and marginalizes them.

For feminists romantic love was not a constant feature of human nature, but was the product of society and culture. It served to tie us to mono-gamous marriage which, given the power relations between men and women and the ways in which femininity and masculinity were constituted, was a relationship doomed to failure. This position was stated forcefully by Lee Comer:

Any glance round society reveals that the sexes are placed on opposite poles, with an enormous chasm of oppression, degradation and misunderstanding generated to keep them apart. Out of this, marriage plucks one woman and one man, ties them together with 'love' and asserts that they shall, for the rest of their lives, bridge that chasm with a mixture of betrayal, sex, affection, deceit and illusion. (Comer, 1974: 227)

Underlying such critiques of the link between love, monogamy and marriage was often a belief in some 'purer' form of love, freed from power relationships and bourgeois institutions, which would be more diffuse, more widely spread throughout our social experience. Firestone and Comer, writing from very different points on the feminist political spectrum, share similar assumptions here. For Firestone romance is love distorted by power. She asks: 'Why has all the joy and excitement been concentrated, driven into one narrow, difficult-to-find human experience and all the rest laid waste?' (1972: 147). She argues for the rediffusion of 'sexual joy and excitement ... over the spectrum of our lives' (147). Similarly, Comer suggests that: 'In rare moments, when the external categories which fragment our emotions fall away, we glimpse the possibility of whole feelings' (1974: 219). These 'whole feelings' involve a plurality of loves directed towards a multiplicity of others. Monogamous, heterosexual love is seen as a false solution to the fragmentation of the self which binds us to oppressive relationships. It is:

> The means by which we are allowed to recompose the fragmentation of our selves into an apparent whole. So that jealousy comes to be regarded as the objective proof of love instead of an excrescence of the emotions. So that sex is legitimized, so that attraction and warmth and affection can be called 'love', which can then be parcelled into marriage. (Comer, 1974: 220)

Compared with more recent feminist analyses of the ways in which our subjectivities are constituted, much of this seems rather naive. The very possibility of 'whole selves' is the product of a particular humanist discourse which now seems highly questionable (Weedon, 1987) and the notion of a pure love uncontaminated by cultural and social structures has become untenable. More than this, the tone of Firestone's and Comer's critiques suggests that quest for love is an illusion which, once 'seen through', can be easily discarded. This simplistic conception of ideology and its relation to subjectivity, the implication that all we needed was an effort of will to break out from the shackles of exclusive romantic love, effectively precluded the possibility of confronting the potency of this emotion and seeking for an explanation of it.

Although flawed, these feminist analyses were more critical than those of conventional social theorists and raised questions which deserve re-examination in the light of more recent theoretical developments – in particular, the idea that 'love' may be a way in which we seek to resolve some of the contradictions of our existence, the exclusivity and potential oppressiveness of the relationships into which it draws us are themes which should be pursued.

What is love?

Most analyses of love, contrary to normal social scientific practice, do not attempt a definition of the object of enquiry. Romantic convention tells us that love is in essence indefinable, mysterious, outside rational discourse. Its meaning is held to be knowable only intuitively, at the level of feeling, and cannot be communicated in precise terms. Social theorists have generally accepted this, thus taking for granted what is part of the cultural construction of love. They have refrained from examining the irrational and unpredictable and have concentrated instead on institutionalized expressions of love. Descriptions of the emotion itself tend to be literary rather than theoretical.

Emotions, in the sense of what is subjectively felt by individuals, are not observable phenomena. 'We have no access either to our own emotions or to those of others, independent of or unmediated by the discourse of our culture' (Jagger, 1989: 148). There is thus no way of exploring love except through the ways in which it is talked and written about. Language, moreover, itself contributes to the cultural construction of emotions and is a means by which we participate in creating a shared sense of what emotions are.

The cultural construction of romantic love is many layered. Its most superficial elements, those most amenable to challenge and change, are such romantic conventions as the celebration of Valentine's day, gifts of red roses or candle-lit dinners. These are customs of recent origin by no means essential to the experience of love. More fundamental is the link between love and 'compulsory heterosexuality' (Rich, 1980) institutionalized in marriage. Here we have a social relationship and legal contract of considerable importance and which most of the population enter into. Yet not all lovers necessarily marry: many are debarred from doing so if they are lesbian, homosexual or already married. The increased incidence of cohabitation indicates that many are choosing not to marry or to postpone marriage. More fundamental and more firmly embedded in our culture are the ideals and hopes of personal fulfilment, contentment, companionship and affection commonly invested in love relationships. This is different again from the mysterious, overpowering emotion of 'falling in love' which is deemed such a potent force. It is being 'in love' which for Weber (1948) is the irrational reaction to rationality, for Barthes (1978) creates a sense of 'disreality', for Macfarlane (1987) possesses a 'compulsive authority'. It is this which I wish to explore further.

The adjectives commonly used to describe the experience of 'falling in love' mark it as very different from other forms of love. Love for parents, children, siblings or friends is not usually thought of as compelling, overwhelming, uncontrollable, inexplicable and ecstatic – nor even is love in long-term sexual relationships. Many of the discussions of the history of romantic love, however, rest on the assumption that conjugal love – lasting affection and companionship – is the outcome of falling in love. A distinction is commonly made in our culture between loving someone and being in love with them, as it was by most of the women in Shere Hite's (1988) study. Only a small minority of those who had been in a relationship for more than two years said that they were 'in love' with their partners, but they nearly all said that they loved him or her. This difference is also noted by other recent commentators on love (Douglas and Atwell, 1988; Macfarlane, 1987; Sarsby, 1983). Macfarlane's account implies that this is in some way functional:

> We need to distinguish between an irrational, passionate love that helps in selecting a partner, and companionate love that maintains a relationship. Choice ... is always difficult ... some external force of desire is needed to help the individual make a choice. Hence passionate love overwhelms and justifies and provides compulsive authority. (1987: 141–2)

Sarsby, however, stresses the contradictions between these two forms of love:

Love is seen as the bolt from the blue against which one cannot struggle, the preordained meeting of twin souls, the compulsion which allows one to break any of society's rules as long as one is faithful to the emotion itself. The extraordinary contradiction lies in the fact that love is the almost prescribed condition for marriage in most of Europe and the United States ... millions of private, potentially socially disruptive, emotional dramas are virtually the only acceptable means of moving towards marriage ... the 'taming' of love into this most conventional of patterns is one of its mysteries. (1983: 5–6)

I would agree that there is indeed a fundamental contradiction here. Love may impel us into monogamous unions but it can equally be a threat to monogamy, a reason for changing partners or engaging in extra-marital liaisons (Lawson, 1988).

But what is the nature of this exotic, exciting passionate compulsion? It is often described, as it is by Weber (1948), as a form of ecstasy akin to a mystical experience or, in Bertilsson's words 'comparable in force and in momentum to a religious conversion' (1986: 28).[4] Yet casting love in such mystical terms as a 'fusion of souls' (Weber 1948: 347) does not help us to comprehend this emotion. Rather, it seems to accord it a special legitimacy by placing it on some higher plane inaccessible to reason or explanation. This, of course, is part of the ideological packaging of romantic love: 'fools give you reasons, wise men [*sic*] never try'.

At a more mundane level, love is represented in popular culture through well established romantic formulae of the 'moonlight and roses' variety. Lucy Goodison says of these:

They may be the pre-formed moulds which society offers us to pour our love into: but they are not its source. These fantasies are pretty, while the central drive of falling in love seems to be more of a blood and guts affair. It is not just glamorous and appealing. More than wanting to cosset the beloved we may feel we want to eat them alive.... Romantic feelings and fantasies may be the blossoms produced by being in love, but its roots lie deeper in the earth, the power it feeds on is not essentially romantic, but one that tears at the innards. (1983: 51–2)

This description may suffer from the essentialist implication that love at root is somehow asocial, but its emphasis on the powerful viscerality of love captures the compulsiveness associated with the emotion in a way which neither banal romanticism nor high flown mysticism can. This is, after all, an emotion which is not only experienced as overwhelming and uncontrollable, but is also often described as violent, even ruthless (Bertilsson, 1986) and so powerful as to be almost unendurable (Haug et al., 1987). Even its more clichéd symptoms – the 'can't eat, can't sleep' syndrome for instance – are more in tune with Goodison's depiction of love than those descriptions which focus on hearts and flowers or unions of souls.

The power attributed to this emotion is far more difficult to account for than the mere link between mutual affection and free choice of marriage partners which has been the main focus of most discussions of the 'romantic love complex'. It can neither be dismissed as the simple product of capitalist or patriarchal ideologies nor should it be accepted as a universal incomprehensible fact of human nature. The capacity to experience this emotion must, like all human experience, be mediated by language and culture. It is also clearly deeply embedded in our subjectivities and must in some way be formed in and through the processes by which our subjectivities are socially constituted. It is an emotion to which both sceptics and romantics can succumb, which is felt by lesbians and gay men as well as by heterosexuals. It is much easier to refuse to participate in romantic rituals, to resist pressures towards conventional marriage, to be cynical about 'happy ever after' endings than it is to avoid falling in love.

Being 'in love'

I now want to specify further what, within Western culture, is understood by being 'in love' and how it is differentiated from other, related experiences. It is necessary here to bear in mind de Beauvoir's dictum that love does not have the same meaning for men and women.[5]

The most obvious way in which romantic love differs from other forms of love is that it is sexual. There are those who consider that this form of love can be equated with sexual desire, that it is merely lust gift wrapped in romantic conventions. A substantial minority of Hite's (1988) respondents, 28 per cent, equated love and lust and saw the former as an excuse for the latter. Certainly for many women love and sexual desire are more closely associated than is reported to be the case among men. Among Lawson's (1988) sample of adulterers, both men and women placed sexual fulfilment ahead of love among their motives for engaging in extra-marital liaisons. Yet for women love came a close second while for men it was far less important. Research with young, adolescent women suggests that the very capacity for sexual arousal may be bound up with understanding this sensation as love (Jackson, 1982a; Lees, 1986). Sexual relations are, for young women in particular, still fraught with anxieties about sexual exploitation (see Jackson, 1982a; Lees, 1986; Leonard, 1980; Thomson and Scott, 1991; Wallace, 1987). In this context 'love' serves to validate sexual activity morally, aesthetically and emotionally. An act which might otherwise be characteristic of a 'slag' is transformed into something beautiful, magical and pleasurable (Jackson, 1982a). Similarly, Leonard says of romantic love that it is:

> ... a means by which women in our society resolve the contradiction between being sexually desirous but not sexually experienced. They sublimate their sexual feelings into a 'courtly love' mould, and thereby ignore the passive, dominated role they must occupy in heterosexual courtship. (Leonard, 1980: 262)

It has been suggested that part of the attraction of romantic fiction lies in the way in which it resolves such contradictions (Finn, 1988; Radway, 1987). It also articulates the strong association between love and sex felt by many women. Romance has been described as 'pornography of the feelings, where emotions replace sexual parts' (Wilson, 1983: 43). Radway's (1987) romance readers certainly seemed to gain pleasure (arousal?) from reading of sexual encounters represented as the consummation of love although, as McRobbie (1991) points out, these women readers reveal little of their sexual desires.

Even so, it is not always the case even for women that lust and being in love are experienced as one and the same, and scepticism about romantic love has been reported even among the very young (see Griffin, 1987; Wallace, 1987). As Goodison (1983) comments, it is possible to feel powerful sexual attraction, 'magnificent lust' without it necessarily being accompanied by the dizzying, stomach churning sensations/emotions associated with being in love. She suggests one peculiar feature of the lust felt while in love: that it is not concerned with purely physical gratification. Ordinary lust or arousal is capable of satisfaction; lust when in love is insatiable.[6]

That love is not really about caring for another, but is a very self-centred emotion, is suggested by a range of theorists from Firestone (1972) to Luhmann (1986). Love has generally been associated with individualism in terms of free choice of partners, but it may also be individualistic in a deeper sense. To be in love is to make one unique other the centre of your universe, but it also demands the same in return. Desire demands that we should be the 'only one' for the other. This exclusiveness may be a product of a culture which encourages us to think of individuals as unique beings who are somehow essentially 'ourselves' independent of the social milieu within which our selves have been forged (see Errington and Gewertz, 1987; Geertz, 1984). Yet paradoxically, the other whom we love, this special person, is frequently our own creation: the 'real' individual we imagine we love may be little more than a pretext around which our fantasies are woven (Wilson, 1983, 1988).

The self-centredness of those in love can be seen as straightforwardly antisocial. Ros Brunt comments that she has never been convinced that all the world loves a lover:

> This most highly prized form of love has a selfish, indulgent and extraordinarily egotistical aspect.... It ... encourages a massive self absorption that 'makes the world go away' to an extent that can be quite disturbing to anyone else in the immediate vicinity, and devastating to what are seen as other, less important social affiliations. (Brunt, 1988: 21)

Being in love in some way places the lover outside the mundane, everyday world. It is this which Barthes calls 'disreality', a state in which 'any general conversation which I am obliged to listen to (if not take part in) appalls me, paralyses me' (Barthes, 1978: 88). As the title of Goodison's (1983) paper expresses it, 'really being in love means wanting to live in a different world'. This, of course, is part of the attraction and excitement of love, what Brunt calls its utopian aspect, which has led others to liken it to a mystical ecstatic religious experience.

> The lover knows himself [*sic*] to be freed from the cold skeleton hand of the rational orders, just as completely as from the banality of everyday routine. (Weber, 1948: 347)

Such ecstasy and self-absorption centred exclusively on a single other renders the lover extremely vulnerable. This vulnerability, often manifested as jealousy, is associated with the chronic insecurity of the lover. If being in love is, as I've suggested, fuelled by a desire that cannot be satisfied, then insecurity may be fundamental to it. This impossible desire is part of the excitement of being in love, an excitement which cannot be allayed so long as the gratification it seeks is denied. Romantic love is played out around themes of 'compulsion and denial' (Wilson, 1983: 42). Love stories end at the moment of final consummation since 'gratification destroys the compulsion little by little' (Wilson, 1983: 42).

Freud was not without insight in arguing that love thrives only when obstacles are put in its way (Freud, 1912). Feeling insecure is not, I think, merely a result of being in love but it is fundamental to its continuance. This is recognized in commonsense folkways in 'playing hard to get' as a means of arousing another's interest. It is why being 'in love' appears to wear off once lovers feel secure with each other (Douglas and Atwell, 1988), and why long-term relationships cannot provide the excitement we prize so highly, leading some, perhaps, to taste the novel, forbidden fruits of adultery (Lawson, 1988). There appears to be something about romantic love as described in both social scientific and literary writings which suggests that it is the product of restriction and unattainability.

Love is often unrequited and rarely balanced. A recurrent theme in Barthes' *A Lover's Discourse* is this imbalance which is played out around the theme of waiting, whether it be the modern Western lover waiting for a telephone call or the Chinese mandarin waiting in the courtesan's garden for the 100 nights to elapse after which she has promised herself to him: on the 99th night he picks up his stool and walks away. For Barthes waiting encapsulates the powerlessness of the lover, being in the power of the other. 'The lover's fatal identity is precisely: I am the one who waits.' The other does not wait (Barthes, 1978: 40).

Yet if love is powerlessness symbolized by waiting, it also holds out the promise of power, of being the loved one, of ensnaring another into this total psychic dependence. This may be part of the specifically powerful attraction that love has for women. It is perhaps the only way in which women can hope to have power over men. This is another common theme of romances and may, as Modleski (1984) suggests, be a way in which women can give vent to some of their anger towards men and a desire for

vengeance. In both fairy tales and romantic fiction love tames and transforms the beast: love has the power to bring him to his knees. The ways in
which such narratives engage with our desires and fantasies is a theme to
which I now turn.

Love stories: the narrative construction of emotion

> Feelings are not substances to be discovered in our blood, but social practices
> organized by stories that we both enact and tell. They are structured by our forms
> of understanding. (Rosaldo, 1984: 143)

Our subjectivities, including that aspect of them we understand as our
emotions, are shaped by social and cultural processes and structures but are
not simply passively accepted by us. As Haug et al. (1987) have argued, we
actively participate in working ourselves into structures and this in part
explains the strength of our subjection to them. We create for ourselves a
sense of what our emotions are, of what being 'in love' is. We do this by
participating in sets of meanings constructed, interpreted, disseminated and
deployed throughout our culture, through learning scripts, positioning
ourselves within discourses, constructing narratives of self. We make sense
of feelings and relationships in terms of love because a set of discourses
around love pre-exists us as individuals and through these we have learnt
what love means. As Ros Brunt comments:

> The script for love has already been written and is being continually recycled in all
> the love songs and love stories of Western literature and contemporary media.
> (Brunt, 1988: 19)

When we fall in love it feels like 'getting to star in your own movie'
(Brunt, 1988: 19). What Brunt is describing here is not a passive internal-
ization of these scripts but an active sense of locating ourselves within them.
The idea of love as a narrative or drama is recognized too in a long-running
advertisement for the 'Dateline' agency, which offers its services as a
chance to be part of 'your own love story'.

Those who feel themselves to be 'in love' have a wealth of novels, plays,
movies and songs on which to draw to make sense of and describe their
passion. This can manifest itself in the half-conscious self-dramatization so
acutely observed by Barthes in a passage where he once again situates the
lover as waiting – this time in a café. The beloved is late:

> In the prologue, the sole actor in the play, I discern and indicate the other's delay
> ... (I look at my watch several times); the prologue ends with a brainstorm: I
> decide to 'take it badly.' I release the anxiety of waiting. Act I now begins; it is
> occupied with suppositions: was there a misunderstanding as to the time, the
> place? ... What is to be done ...? Try another café? Telephone? But if the other
> comes during these absences? ... Act II is the act of anger; I address violent

reproaches to the absent one.... In Act III I attain to ... the anxiety of abandonment ... the other is dead: explosion of grief.... That is the play.... (Barthes, 1978: 37–8)

Here we have a sense that emotions can be managed in accordance with certain conventions (he decides to 'take it badly'), that there is some intentionality involved in the expression of emotion (see also Hochschild, 1983; Jagger, 1989). That Barthes' scenario can be recognized by many as typical of a lover's experience suggests that this emotion called 'love', so often represented as uniquely personal and inexplicable, follows culturally prescribed patterns. Barthes' *A Lover's Discourse* (1978) is constructed from what he terms 'fragments' of others' writings on love. His invitation to his readers to position ourselves within this discourse is something most of us can readily accomplish because, as he assumes, we can recognize ourselves and our own experiences in at least some of the fragments he offers us. This is not because the Western literary tradition has simply recorded some pre-existing emotion, some essential human 'truth', but because that tradition supplies us with narrative forms with which we begin to be familiarized in childhood and through which we learn what love is. Throughout our lives we are exposed to, and participate in, the sort of drama Barthes describes.

Within our culture public and private narratives often overlap and intermesh. Private narratives become public, for example, in magazines through readers' letters, problem pages and features based on 'real life' emotional dramas. Television and radio stations also offer similar opportunities for narrative disclosure through chat shows, phone-ins and so on. Radio One's regular morning feature 'our tune' is a case in point (see Montgomery, 1991). With the theme music from Zefferelli's film of *Romeo and Juliet* playing in the background, a story of an emotional turning point in a listener's life is recounted, usually (although not always) focusing on heterosexual romance. Through these sorts of media products we are invited to construct narratives and to make use of narrative strategies already available through those same media. Often comparisons are made between such fictional narratives as TV soaps and dramas and 'real life' by offering us glimpses of the private lives of their stars, drawing parallels or contrasts between the actors' lives and those of the characters they play. Implicitly or explicitly we are prompted by such stories to make sense of our own lives and others' lives through narrative.

Narratives are thus not merely a form encountered in novels, plays and films. They are very much a part of everyday cultural competencies. We constantly tell stories: events we have witnessed or participated in are recounted to others in narrative form and in our fantasies we tell ourselves stories. We learn to do this from an early age and in so doing we also learn to construct and reconstruct our own biographies in narrative form. Hence our subjectivities are in part constituted through narrative (Johnson, 1986). As Rosaldo (1984) suggests, the stories we enact and tell structure past and present experience and allow us to project future experience.

Where love is concerned such narratives are also differentiated by gender, discursively constructing for us gender specific subject positions. This may be important to men's and women's different experiences of love. To be overly emotional for a Western male, particularly within Anglo-Saxon culture, is to bring his masculinity into question. Most discourses around gender, sexuality and love represent women as the more emotional gender: not only as being more nurturant and expressive but also as more deeply emotive beings. Hence, as Hollway (1984a) notes, men's ability to displace fear of their own emotional needs on to women and their tendency when talking about heterosexual relationships to articulate a certain anxiety centred on a fear of commitment. In talking about their sexual and emotional relationships with women, the men Hollway interviewed drew on two discourses. Within the 'male sexual drive discourse', constructed around physical desire rather than love or affection, men cast themselves as subjects and women as objects. Within the 'have-hold discourse', however, men positioned themselves as objects in danger of entrapment by the emotionally needy female subject. Men's distancing of themselves from emotion, their fear of loss of control, has been noted by a number of writers and is experienced by women as a problematic aspect of heterosexual relationships (see, for example, Cancian, 1990; Hite, 1988; Mansfield and Collard, 1988; Rubin, 1983).

Western masculinity is not constituted as wholly unemotional; rather, boys and men are not encouraged to develop competence in locating themselves within discourses of the emotions. The narratives woven around love and romance are available to both women and men within our culture, but not equally so. Being constituted as feminine involves girls in discourses of feeling and emotion and, more specifically, the culture of romance, from which boys are more often excluded or from which they exclude themselves in order to construct a sense of their own maleness. It is through the idiom of sexual bravado and conquest, not the language of romance, that masculinity is asserted (Wallace, 1987; Wood, 1984).

Children learn the standard pattern of romance narrative very early in life from such sources as fairy tales. Bronwyn Davies' (1989) study of Australian pre-school children demonstrates that young children of both sexes have learnt romantic convention to the extent that they are dismayed when it is flouted. Neither boys nor girls were impressed by the ending of a feminist fairy-tale in which the princess decides that the prince is not worth bothering with and skips off into the sunset alone. Girls tended to view the clever resourceful princess more positively, and the spoilt selfish prince more negatively, than did the boys, but they still wished for a conventional conclusion to the story. This perhaps presages the preference of teenage and adult romance readers for spirited heroines who nonetheless do not step far enough outside the bounds of acceptable femininity to alienate the hero (Christian-Smith, 1991; Radway, 1987).

Reading matter marketed for girls continues this acculturation into romance. Even comics for young girls with no romantic or sexual content, as Walkerdine (1984) notes, construct narratives around feminine self-sacrifice and the good-girl/other-girl dualism which continues into teenage and adult romance fiction. Through such media sources, as well as through conversations with other girls and adult women, girls are learning nuances of meaning through which they make sense of emotions and relationships.

This is certainly culturally specific. The anthropologists Errington and Gewertz's account of the gulf of understanding which separates their teenage daughter Alexis from Lucy, a young New Guinea Chambri woman with whom she had been close friends in childhood, illustrates this. Alexis, who had been reading *Jane Eyre* and *Wuthering Heights*, found it 'incomprehensible' that Lucy, having chosen to remain with her own kin rather than live with the father of her child, 'was neither distraught nor even distressed by the loss of her Heathcliffe' (Errington and Gewertz, 1987: 128). They note that such novels are not simply a means by which we make sense of our own and others' experience, 'but are among the many cultural mechanisms which lead individuals to regard themselves and others as having a subjective self' (Errington and Gewertz, 1987: 166). This sense of individual subjectivity was alien to Chambri culture, where people saw themselves in terms of their position within social networks, rather than in terms of assumed interior feelings and motives. The sense of a unique individual essence identified as central to Western post-Enlightenment thought could, then, be a prerequisite for romantic narrative which hinges on the idea of two such unique individuals being made for each other.

This learning of romance narrative, which Alexis shares with many of her Western contemporaries, is not a process where girls are passive recipients of inculcation into romanticism, rather it is a resource they draw upon in making sense of their emotional and social world. As Christian-Smith (1991) found, for young teenage girls romance fiction may be quite explicitly read in an attempt to learn the scripts and conventions of heterosexual relationships. She also suggests, importantly, that romance reading may be for girls a form of literary consumption about which they can demonstrate knowledge and competence. Romantic fiction, soap operas and other feminine genres are not something girls merely consume: they are narrative forms which they can learn to manipulate, second guessing the plots of what they read or see (Christian-Smith, 1991), using similar narrative structures and devices in what they themselves write (Moss, 1989) or employing them to construct their own private fantasies (Thompson, 1984). The decline in romantic fiction in teenage magazines noted by McRobbie (1991) is unlikely to herald the decline of the culture of romance. The features in many of these magazines, especially those concerning the stars of popular music, may well be providing the material for personal romantic fantasies which girls find preferable to the stilted photo-stories they are offered (Thompson, 1984).

What is being created in these narratives and shared in the feminine culture of girls and women is a certain form of emotional literacy which men rarely acquire. Women often find men emotionally illiterate precisely because men have not learnt to construct and manipulate romance narratives or wider discourses of emotion. Men are generally aware of the more superficial conventions of romance, but not its more complex aspects. Women may find this annoying and often hurtful, but they also make allowances for it. Part of the culture of romance consists in women's shared knowledge that men are creatures with emotional disabilities which we can help them overcome, that they have a more emotional side buried under their masculine posturing (Radway, 1987). This shared feminine knowledge is not merely a product of romance narrative, though it is central to it, it is also bound up with the material realities of gender, the fact that men rely on women, rather than each other, for nurturance.

It is in these terms that Radway accounts for the specific pleasures of reading romance – it satisfies a need for nurturance which women do not receive in everyday life. The heroes of the romances which Radway's sample of readers most enjoyed were 'spectacularly masculine' (Radway, 1987: 128), but with a hint of something softer beneath the hard exterior. The hero behaves in characteristically masculine ways, hurting and humiliating the heroine. In the end, however, his cruelty is explained as resulting from misunderstanding: eventually, with the help of the heroine, his softer side is revealed as he declares his love for her. Radway sees this form of narrative structure as a means by which women can deal with their anxieties about masculinity, explaining its negative consequences for them, without fundamentally challenging it. They gain pleasure from identification with a heroine who is finally nurtured by the hero and whose identity is confirmed by his love for her.

But where is the passion, excitement and eroticism in this account of romance? The ideal romances which Radway describes do not simply represent the heroine as the recipient of affection, but as the object of uncontrollable passion. The hero often rapes the heroine in these novels. This is constructed not as an act of violence but as the result of overwhelming desire. Again Radway suggests that women are thus enabled to deal with real fears about male violence without questioning the patriarchal society and culture which produces it. This may be the case, but it does not explain why women find pleasure and excitement in this eroticization of male power, and this is implied in her account of romance readers. It is also a feature of Helen Taylor's (1989b) study of *Gone With The Wind* fans, many of whom found the scene in which Rhett rapes Scarlett highly erotic. They do not, however, generally describe this scene as a rape: rather, Rhett is seen as 'driven mad' by his love for Scarlett and his actions are read as resulting from *her* power over him. The meaning of the quintessential male enactment of power over woman is thus reversed. This may be suggestive of the excitement which romance offers women: the excitement of a form of power over men (see Modleski, 1984). The attraction of romance for women may well lie in their material powerlessness.

Radway's (1987) account conflates the two forms of love which those who inhabit our Western culture habitually distinguish between. One is a felt need for nurturance which could be satisfied but which, for heterosexual women, frequently is not, the other is romantic desire experienced as overwhelming, insatiable. This is precisely what romantic narrative and the ideology of romantic love do: they assume that the former is the outcome of the latter. The 'happily ever after' conclusion of fairy tales and romances papers over the contradictions between these two forms of love.

The narrative closure effected at the moment of passion's consummation indicates that the excitement lies in the chase, not in the 'happily ever after'. Many of the 'great' romances of Western cultural tradition end in death, thus refusing routinization (Wilson, 1983). The attraction of romance narrative in part lies in the ability to relive the chase over and over again. Have we learnt too well that the story ends when mutual love is established, that once past that point the narrative has no direction? Or is there something else which predisposes us to pursue a form of love which evaporates almost as soon as we think we have captured it?

Conclusion

All this raises far more questions than can be answered. Ideas I think worth pursuing are clear: the idea that narratives of self are something we actively construct through accessing certain discourses and narrative structures existing within our culture, the notion that subjectivity, indeed the very idea that we are individual subjects, is discursively constructed. I would not wish to rule out the possibility that certain felt emotional needs and desires are constituted through our early experiences of nurture and through our entry into a particular culture, but any account of this must recognize the historical and cultural specificity of these experiences and should not assume that our emotional needs are irreversibly fixed at some point in childhood. Since gender differences are so crucial a factor in understanding the culture of romance, it is also important to remember the material power differences between women and men: women's historic economic dependence on men, the emotional and physical labour they perform for men within households and families underpin published and broadcast romance narratives and the narratives we construct around our own experience of romantic and domestic attachments.

Notes

1 As Rosaldo (1980) reminds us, we cannot assume when making cross-cultural comparisons (and the same applies to historical ones) that we are comparing like with like. When we think we recognize a social phenomenon as familiar, it may only be because we have imposed meanings derived from our own society on the cultural patterns of another.
2 In drawing out common themes in the work of representative feminist thinkers, I am necessarily glossing over differences. For example, where de Beauvoir

emphasizes women's tendency to worship and idealize men, Firestone sees men as more prone to romantic idealization. Both of these theorists stress women's powerlessness in love relative to men, while Comer focuses on love as a means of binding both men and women into monogamous marriage. I have also confined myself to considering only these three writers and have thus excluded some well-known analyses such as that of Greer (1970). It should also be noted that none of these writers mounts a sustained critique of heterosexuality itself.

3 That this accords with many women's experience of heterosexual love is suggested by more recent work such as that of Rubin (1983), Radway (1987), Hite (1988), Mansfield and Collard (1988) and Cancian (1990).

4 Even feminist accounts, otherwise firmly grounded in material reality, sometimes slide towards such mysticism (see, for example, Haug et al., 1987: 278–9).

5 I am aware of the problems of essentializing the categories 'women' and 'men'. It should be clear that my comments on gender differences in love refer to culturally constituted masculinity and femininity, not to some essential differences, and are offered in the spirit of sociological generalization rather than implying some absolute dichotomy.

6 There is a parallel here with the psychoanalytic distinction between a need, which is capable of gratification, and desire, which is not (see Chapter 8).

8 Women and Heterosexual Love: Complicity, Resistance and Change

This chapter is a further development of my ideas on love. It originated as a paper delivered at a conference on the theme of 'romance revisited' held at Lancaster University in 1993 and was later published in a book of the same title (Pearce and Stacey, 1995). Whereas the last chapter was framed from within sociology, this one addressed a specifically feminist audience and was more explicitly concerned with heterosexuality.

Romantic love has been somewhat neglected by feminists, despite the considerable attention that has recently been paid to its fictional representation. Research on women as readers and viewers of romance, however, does reveal that it has considerable emotional resonance for them. In order fully to appreciate both the appeal of such fiction and the place of romantic love in women's daily lives, we need an analysis of love itself, the ways in which it is made sense of as an emotion and how it figures in women's understanding of their own and others' relationships. In particular, rather than treating romantic desires as given, we should consider the ways in which they are culturally constructed.

In this chapter I will suggest some lines of enquiry that might be pursued and indicate some of the theoretical and political questions which love and romance raise for feminists. My remarks are directed towards heterosexual love, since it is here that the political issues are brought into sharpest relief. It is in heterosexual relationships that romantic love has been institutionalized as the basis of marriage, and it is heterosexual love which dominates cultural representations of romance. Yet it is clear that contemporary ideals of romantic love, framed within the context of a heterosexual and patriarchal social and cultural order, also impinge on those who resist the constraints of compulsory heterosexuality.

There is nothing new in feminist critiques of love, which had their origin in the period of first wave feminism. For example, the Russian revolutionary, Alexandra Kollontai, was fiercely critical of the individualism, possessiveness and exclusivity of romantic love (1972). Later Simone de Beauvoir (1972) provided foundations for analyses of romantic love developed by early second wave feminists such as Comer (1974), Firestone (1972) and Greer (1970). These accounts were unambiguously critical of romantic love (see Chapter 7). It was the bait in the marriage trap; it served to justify our subordination to men and rendered us complicit in that subordination; it involved an unequal emotional exchange in which women gave more than they received; its exclusivity was taken as indicative of the emotional impoverishment of our lives; it diverted women's energies from more worthwhile pursuits. Where these writers considered romantic fiction, as in the case of Greer, it was represented simply as 'dope for dupes' – a means of brainwashing women into subservience. The emphasis, then, was unequivocally on the dangers of love and romance for women.

Since that time feminists have developed new perspectives, which take women's pleasure in romantic fiction more seriously and which offer more sophisticated accounts of women's reading practices. This shift in focus from the dangers of romance to its pleasures, however, risks clouding our critical vision. Part of the problem, as I see it, is that love itself has moved out of the picture. The emotion which romantic fiction represents and which is so central to its readers' responses to it remains relatively unexplored. Subjecting love itself to analysis may serve to sharpen our critical faculties.

I want to state very firmly that retaining a critical perspective on love and romance need not be simplistic. You do not have to see romance readers as cultural dupes in order to argue that romance is implicated in maintaining a cultural definition of love which is detrimental to women. Nor need we resort to a moralistic sackcloth-and-ashes feminism which enjoins strict avoidance of cultural products and practices which are less than ideologically sound. It is not necessary to deny the pleasures of romance or the euphoria of falling in love in order to be sceptical about romantic ideals and wary of their consequences. It is possible to recognize that love is a site of women's complicity in patriarchal relations while still noting that it can also be a site of resistance.

The cultural construction of emotion

In saying that we should give greater consideration to romantic love as an emotion, I am not implying that there is something called 'love' that exists outside society and culture. Indeed, I think it vitally important that as feminists we should contest ideological constructions of love which represent it as 'natural'. On Valentine's day 1993, BBC2 screened an evening of programmes on love, including one on the writing and marketing of Mills and Boon romances. We were told that the books sell millions all over the world and are translated into dozens of languages – proof that they speak to a universal feminine concern, that romantic love is a transhistorical, transcultural phenomenon. Feminists have learnt to be sceptical of such universalizing, naturalizing claims. These romances derive from a specifically Western cultural tradition – if they are being consumed world-wide we need to know why and how they are being read. It cannot simply be assumed that all women everywhere make sense of them in exactly the same way (Taylor, 1989a). We therefore need to develop analyses of love as a culturally constructed emotion and to explore its linkages to specific social orderings of intimate relationships.

Emotions should not be regarded as pre-social essences, but as socially ordered and linguistically mediated (Hochschild, 1983; Jagger, 1989) (see Chapter 7). This means that they are also culturally variable. Recent anthropological work suggests that particular constructions of emotion and, indeed, the category 'emotion' itself, are culturally specific (Lutz and Abu-Lughod, 1990; Rosaldo, 1984). As yet there has been little exploration of love from this perspective, but some of the insights of anthropologists are suggestive of possible interconnections between modern Western ideas of the self and of emotionality which might have implications for an analysis of love.

Individualism is a key issue here: in particular the way in which Western introspection about our 'feelings' is linked to a definition of individuals in terms of unique subjectivities (Abu-Lughod, 1990; Errington and Gewertz, 1987; Lutz, 1986). This is particularly pertinent to the emotion we call romantic love since it assumes a coming together of two such unique subjects, each of whom should be the 'only one' for the other. While ideal love is often thought of as a merging of selves, it presupposes the prior existence of two distinct selves. Moreover, to be 'in love' is not only to be intensely preoccupied with one's own inner feelings, but with those of the beloved (does s/he really love me, does s/he feel as I do?). Such concerns, taken for granted within Western discourses of the emotions, may be quite alien elsewhere (Abu-Lughod, 1990; Errington and Gewertz, 1987).

The construction of the self in terms of inner psychic processes may well be historically as well as culturally specific (Foucault, 1988; Rose, 1989). Moreover, the discourses around individual subjectivity which have emerged over the last few centuries have also been discourses around gender. Emotionality in general has been associated with the feminine, counterposed to masculine rationality (Lutz, 1990), while love in particular has been defined as part of the feminine sphere (Cancian, 1990). Whereas the link between romantic love and individualism was once discussed primarily in terms of free choice of marriage partners (see Chapter 7), more recently attention has been paid to shifting definitions of love itself, to its interconnections with ideals of self-realization and to the gendered character of both love and the self (Cancian, 1990; Giddens, 1992; Seidman, 1991). This recent work draws extensively on feminist scholarship even where it is not directed by explicitly feminist agendas. What does emerge from the very different perspectives offered by Cancian, Giddens and Seidman, however, is that 'love' is not a fixed, unchanging emotion and that its shifting meanings are the outcome of gendered struggles. In particular, love has been, for the last two centuries, a locus both of feminine complicity in and resistance to male domination.

Love, like all emotions is not directly observable. We can, in the end, analyse only the ways in which it is talked and written about – the discourses around romantic love which circulate within our culture – but these I would argue construct our experience and understanding of love. This is not to deny that emotions are deeply, subjectively felt as embodied experience (see Lutz and Abu-Lughod, 1990: 12), nor that such discourses are embedded in observable social practices and material social realities. Whereas a strictly Foucauldian use of the term 'discourse' counterposes it to ideology (Foucault, 1980), I would argue that feminists need to retain a conceptualization of discourses as ideological in their effects in that they can work to conceal, legitimate or render palatable relations of subordination and domination (see Chapter 1). Such discourses can also be internally contradictory while at another level serving to hide such contradictions. This process is evident in modern romantic ideals.

Love's contradictions

Romantic love hinges on the idea of 'falling in love' and this 'fall' as a means for establishing an intimate and deep relationship. Yet being 'in love' is also seen as radically different from other forms of love – mysterious, inexplicable, irrational, uncontrollable, compelling and ecstatic. Even feminists often resort to mystical language to describe it. Haug et al., for example, see love as a means of retrieving 'the buried and forgotten stirrings of the soul' (Haug et al., 1987: 278). It appears to be experienced as a dramatic, deeply felt inner transformation, as something that lifts us above the mundane everyday world – which is of course part of its appeal and has led some feminists to defend it against its critics (see, for example Baruch, 1991; Person, 1988). It is different in kind from lasting, longer term affection and widely recognized as more transient.

There are fundamental contradictions between passionate, romantic attraction and longer term affectionate love, yet the first is supposed to provide the basis for the second: a disruptive, tumultuous emotion is ideally supposed to be the foundation of a secure and durable relationship. Feminists from Kollontai (1972) to Firestone (1972) – as well as mainstream social theorists – have suggested that romantic love is not really about caring for another, but is self-centred and individualistic. There is a strong suggestion in literary, psychoanalytic and social scientific writings that the excitement of love thrives only when obstacles are put in its way. Again this makes it an unlikely basis for a committed relationship. So too does the oft noted tendency to romantic idealization – the other we pursue so compulsively is frequently the product of our own imagination (Baruch, 1991; Wilson, 1983). Hence the transformative power of love, its ability to turn frogs into princes. One of the most obvious appeals of romantic fiction is that it enables readers to relive the excitement of romantic passion without having to confront its fading and routinization. In real life we all too often discover that our prince was only a frog after all.

The passionate compulsiveness of love raises the issue of eroticized power and violence – a persistent theme both of pornography and romantic fiction. This is suggestive of an articulation between love and violence which is rarely explored, although the related linkages of sexuality with violence and love with sexuality have received considerable attention. Although the concept of love in some senses carries connotations antithetical to violence, in its passionate, romantic form it is not a gentle feeling. It is often characterized as violent, even ruthless (Bertilsson, 1986). 'More than wanting to cosset the beloved we may feel we want to eat them alive' (Goodison, 1983: 51–2). It can also be a pretext for violence which, if provoked by a jealous rage, can be read as proof of love – as can rape. Good reason, I think, to maintain our critical stance on the romantic construction of love, particularly since many of us are well aware of the painful experiences of women abused by those they had loved.

Although love relationships are often seen as egalitarian, the compulsiveness and insecurity of romantic passion imply a struggle for power. To be in love is to be powerless, at the mercy of the other, but it also holds out the promise of power, of enslaving the other. It thus offers women the hope of gaining power over a man: a common theme of romance narrative is the idea that women can tame the male beast by snaring him in the bonds of love (Modleski, 1984; Radway, 1987). Here the themes of complicity and resistance come into play – the desire for power over a man might be read as resistance. The power it delivers is, of course, illusory. It only lasts while the man is in the throes of romantic passion, after which the beast is likely to reassert himself (Langford, 1992). He may continue to be dependent on a woman's nurturance and she may continue to gain a sense of power providing it – but the structural bases of power and inequality in heterosexual relationships remain untouched. What she is providing is emotional labour which, like domestic labour, may offer her a sense of self-worth while simultaneously being exploitative (Bartky, 1990; Delphy and Leonard, 1992).

Love's discontents

Once heterosexual love is routinized within a committed relationship, then, the asymmetry of gender may become all the more apparent. This again raises the question of women's resistance. Dissatisfaction with a lack of emotional reciprocity, with men's incapacity to give or display love, has emerged as a source of women's discontent in numerous studies of marriage and long-term heterosexual relationships since the 1960s (see, for example, Duncombe and Marsden, 1993; Komarovsky, 1962; Mansfield and Collard, 1988; Rubin, 1976, 1983). It has also been used to explain the attraction of romantic fiction for women (Radway, 1987). This may be a way in which the ideal of companionate marriage based on romantic love sows the seeds of its own destruction – or at least the destruction of a specific relationship. Women appear to be more dissatisfied with the emotional than the material inequities of marriage and heterosexual relations (Duncombe and Marsden, 1993; Mansfield and Collard, 1988).

One potentially subversive aspect of romance fiction suggested by Radway (1987) is that it is a means by which women provide themselves with the nurturance lacking in their relationships with men (see Chapter 7). It also clear from ethnographic studies like Radway's that, when women talk about their reading and viewing preferences, this can be an occasion for discussing gender differences, highlighting men's distance from the feminine emotional world and voicing their criticisms of the men in their lives (see also Gray, 1992). Rarely, however, does this lead to any explicit critique of heterosexual relationships. As Radway herself notes, the consumption of romantic fiction is an adaptation to discontent not a challenge to its source. It also sustains the ideal of romance which produced the discontent in the first place.

There is a further issue here. It is all too tempting to simply accept that men are emotional inadequates and thereby treat women's emotional desires and capacities as given, or even as a form of feminine superiority, particularly since women have for so long been undervalued because of our imputed emotionality. We should be very wary indeed of falling into such an essentialist stance for two reasons. First, what we are dealing with is not merely an imbalance of values, but a material, structural imbalance. Our nurturant capacities are closely interwoven with our location within patriarchal relations – we should be cautious of revalorizing what might be symptomatic of our subordination. More generally, we should not treat emotions as given. Hence, whether we are talking about nurturant caring love or passionate romantic love, we need an explanation of the ways in which these emotions are constructed at the level of our subjectivities.

Earlier feminist accounts recognized that women's romantic desires were not merely an expression of some innate feminine proclivity, but often underestimated how deeply rooted in our psyches these desires were. Romance was a confidence trick which, once seen through, could be avoided, but which continued to dupe and ensnare less enlightened women. More recently the cultural dupe notion has been challenged, particularly in relation to romantic fiction.

Readers of romance are of course perfectly aware that it is not a realistic representation of the social world – indeed, that is part of its attraction (Fowler, 1991; Radway, 1987). They know what they are reading and they know they cannot hope to achieve this fantasy in reality. It is also the case, as numerous sociological studies tell us, that romantic aspirations in choice of life-partners are tempered with realism. The point, however, is that romanticism and realism can coexist at different levels of our subjectivities. It is perfectly possible to be critical of heterosexual monogamy, dismissive of romantic fantasy and still fall passionately in love: a fact which many feminists can themselves testify to (Gill and Walker, 1993; Jackson, 1993a). This should not surprise us since it is now widely recognized that our subjectivities are not coherent and consistent.[1] It is the awareness of such contradictions which has inspired much feminist writing on love and romance. Gradually feminists have broken the silence which surrounded our continued experience of 'unsound' desires, have been willing to 'come out' as secret fans of romance (Kaplan, 1986; Modleski, 1991; Taylor, 1989b). Romantic ideals can be deeply embedded in our subjectivities even when we are critical of them.

Love, romance and subjectivity

Here I find myself confronting what seems to me a major gap in feminist theory – the lack of a convincing theory of subjectivity. It has become almost conventional to introduce psychoanalytic explanations at this point. Various versions of psychoanalysis have indeed been used to explain the attractions of romance reading for women. Radway's use of Chodorow's (1978) framework may provide a coherent explanation of why women wish to be nurtured and why men are incapable of providing that nurturance, but it doesn't explain why women are so attracted to tales of passionate, even violent, desire.[2] Lacanian accounts certainly tackle desire in a way which is congruent with some of the features of romantic love which I have identified. Desire is constituted through lack, an inevitable product of our entry into language and culture and is intrinsically incapable of satisfaction (Mitchell and Rose, 1982). Since this is conceptualized in terms of entry into language and culture per se, not of entering a specific culture (see Chapter 1), the implication is that 'desire' is an essential part of human social nature. Lacanian psychoanalysis does not admit of the possibility of emotions being structured differently in different cultural settings and thus imagines the whole world to be beset by the same desire – an assumption that anthropologists would make us wary of (Errington and Gewertz, 1987; Lutz and Abu-Lughod, 1990; Rosaldo, 1984).

I am not convinced, either, that the Lacanian account can deal with the specifics of the ways in which language structures emotional and sexual experience even within Western culture. Emotions are not simply 'felt' as internal states provoked by the unconscious sense of lost infantile satisfactions – they are actively structured and understood through culturally specific discourses. These discourses differentiate between love as nurture, being 'in love', lust and sexual arousal – all of which are conflated in the psychoanalytic concept of desire. Even if we were to accept that desires are shaped at an unconscious level, that this is what surfaces in our romantic imaginings, this cannot account for the specific content of our desires and fantasies. Fantasies do not emerge fully formed into our consciousness. They are actively constructed by us, in narrative form, drawing on the cultural resources to hand.

Lacanian psychoanalysis, while ostensibly an account of the cultural construction of emotion, locates 'desire' as an inner state and thus precludes the possibility of linking the experience of 'love' to specific cultural contexts and to the specific discourses and narratives which give shape to our emotions. Feminist accounts of the pleasures of romance reading within this type of psychoanalytic framework, for example Alison Light (1984) on *Rebecca* and Cora Kaplan (1986) on *The Thorn Birds*, seem to me to suggest that romantic fiction reflects, gives voice to or is constructed around a set of emotions which already exist. I would argue, on the contrary, that romantic narrative itself contributes to the cultural construction of love. I do not maintain, as some early critics of romance did, that it is simply a means of brainwashing women into subservience. Rather, I am suggesting that this is but one of the resources from which we create a sense of what our emotions are.

What I would suggest, and have discussed in more detail in Chapter 7, is that we explore further the possibility that our subjectivities – including our emotions – are shaped by the social and cultural milieu we inhabit through processes which involve our active participation. We create for ourselves a sense of what our emotions are, of what being in love is, through positioning ourselves within discourses, constructing narratives of self, drawing on whatever cultural resources are available to us. This perspective allows us to recognize the constraints of the culture we inhabit while allowing for human agency and therefore avoiding the 'cultural dupe' syndrome, of admitting the possibility of both complicity in and resistance to patriarchal relations in the sphere of love.

Conclusion: resistance, complicity and change

If, as I have suggested, emotions are culturally constructed, they are not fixed for all time. Recent accounts of love suggest that it has indeed changed its meaning over time and that this has come about in part because personal life has been the object of political, especially feminist struggle (Baruch, 1991; Cancian, 1990; Giddens, 1992; Seidman, 1991). Where these writings comment on current trends and begin to predict future changes, however, they frequently overestimate the changes which are occurring.

A common strand running through these analyses is the claim that romantic love is being undermined as a result of changing sexual mores and women's demands for more equal relationships. For Baruch (1991) romantic love might meet its end once the denial it feeds upon gives way to too easy gratification of sexual desire, but may yet be revived by the anti-permissive climate consequent upon the spread of AIDS. While Seidman (1991, 1992) espouses a more libertarian and less romantic ethic than Baruch, he shares her view that libertarianism and romanticism are antithetical to each other, and that we are now witnessing a struggle between these opposing social currents. He argues that the progressive sexualization of love during the 20th century created the preconditions for its demise by valorizing sexual pleasure in its own right and therefore breaking the linkage between love and sexuality. Giddens (1992) sees these same trends as leading away from the romantic quest for the 'only one' with whom to share one's life towards the ideal of the 'pure relationship', more contingent than lifelong monogamy, lasting only as long as it is mutually satisfying. Women are leading this trend because they are refusing to continue to service men's emotional needs at the expense of their own. Similarly, Cancian (1990) detects a move away from 'feminized' love, to a more androgynous form, where men take more responsibility for the emotional well-being of their partners.

A less restrictive sexual morality does not, in itself, indicate that romantic love is losing its emotional salience, although it may well mean that love is less often regarded as a precondition for physical intimacy. Romanticism and libertarianism are not as mutually exclusive as Baruch and Seidman imply. It is not only moral strictures which place barriers in the way of the gratification of our desires, and romantic love is not in any case reducible to sexual desire. A libertarian ethic may be antithetical to a prescriptive form of romanticism which enjoins lifelong monogamy on lovers, but need not preclude falling in love. Young women's increased heterosexual activity is not necessarily evidence of an absence of romantic desires, although it may indicate a higher degree of realism about the durability of relationships founded upon them. Higher divorce rates, adultery and serial monogamy may indicate a continued search for romantic fulfilment rather than the abandonment of that quest. It may be the case that women are expecting more out of heterosexual relationships and are less likely to remain in them if these expectations are not realized. This does not mean, however, that in their search for the 'pure relationship' they regard their love for their partner as contingent and conditional at the outset, or that they have ceased to entertain romantic hopes. Given the lack of evidence that women's demands are currently being met, claims that a more egalitarian form of love is emerging seem absurdly over optimistic and wilfully neglectful of the continued patriarchal structuring of heterosexuality.

It is erroneous to assume too close a correspondence between changes in patterns of sexual relationships and transformations of romantic desire. What may be happening is that the contradictions of romantic love are becoming more apparent with the partial erosion of its institutional supports. Now that premarital chastity and lifelong monogamy are no longer expected of women, it becomes obvious that romantic love does not guarantee lasting conjugal happiness – but then it never has. This may lead us to modify our expectations of intimate relationships, may render them less durable, but it does not yet herald the demise of romantic desires.

Certainly the purveyors of romantic fiction are not suffering a contraction of their markets. Rather, they are adapting their plots to suit shifts in sexual mores – but their more assertive, less virginal heroines are still seeking Mr Right. There are, moreover, new markets being created, notably through book series for young readers. If, as I have suggested, the attraction of such romances both requires and helps constitute particular emotional responses, reports of the death of romantic love are certainly exaggerated.

Notes

1 This insight is usually attributed to psychoanalytic and poststructuralist perspectives, but I would argue that most feminists have – at least implicitly – long recognized that this is the case (see Jackson, 1992b).

2 *Editorial note*: Chodorow's psychoanalytic account explains gender difference in terms of the differential experience of mothering undergone by boys and girls. Because of the strong bonds of identification between mothers and daughters, girls do not develop a strong sense of autonomous selfhood, but rather define themselves in relation to others. This creates both a capacity to nurture and a need for nurturance. In order to become masculine a boy must distance himself from his mother, and from all that is feminine, and thus develops a sense of himself as separate and apart and in the process denies the possibility of emotional connection to another.

9   Gender and Heterosexuality: a Materialist Feminist Analysis

In Britain the feminist debate on heterosexuality was re-opened by the publication of a special issue of the journal Feminism & Psychology *in 1992 and its subsequent re-issue, in an expanded form, as an edited book (Wilkinson and Kitzinger, 1993). Like many heterosexual feminists, I had reservations about the way in which the discussion was framed, but I welcomed the chance to revisit past feminist controversies in a new theoretical and political context. This chapter was one of a series of interlinked contributions I made to the ongoing debate (Jackson, 1994, 1995b, 1995c, 1996a, 1996b, 1996c). I have chosen to reproduce this particular piece since it was here that I explored the materialist feminist basis of my argument in greatest detail and made my position on the relationship between gender and sexuality most explicit. Some of the material from my other work on heterosexuality has been incorporated into Chapters 1 and 12.*

This chapter is a response to the recent resurgence of debate on feminism and heterosexuality. Although positions within this debate are not as polarized as they were in the early 1980s, there is still a large gulf between radical lesbian feminist critics of heterosexuality (Kitzinger and Wilkinson, 1993) and heterosexual feminists seeking to defend their sexual practices (Hollway, 1993; Segal, 1994). I find myself caught in the middle, dissatisfied with both sides – a white, heterosexual radical feminist, wanting to problematize heterosexuality without damning myself as a failed feminist. I have therefore been looking for means of theorizing heterosexuality critically, exploring the ways in which it is implicated in the subordination of women, but without conflating heterosexuality as an institution with heterosexual practice, experience and identity. I have found a useful starting point in the analyses of gender produced by French materialist feminists, especially Christine Delphy (1984, 1993). In developing this perspective, I shall argue that gender – as a socially constructed product of patriarchal hierarchies – is fundamental to an analysis of sexuality.

The concept of gender has not been uncontested within feminism: the usual distinction between 'sex' as biological difference and culturally constructed 'gender' has proved particularly problematic. There have always been some feminists who disliked this distinction. Psychoanalytic theorists, for example, maintain that sex, gender and sexuality are inextricably linked and cannot be disentangled from each other (Mitchell, 1982). This is the case both for those who see femininity and masculinity as culturally constructed and those who assume that some essential difference exists prior to cultural influences. Feminists interested in asserting women's 'difference' – whether from a psychoanalytic perspective or not – often object to the sex–gender distinction because they see it as denying the specificity of women's bodily experience (Brodribb, 1992; Gatens, 1983; Irigaray, 1985, 1993).

On the other hand, there are those who question the sex–gender distinction on the grounds that its challenge to essentialism does not go far enough: it still assumes a natural sex on to which gender is grafted. This can all too easily lead to the assumption that heterosexual relations between anatomical males and anatomical females belong in the realm of nature. Hence it is argued that we should question the very existence of gender categories themselves and ask why and how the social world is divided into the two groups we call 'women' and 'men'. This position is often associated with recent writings by poststructuralists and postmodernists, such as Butler (1990a), and Riley (1988), but as far back as the 1970s French radical feminists were arguing that sex categories are themselves social, that there could be no concept of 'woman' which was 'unrelated to a social context' (Questions Féministes Collective, 1981: 214). These materialist radical feminists differ from poststructuralists and postmodernists in one very crucial respect. The latter see the meaning of social categories as fluid and shifting, constantly being contested and renegotiated. Materialists, while accepting that these categories can and must be challenged, see them as rooted in social practices and structural inequalities which are built into the fabric of society. 'Men' and 'women' are not simply discursive constructs, but are materially existing social groups founded upon unequal, exploitative relationships (see Delphy, 1993; Guillaumin, 1995; Wittig, 1992). It is this perspective that I wish to explore further.

Materialist feminist perspectives

Materialist feminism is a form of radical feminism which has been an established current in France since the 1970s. Its exponents include Christine Delphy and Monique Wittig; others, such as Nicole-Claude Mathieu and Colette Guillaumin, are less well known outside France. In the period from 1977–80 this theoretical tendency found expression in the journal *Questions Féministes* (*QF*). This journal was dedicated to the analysis of patriarchy as a social system in which men and women constitute classes with opposing interests. This was the starting point for their analysis of men and women as social categories: a radically anti-essentialist perspective on gender.[1]

The form of theory these thinkers have generated confounds popular stereotypes of both radical feminism and 'French Feminism'. The former is frequently misrepresented as championing 'women's values' as if they were essential feminine attributes – a position to which materialist feminism is fundamentally opposed. The latter, 'French Feminism', has come to denote something quite different from feminism in France. It is largely an Anglo-American invention which canonizes some French theorists while completely ignoring others (a misrepresentation perpetuated by some influential anthologies, for example, Fraser and Bartky, 1992; Jardine and Smith, 1987; Marks and Courtivron, 1981). Within France, those engaged in psycho-analytic theorizing about femininity, exploring women's relationships to their body and 'feminine' language, have not generally defined themselves as feminists. Yet this is what is called 'French Feminism' outside France, the 'holy trinity' being Hélène Cixous, Julia Kristeva and Luce Irigaray (Landry and MacLean, 1993: 54).[2] 'French Feminism' can also mean work which draws on the writings of certain male theorists, such as Lacan, Foucault and Derrida. The boundaries of 'French Feminism' are thus strangely constructed: some men fall within its definition, as do women who do not call themselves feminists, but those who have always called themselves feminists are excluded. This, as Delphy has pointed out, is a form of imperialism whereby women from outside France define what 'French Feminism' really is, while feminists within France are denied the right to be heard (Delphy, 1995: 213–221).

French radical feminism, in particular, suffers from this silencing. Some-times French radical feminism is reinvented: Chris Weedon even goes so far as to identify the 'trinity', and Irigaray in particular, with radical feminism (Weedon, 1987: 9) – apparently because she assumes that anyone asserting women's essential 'difference' must be a radical feminist! Those in France who name themselves radical feminists have always vigorously opposed this point of view. For example, much of the editorial of the first issue of *QF* was devoted to a polemic against this doctrine of 'neo-femininity'.

If, as materialist feminists argue, relations between women and men are class-like relations, then gender divisions have nothing to do with nature but are the product of social and economic structures. Patriarchal domina-tion is not based upon pre-existing sex differences, rather gender exists as a social division because of patriarchal domination. Hence hierarchy pre-cedes division (Delphy, 1993; Delphy and Leonard, 1992). As Delphy and Leonard put it:

> For us 'men' and 'women' are not two naturally given groups who at some time fell into a hierarchical relationship. Rather the reason the two groups are distinguished socially is because one dominates the other. (Delphy and Leonard, 1992: 258)

This argument is in keeping with the Marxist method of analysis adopted by materialist feminists. For Marxists classes only exist in relation to one another: there can be no bourgeoisie without the proletariat and vice-versa. Similarly 'men' and 'women' exist as socially significant categories because of the exploitative relationship which both binds them together and sets them apart from each other. Conceptually there could be no 'women' without the opposing category 'men', and vice-versa. As Wittig says: 'there are no slaves without masters' (1992: 15).

Because they analysed women's oppression in terms of class, French radical feminists emphasized the social aspect of sex categories. From the 1970s they began to speak of social men and social women as distinct from biological males and females (see, for example, Delphy, 1984; Guillaumin, 1987; Mathieu, 1977; Wittig, 1992). The implications of treating 'men' and 'women' as social categories were elaborated in the editorial to the first issue of *Questions Féministes* in November 1977, in which members of the collective spelled out their position on sex differences in some detail. They argued that opposition to naturalistic explanations of sexual difference is a basic tenet of radical feminism. Women's oppression derives from a patriarchal social system and 'in order to describe and unmask this oppression, arguments that have recourse to "nature" must be shattered' (Questions Féministes Collective, 1981: 214). Ideas of feminine 'difference' embraced by adherents of 'neo-femininity' derive from patriarchal reasoning which claims that women are different in order to justify and conceal our exploitation. In order to counter this ideology, the Collective argues, radical feminism must refuse any notion of 'woman' that is unrelated to social context:

> The corollary of this refusal is our effort to deconstruct the notion of 'sex differences' which gives a shape and a base to the concept of 'woman' and is an integral part of naturalist ideology. The social mode of being of men and of women is in no way linked to their nature as males and females nor with the shape of their sex organs. (1981: 214–15)

The consequences of this are indeed radical. The political goal envisaged is not the raising of women's status, nor equality between women and men, but the abolition of sex differences themselves. In a non-patriarchal society there would be no social distinctions between men and women, nor between heterosexuality and homosexuality:

> On the level of sexual practices, the distinction between homo- and heterosexuality will be meaningless since individuals will meet as singular individuals with their own specific history and not on the basis of their sexual identity. (1981: 215)

To be biologically male or female would no longer define our social or sexual identities. This does not mean women becoming like men 'for at the same time as we destroy the idea of the generic "Woman", we also destroy the idea of "Man"' (1981: 215). It cannot be otherwise since the terms woman/women and man/men are defined in relation to each other, they have no meaning outside this relation. The difference denoted by these terms derives from hierarchy, so that the destruction of sexual hierarchy will bring about the destruction of sexual difference.

While the Collective agreed on these basic premises, its members did not agree on the political consequences of their analysis, particularly for sexuality. In 1980 *QF* ceased publication after an acrimonious dispute over radical lesbianism and heterosexual feminism. This conflict was by no means confined to the QF Collective – it divided radical feminists as a whole. Nor was this a peculiarly French issue, but was being debated in many Western countries, including Britain (see Chapter 1). In France, public debate on this issue was initiated by the publication of two articles in *Questions Féministes* in February 1980. The first of these was Monique Wittig's 'The straight mind', in which she challenged the heterosexual thinking she saw as underlying patriarchal culture. The category 'woman', she argued, had no meaning outside 'heterosexual systems of thought'. She concluded that, because they live outside heterosexuality, 'lesbians are not women' (1992: 32). The other article, 'Heterosexuality and feminism' by Emmanuèle de Lesseps, argued against the politics of radical lesbianism. Lesseps acknowledged the contradictions that heterosexual feminists face, but rejected the idea that all feminists should become lesbians or that feminism should exclude heterosexual women. This she saw as turning the feminist movement, which began from women's common experience, against women (cited in Duchen 1987: 78–79).

Each side defended its position as deriving in terms of the central tenet of radical feminism: that 'men' and 'women' are classes. As the radical lesbians saw it, they were pushing 'the logic of radical feminist analysis to its logical conclusion' and identified with 'a lesbian political analysis which considers the *class of men* to be the main enemy' (in Duchen, 1987: 85, emphasis in original). If men are the class enemy, they argued, feminists should withdraw from any personal relationships with them, should refuse to service them sexually or otherwise and should devote all their energies to the liberation of women. Heterosexuality was 'antagonistic to feminist commitment' (1987: 85) and those who did not see this were at best reformist and at worst class 'collaborators' (1987: 87). Those who opposed the radical lesbian position, Delphy and Lesseps, subsequently launched *Nouvelles Questions Féministes*. In its first editorial they countered the arguments of the radical lesbians, which they saw as incompatible with the premises of radical feminism: the recognition that women constitute an oppressed class, that we are all oppressed by men as a class and that feminism is the struggle against this *common* oppression of women (in Duchen, 1987: 81). While accepting the need for a critique of heterosexuality, they insisted that this should be dissociated from a 'condemnation of heterosexual women' (Duchen, 1987: 82).

Since then, theorists on both sides of the debate have held to the position that the categories 'women' and 'men' are the product of class relations, but with differing consequences for the analysis of both lesbianism and heterosexuality (see Delphy, 1984, 1993; Wittig, 1992). It is Delphy's analysis that I am following here, particularly her continued insistence that it is gender division itself, and not just the content of gender categories that should be the object of scrutiny (Delphy, 1993).

Materialist and postmodern perspectives

Although it remains controversial, such radical anti-essentialism has now become more academically fashionable – particularly among poststructuralists and postmodernists. These theorists frequently take their inspiration from the Anglo-American version of 'French Feminism' – although Wittig's work has had some influence on theorists such as Diana Fuss (1989) and Judith Butler (1990a), who are concerned with the interconnections between gender and sexuality. Reading Wittig in isolation from other materialist feminists, however, leads to interpretations of her work which undermine its materialist foundations. Exploring these perspectives will help to elucidate the differences between postmodern and materialist deconstructions of gender as well as the debates within materialist feminism itself.

Wittig endorses the materialist feminist view that there are no natural sex categories pre-existing hierarchy. 'It is oppression that creates sex and not the contrary' (1992: 2). Like Delphy she sees men and women as social classes and sexual divisions as a product of this class relationship, but places particular emphasis on heterosexuality as the locus of women's oppression. 'The category of sex is the political category that founds society as heterosexual' (1992: 5).[3] Where she differs radically from Delphy is in her assertion that lesbians, fugitives from the heterosexual contract, escape from the category 'women', and thus are not women (Wittig, 1992). Both Fuss (1989) and Butler (1990a) are critical of the essentialism implied by treating lesbianism as lying outside the cultural construction and regulation of gender and sexuality. This is an argument with which Delphy would concur, given that she sees heterosexuality and homosexuality as culturally constructed in the same way as gender – in line with the position originally outlined in *QF*.

Butler's (1990a) radical deconstruction of gender owes a great deal to materialist feminism, but is not itself materialist. She does not read Wittig in the context of the thinkers whom Wittig herself (1992: xiv) names as her chief political influences, such as Mathieu, Delphy and Guillaumin, but in conjunction with Foucault, Lacan, Derrida, Kristeva and Irigaray. As a result, she filters out much which is fundamental to materialism. In the first place Butler over-sexualizes Wittig's conceptualization of heterosexuality. According to Butler, Wittig sees the binary sexual divide as 'serving the reproductive aims of a system of compulsory heterosexuality' (1990a: 19), and as restricting 'the production of identities along the axis of heterosexual desire' (1990a: 26). Now it is true that Wittig places great emphasis on women's sexual servicing of men, but she also makes it clear that the heterosexual contract involves a good deal more than coitus and reproduction:

> The category of sex is the product of a heterosexual society in which men appropriate for themselves the reproduction and production of women and also their physical persons by means of . . . the marriage contract. (Wittig, 1992: 6)

This contract 'assigns the woman certain obligations, including unpaid work' (1992: 7). Wittig goes on to argue that it determines control of a woman's children and where she should live, makes her dependent on her husband, subject to his authority, and denies her the full protection of the law if he assaults her. Elsewhere she explains that what lesbians escape from is a relation 'which implies personal and physical obligation as well as economic obligation' (1992: 20). All this bears comparison with Delphy's (1984) analysis of the class relation between men and women and with Guillaumin's work on sexual difference and on the private and collective appropriation of women's labour (Guillaumin, 1981, 1987). Butler, however, ignores these material social relations which underpin the category of sex.

Butler does appear to understand that 'materialism takes social institutions and practices . . . as the basis of critical analysis' (1990a: 125), but she fails to recognize that, for materialists, this implies a system of structural inequalities. Because Wittig's references to such structural inequalities are absent from Butler's summary of her work, we are left with the impression of sexual difference as oppressive, yet not clearly hierarchical. 'Wittig understands "sex" to be discursively produced and circulated by a system of significations oppressive to women, gays and lesbians' (1990a: 113). Wittig's work is thus shaped to fit Butler's own contention that gender is a 'regulatory fiction' to which both women and men are subject, but which is sustained – and can be subverted – through performance.

The association of this deconstruction of gender and sexuality with postmodernism and queer theory explains some feminists' resistance to it – particularly because queer theory ultimately displaces patriarchal gender hierarchy in favour of heterosexuality as the primary regulatory system. It is vitally important for feminism that we see heterosexuality as a gendered hierarchy and not just a normative construction of cross-sex desire. For materialist feminists heterosexuality is not simply a matter of the sex–gender–desire matrix which Butler outlines; it certainly includes this, but heterosexuality is founded not only on a linkage between gender and sexuality, but on the appropriation of women's bodies and labour.

Heterosexuality: institution and identity

Feminist discussions of heterosexuality frequently distinguish between heterosexuality as institution and as practice or experience (Richardson, 1993; Robinson, 1993). Such distinctions are necessary if we are to deal with the complexities of heterosexuality and not treat it as a monolithic entity. They also help us to avoid conflating the critique of heterosexuality with personal criticism of heterosexual feminists – a problem apparent in earlier debates in Britain, France and elsewhere (Jackson and Scott, 1996). I would suggest that, in the light of recent debates, we need to add a further dimension: the social and political identities associated with heterosexuality.[4] Such distinctions are, of course, analytical ones which, as heterosexuality is lived, intersect and interrelate. I would also argue that we should not over-privilege sexuality in relation to other aspects of social life: as institution, identity, practice and experience heterosexuality is not merely sexual. Moreover, while heterosexuality's central institution is marriage, the assumption of normative heterosexuality operates throughout society and even its specifically sexual practice is by no means confined to the private sphere (see, for example, Hearn et al., 1989).

As it is institutionalized within society and culture, heterosexuality is founded upon gender hierarchy: men's appropriation of women's bodies and labour underpins the marriage contract (Delphy and Leonard, 1992). The benefits men gain through their dominant position in the gender order are by no means reducible to the sexual and reproductive use of women's bodies. Men may say that 'women are only good for one thing' but, as Delphy (1992) points out, this is no reason why we should accept this at face value. In marriage, for example, the home comforts produced by a wife's domestic labour are probably far more important to a man's well-being and his ability to maintain his position as a man than the sexual servicing he receives. Nonetheless, a man does acquire sexual rights in a woman by virtue of marriage and a woman who is not visibly under the protection of a man can be regarded as fair sexual game by others (Guillaumin, 1981). Fear of sexual violence and harassment is also one means by which women are policed and police themselves through a range of disciplinary practices – from restricting their own access to public space, to where they choose to sit on a bus or train, how they sit and who they avoid eye contact with (Bartky, 1990). Here the macro level of power intersects with its micro practices. The institutionalization of heterosexuality also works ideologically, through the discourses and forms of representation which define sex in phallocentric terms, which position men as sexual subjects and women as sexual objects.

The question of sexual identity, in particular lesbianism as a political identity, has been much debated by feminists. Heterosexuality, however, is still infrequently thought of in these terms and the vast majority of heterosexual women probably do not define themselves as such. Nonetheless, many of the identities available to women derive from their location within heterosexual relations – as wife, girlfriend, daughter or mother. Attachment to these identities affects the ways in which women experience the institution and practices of heterosexuality. For example, women's ambivalent feelings about housework, their unwillingness to be critical of the appropriation of their labour, even when they are aware of the inequity of their situation, springs from their feelings about those they work for and from their desire to be good wives and mothers (Oakley, 1984; Westwood, 1984). In sexual terms, too, women's identities are likely to be shaped by heterosexual imperatives – the need to attract and please a man. The desire to be sexually attractive appears to be profoundly important to women's sense of self-worth and closely bound up with the gendered disciplinary practices through which docile, feminine bodies are produced (Bartky, 1990). Hence heterosexuality, while uninterrogated, is pivotal to conventional feminine identities.

To name oneself as heterosexual is to make visible an identity which is generally taken for granted as a normal fact of life. This can be a means of problematizing heterosexuality and challenging its privileged status, but for women being heterosexual is by no means a situation of unproblematic privilege. Heterosexual feminists may benefit from appearing 'normal' and unthreatening, but heterosexuality as an institution entails a hierarchical relation between (social) men and (social) women. It is women's subordination within institutionalized heterosexuality which is the starting point for feminist analysis. It is resistance to this subordination which is the foundation of feminist politics. It is hardly surprising, then, that heterosexual feminists prefer to be defined in terms of their feminism – their resistance – rather than their heterosexuality, their relation to men (Swindells, 1993). Resisting the label heterosexual, though, has its problems. It can imply a refusal to question and challenge both the institution and one's own practice; it can serve to invalidate lesbianism as a form of resistance to patriarchy and to deny the specific forms of oppression that lesbians face. For these reasons Kitzinger and Wilkinson are sceptical about those who 'call for the dissolution of the dichotomous categories "lesbian" and "heterosexual"' (1993: 7).

Questioning this binary opposition, however, need not be a way of avoiding the politics of lesbianism or getting heterosexual feminists off the hook, but can represent an honest attempt to problematize heterosexuality (see Gergen, 1993; Young, 1993). Nor is it only heterosexual feminists who are engaged in this deconstructive enterprise, but also lesbian queer theorists such as Diana Fuss (1991) and Judith Butler (1990a; 1991). When such arguments are framed from a postmodernist stance, this does make it difficult to account for the systematic structural bases of any form of oppression (see Jackson, 1992b). Nonetheless, treating the categories 'lesbian' and 'heterosexual' as problematic is by no means antithetical to radical feminism – indeed, I would argue that it is essential. This is not merely a matter of competing identities, but is fundamental to an appreciation of the social construction of gender and sexual categories.

The categories heterosexual, homosexual and lesbian are rooted in gender – they presuppose gender divisions and could not exist without our being able to define ourselves and others by gender. If we take Delphy's (1984, 1993) argument that 'men' and 'women' are not biologically given entities but social groups defined by the hierarchical and exploitative relationship between them, then the division between hetero- and homosexualities is, by extension, also a product of this class relation. Within this perspective it is possible to see gender and sexual categories as both social constructs and material realities. 'Women' are a social rather than natural category defined by their relation to men. Lesbianism, by virtue of its location in relation to patriarchal heterosexuality, also has a real social existence. This does not mean, as Wittig (1992) would have it, that lesbians are not women – we are all defined by our gender and there is no escaping the patriarchal hierarchy within which we are positioned as women.

Heterosexual eroticism: practice and experience

Recent analyses of heterosexuality, whether attacking it (Kitzinger, 1994; Kitzinger and Wilkinson, 1993) or defending it (Hollway, 1993; Segal, 1994), have tended to focus on sexual experience and practice, particularly on desire and pleasure. These debates have been centrally concerned with power – its structural underpinnings and its micro practices, the implications of its erotic dimensions and the degree to which women can subvert or challenge it within heterosexual relations. It should be noted that, for materialist feminists, the experience and practice of heterosexuality is not just about what does or does not happen between the sheets, but about who cleans the bathroom or who performs emotional labour for whom. Because of the prominence of heterosexual eroticism in recent debates, however, I will consider the potential of materialist feminism for furthering our understanding of desire, pleasure and displeasure in heterosexual sex. I will begin from the premise that gender is fundamental, that as desiring subjects we are gendered, as are the objects of our desire. This is as true of lesbian sexuality as it is of heterosexuality.

To desire the 'other sex' or indeed to desire 'the same sex' presupposes the prior existence of 'men' and 'women' as socially – and erotically – meaningful categories. What is specific to heterosexual desire is that it is premised on gender *difference*, on the sexual 'otherness' of the desired object. From a materialist feminist perspective this difference is not an anatomical one but a social one: it is the hierarchy of gender which 'transforms an anatomical difference (which is itself devoid of social implications) into a relevant distinction for social practice' (Delphy, 1984: 144). Since it is gender hierarchy which renders these anatomical differences socially and erotically significant, it is hardly surprising that heterosexual eroticism is infused with power. However, this eroticization of power is not reducible to the mere juxtaposition of certain body parts. There is nothing intrinsic to male and female anatomy which positions women as passive or privileges certain sexual practices above others. There is no absolute reason why the conjunction of a penis and a vagina has to be thought of as penetration, or as a process in which only one of those organs is active. The coercive equation of sex = coitus = something men do to women is not an inevitable consequence of an anatomical female relating sexually to an anatomical male, but the product of the social relations under which those bodies meet. Those social relations can be challenged. Even the most trenchant critics of heterosexuality and penetrative sex such as Jeffreys (1990) and Dworkin (1987) recognize that it is not male and female anatomy nor even, in Dworkin's case, the act of intercourse itself which constitute the problem, but rather the way in which heterosexuality is institutionalized and practised under patriarchy.

For some feminists anatomical difference, or indeed any form of difference between lovers, is seen as a potential source of power imbalance. Hence they strive to 'eroticize sameness and equality' (Jeffreys, 1990: 315). But is 'sameness' necessary for equality? From a materialist feminist perspective it is not difference which produces hierarchy, but hierarchy which gives rise to socially significant differences. All of us are 'different' from each other: no two human beings are 'the same' and a lover is always someone 'other'. The point is that there are some differences which are of little social relevance – such as the colour of our hair – and others which are constructed as socially significant by virtue of hierarchy – such as the configuration of our genitals or our skin pigmentation. Given that gender difference remains a material fact of social life, does this mean that power is an inescapable feature of heterosexual eroticism?

To argue that the power hierarchy of gender is structural does not mean that it is exercised uniformly and evenly at the level of interpersonal sexual relations, nor that our practice and experience is wholly determined by patriarchal structures and ideologies. There is some room for manoeuvre within these constraints. To deny this is to deny heterosexual women any agency, to see us as doomed to submit to men's desires whether as unwilling victims or misguided dupes. Heterosexual feminists, here as elsewhere in their lives, have struggled against men's dominance. We have asserted our right to define our own pleasure, questioned phallocentric models of sexuality, tried to deprioritize penetration or reconceptualize it in ways which did not position us as passive objects (Campbell, 1980; Jackson, 1982b; Robinson, 1993). More recently some have admitted – cautiously or defiantly – that even penetrative sex with men can be enjoyable and that its pleasure is not merely eroticized submission (Hollway, 1993; Robinson, 1993; Rowland, 1993; Segal, 1994).

Critics of heterosexuality are unimpressed by such claims. Kitzinger and Wilkinson, for example, are scathing about heterosexual feminists' attempts to develop egalitarian sexual practices and to change the meaning of penetration. Such strategies, they say, 'obscure the problem of the *institutionalization* of penile penetration under heteropatriarchy' (1993: 21). They see the institution as a totally determining practice so that each and every instance of penetration is an enactment of men's power. While it is the case that penetration within patriarchy is loaded with symbolic meanings which encode male power and is often in fact coercive, it cannot be assumed that it invariably carries this singular meaning. To argue that it does is to treat the physical act as meaningful in itself, as magically embodying male power without any intervening processes. It is thus assumed that the micro-processes of power can simply be read off from the structural level. It certainly cannot be assumed that if women like heterosexual sex we must all be wallowing in a masochistic eroticization of our subordination – the consistent message of the radical lesbian position (Jeffreys, 1990; Kitzinger, 1994; Kitzinger and Wilkinson, 1993).

We need to retain a critical perspective on heterosexual pleasure, but one which is more subtle and less condemnatory. However, we should not underestimate the pervasiveness of male power either. Even if, as Lynne Segal suggests, 'sex places "manhood" in jeopardy', threatening the 'masculine ideal of autonomous selfhood' (1994: 255), the hierarchical ordering of gender and sexuality is not as easy to subvert as she implies. Power operates at a variety of levels. Although we can contest it at the level of individual practice (and enhance our sexual pleasure in the process), this may have little effect elsewhere. There are, moreover, very real material constraints on seeking heterosexual pleasure and for many women it remains elusive (Ramazanoglu, 1994). Women often still discipline themselves to fit a model of sexuality which prioritizes male desires and defines women's fulfilment in terms of 'love' and the giving of pleasure (Holland et al., 1994). This attribute of femininity is hardly confined to sexuality: the ethic of service to men is fundamental to other aspects of gender relations, to men's appropriation of women's labour as well as their bodies.

It is difficult to imagine a truly egalitarian form of heterosexuality while gender division persists; and if that division were eradicated heterosexuality would no longer exist in any meaningful sense – and nor would lesbianism. Materialist feminism enables us to see that both heterosexuality and lesbianism depend for their existence on the hierarchy of gender. Sexuality is one site of struggle against that hierarchy, but it is by no means the only one. Nor is sexuality the sole basis of women's subordination. To give too much weight to sexual desire, practice and identity may deflect our attention from the myriad other ways in which the patriarchal ordering of the world into 'men' and 'women' is perpetuated. Heterosexuality helps to sustain that order, but it should be remembered that heterosexuality itself is not merely a sexual institution.

Notes

1 It should be noted that Delphy alone among these theorists used the term 'gender'. As well as being a term which originated in Anglophone theory, French radical feminists felt that, because it was defined in relation to biological sex, it too readily implied a natural distinction which pre-existed the social division of gender (see, for example Wittig, 1992: xvi). Delphy, on the other hand, prefers to use the concept of gender because 'sex' cannot easily be divested of its naturalistic connotations (1993).
2 Of these three, only Irigaray has ever identified as a feminist.
3 *Editorial note:* Since Wittig prefers the term 'sex' rather than 'gender' to denote the division between women and men, I followed this usage in discussing her work.
4 Elsewhere, I have also distinguished between practice and experience (Jackson, 1994, 1996a).

10   Lost Childhood or Sexualized Girlhood?

This chapter was originally published in Trouble & Strife *as 'Ignorance is bliss, when you're just seventeen'. While this is a witty play on the names of teenage magazines,[1] I have decided to revert to my original, more mundane, title since it more accurately reflects the argument I am making here. I wrote this piece in response to media coverage of sex in teenage magazines and the phenomenon of child beauty contests. The latter became more of a major issue some months after this article was written; at the end of the year, on Boxing Day 1996, a six-year-old star of the child pageant circuit, JonBenet Ramsey, was found murdered in Boulder, Colorado. This provoked extended media coverage in the first few months of 1997 which, once again, revolved around variations on the theme of lost innocence (see Scott et al., 1998).*

Although this chapter in concerned with specific, historically located, political and media events, the issues these raise are of wider relevance, revealing something of the troubled and troubling relationship between childhood and sexuality in late modern Western societies. This has been a long-standing and continuing interest of mine (see Jackson, 1982a, 1990, 1993c), evident in my discussion of sex education in Chapter 4. Some of the ideas presented here have recently been developed further in collaboration with Sue Scott and Kathryn Backett-Milburn (Scott et al., 1998).

On 6 February 1996 a Bill was introduced into the House of Commons proposing that a minimum age recommendation be printed on the covers of teenage girls' magazines, a move which followed publicly aired concern about their sexually explicit content.[2] A week earlier, BBC2 screened a documentary in its 'Under the Sun' series about five-year-old beauty queens in the Southern USA. The *Radio Times* carried a feature article on the programme – 'Made up, dressed up, fed up' written by Alison Graham (1996). The media was suddenly full of discussion about children and sexuality or, more specifically, about girls and sexuality. As usual, public debate missed what feminists might see as the main issues, the perpetuation of compulsory heterosexuality and the construction of female sexuality in terms of objectification and pleasing men. Instead the focus was on the threat posed to childhood.

What struck me about the media coverage of these events was the prominence of the concept of 'innocence'. For example, on the morning of 6 February, Radio 4's regular phone-in focused on sex in teenage magazines, framed by the question 'Whatever happened to childhood innocence?' 'Innocence' appears to be taken for granted as a defining feature of childhood, so that anything which threatens it is seen as a danger to childhood itself. Hence a recurrent theme in media discussions of both young women's magazines and child beauty queens was the idea of lost or stolen childhood. It is not, however, just asexual innocence which is seen as threatened, but the supposed golden age of freedom from the pressures of adult life. Thus Alison Graham says of the little beauty queens: 'childhood is forgotten in a whirl of singing lessons, modelling tutorials, photo sessions and hairdresser's appointments' (1996: 22). Yet asexuality is nonetheless thought of as central to this age of innocence – Graham makes it clear that sexuality is something which such young children should know nothing about.

Where have we heard all this before? One arena where the concept of innocence has been deployed in the media is in coverage of child sexual abuse. Jenny Kitzinger (1988) has argued that feminists should be critical of the way this concept is used to evoke public revulsion against sexual abuse. She points out that 'innocence' itself is seen as titillating and is eroticized as a sexual commodity, and that the ideal of innocence is used to stigmatize the sexually knowing child, to make her a potentially legitimate victim. Moreover, in the name of protecting 'innocence' adults deprive children of access to sexual information which might help them avoid sexual abuse and exploitation. Meanwhile, those who have worked to put child sexual abuse on the political agenda are themselves accused of destroying the 'age of innocence'.

We should be equally sceptical about the application of this concept to child beauty queens or the issue of sex in teenage magazines. In *Childhood and Sexuality* (1982a) I argued that the idea of 'innocence' is a means of depriving children of knowledge and justifying their powerlessness. I still stand by that view and, like Kitzinger (1988), would suggest that we need to think critically about the power which adults wield over children, the power that makes child abuse possible and which gives individual parents exceptional rights over their children. In so doing, of course, we need to pay attention to the intersection between parental power and patriarchal power. Feminists are unlikely to lose sight of patriarchal power but we are, as Christine Delphy (1992) has pointed out, sometimes guilty of neglecting the power that mothers wield over children.

In the recent public debates on childhood sexuality the wider context of both adult power and the construction of gender have, for the most part, been ignored. In all this discussion of children and sex, it is rarely made explicit that gender is an issue – yet in both the case of the beauty pageants and the magazines the children who are the objects of concern are *girls*. This makes a difference, since discourses on both childhood and sexuality which underpin these discussions are profoundly gendered. This neglect of gender has meant that the emphasis is on what is deemed extraordinary, the challenge to idealized models of childhood, rather than on what is depressingly and predictably ordinary – the cultural construction of sexualized femininity.

Of Barbie dolls and beauty queens

Like most women I know who watched the BBC documentary on child beauty queens, I was both fascinated and appalled. And yes, part of what appalled me was what was being done to these children, their whole lives governed by their parents' desire for their success in competition. Clearly the children did not have much choice in the matter. The documentary followed two rivals preparing for a major contest, concentrating on the one who finally won. She was certainly not happy – most of the time she seemed bored, fretful and sulky – only on stage did she come alive. Her rival seemed to be going along with the whole thing much more cheerfully.

The issue for me, though, was not that the discipline and sexualization enforced on these children was robbing them of their childhoods – rather it seemed an extreme manifestation of the ways in which children in general and girls in particular are treated. Children are defined as dependants subject to parental authority and, within limits, parents have the power to rear them as they choose. Childhood is also remarkable for the degree of control exercised over the body by others. Children's appearance, deportment, posture and movement are regulated, they are touched, kissed and fussed over and are more likely to be subject to physical punishment than any other category of person. This control of the body is more rigorously imposed on little girls (see Haug et al., 1987), one facet of the intersection of gender with the more general powerlessness of children.

These five-year-old beauty queens are young enough and small enough to be physically coerced. They are inexperienced enough not to know that any other mode of life is possible, since they live their lives competing on a relatively small circuit against the same opponents. Like all children, constrained to live their lives according to their parents' choices, they are forced to go along with what parents think best for them, whatever it is. What their parents think is best for these children is to win the contests, be the prettiest girl in town, or in the whole of the South.

A degree of 'femininity' is being imposed on these children which might well seem excessive even by non-feminist standards. Just when little girls are beginning to escape from the confines of frilly frocks and restrictive injunctions to be 'feminine', this programme came as a reminder that there are still sections of the population imposing very rigid and traditional ideals of femininity on their daughters. This is carried to extremes for the contestants in beauty pageants. These girls are being taught very deliberately, rigorously and systematically that the only thing about them of value is their prettiness and their ability to carry off a carefully managed performance of stereotypical femininity. This form of feminine attractiveness is culturally specific: blonde is beautiful, white is beautiful. In one section of the contest the girls are dressed as 'Southern Belles'. Not surprisingly, there is not a black child in sight – the racist standards of beauty noted in adult contests are also evident in those for children.

This commodification of a specific form of feminine attractiveness merges with the reduction of children to objects owned by their parents. With little girls this has often led to them being treated as dolls to be dressed up and displayed. During the documentary on children's beauty contests, one doting mother said of her daughter that, when dressed up and made up in her stage costume, she 'looks just like Barbie'. Like many girls her age, this one owned a collection of Barbie dolls. These dolls are hugely popular with little girls, a means of playing at a form of adult femininity; *Barbie* magazine is read by 14 per cent of girls aged 7–10 in the UK (Central Statistical Office, 1994). The little beauty queens have the opportunity (or misfortune) to act out the fantasy.[3]

What impressed me was not how grown up these little girls looked in their adult clothes, hair-dos and make-up – but how infantilized is the form of adult femininity they are emulating. I've always thought that extreme 'femininity' is a form of childishness – a sexualized gloss on the vulnerability and powerlessness of children. This is underlined by the performance of these children, already able to be feminine in these terms. Yet in the way that the girls were talked about in both the programme and the *Radio Times* article, these superficial signs of adult 'maturity' are taken as some sort of real difference between little girls and adult women. In the *Radio Times* there was a photo of one of them captioned 'Look, no make up ... Brooke as she really is.' The authentic child is one without make-up – no-one says this of adult women. Imagine this said, say, of a super model. For adult women, make-up and all other aids to 'femininity' are advertised as 'bringing out' the 'real woman' within. The dividing line between authentic childhood and authentic womanhood in this discourse, it seems, is a thin veneer of 'sophistication' symbolized by the presence or absence of make-up.

Yet the sexualization of childhood is not new. Little girls have long been taught to cultivate prettiness and coquetry, to get what they want by sexualizing themselves – and know they are failures if they don't match up. Beauty pageants can be seen as just a logical extension of this. For generations little girls have aspired to be 'May queens' or local carnival queens. The beauty contests are just a more commercialized and professionalized version. Even this is not a recent invention: beautiful baby contests are something I remember from my childhood. I also recall that Pears soap sponsored a 'Miss Pears' competition, the winner of which then featured in advertisements. It might be said that these represented properly innocent, asexual childhood. If so then these images illustrate Kitzinger's point that innocence itself is often sexualized. Judith Ennew (1986) suggests that such representations have distinct parallels with pornography. One example is a painting by Munier called 'Playmates', used by Pears Soap advertisements in 1903 (pre-dating Miss Pears) which features a scantily clad child in a distinctly sexual pose. She also places the famous photograph of Marilyn Monroe with her skirts blowing up around her next to an Oxo advertisement featuring a similar depiction of a small girl, suggesting that both represent the same fantasy (1986: 132–3).

What separates the beauty queens from past generations of Miss Pears or hundreds of 'cute' little girls featured in advertisements, how do we tell the Barbie dolls from the baby dolls? Partly the difference derives from the superficial effects of make-up and more adult clothes and hairstyles. It also, however, derives from something called 'sexuality', something antithetical to authentic childhood which is in part produced by dressing up for this 'adult' performance. It is also, however, about gestures, movements, a particular turn of the head, the knowing look or wink – all of which the competitors in the beauty pageants were being explicitly taught. They were being deliberately schooled in the performance of a sexualized femininity. The result, according to Alison Graham (1996: 24) is a little girl who 'imitates a sexuality she should know nothing about'. This phrase presupposes that sexuality is in itself improper for children and, more importantly, it hinges on the idea that female sexuality is reducible to how one looks, to a performance of sexual desirability and availability. Women's 'sexuality' is talked about in these terms, too – even by some feminists (see, for example, Coward, 1982). It is not an autonomous female sexuality which is meant here, but the process of self-objectification.

The little girl who 'imitates a sexuality she should know nothing about' is just acting out a more stylized version of the usual little girl performance – and in one sense knows nothing about sexuality while in another knows a great deal. She is probably ignorant about the mechanics of heterosexual sex, yet she knows that being attractive, flirtatious and cute wins a positive response from adults – and little girls know this even if they don't enter beauty contests. Again, this is not a new phenomenon: Simone de Beauvoir noted it nearly 50 years ago. In *The Second Sex* she argues that the little girl 'soon learns that in order to be pleasing she must be "pretty as a picture"; she tries to make herself look like a picture, she puts on fancy clothes, she studies herself in the mirror, she compares herself with princesses and fairies.' Through engaging in 'childish coquetry' she will seek to be the centre of attention (de Beauvoir, 1972: 306). This is not so far away from the five-year-old contestant in a beauty contest who announces to the approval from all around her 'I'm a queen every day' (Graham, 1996: 24).

This knowing but not knowing – being encouraged to sexualize themselves as objects without knowing the response this produces in adult men – is a dangerous game for girls. Paradoxically, the same parents who encourage their daughters to behave like this would, I'm sure, think it terrible for them to know about the realities of sex. It is this anxiety which underlies recent concern about teenage magazines. On the one hand these publications encourage aspects of femininity which are socially approved – interest in fashion, make-up and being attractive – while in another they appear to pose a threat of a more knowing and active female sexuality. It is the issue of sexual knowledge and how much of it should be available to young women which is the central issue at stake in public debate and in the attempt to regulate teenage girls' reading.

Sex and the teenage girl

Even if there were a law printing minimum reading ages on the covers of magazines, I cannot seeing this stopping young women from wanting to read them – though it might enhance parents' ability to police what their daughters are reading. The most popular magazine among boys aged 11–14 – *Viz* – does carry on its cover the message 'not for sale to children'. According to the Central Statistical Office's publication *Social Focus on Children* (1994), over a quarter of boys in this age group read it. I find this far more worrying than the magazines girls are reading, but boys' reading habits have not come under public scrutiny – a point I will return to later.

We might want to consider why a magazine called *Just Seventeen* is the most popular purchase among 11- to 14-year-olds in the first place, or why *19* is read by girls in their mid-teens. Part of the appeal of these magazines is that they speak to those who are still classed as children, still lacking the rights of adulthood but whose dreams and aspirations are for the maturity and status that young womanhood seems to offer them. Girls of this age often want to be older, want to be treated as adults, want what they are debarred from on the grounds of age. Wanting the forbidden does not necessarily mean that they all want to rush out and have sex, but they do want the right to know about it.

More sensible commentators, such as Claire Rayner, quoted in the *Guardian* (Weale, 1996), have pointed out that teenage interest in sexuality is nothing new. I entered my teens in the early 1960s when teenage magazines had lots of romance and no explicit sexual content (it was *Mirabelle* and the like in those days, even *Jackie* had yet to be launched). In the stories a kiss was the culmination of every romantic encounter. I and my peers were desperate to know more but were starved of likely sources. At the age of 11 or 12 we were reduced to reading out 'the dirty bits' from James Bond novels (it was that bad!). I recall great excitement when someone got hold of a copy of *Lady Chatterley's Lover*. At 14, continuing this communal reading practice, I and three friends were nearly expelled from school having been caught with *The Perfumed Garden*. Following this incident my father forbade me even to *talk* to boys – assuming, rather like some of those pontificating about teenage magazines today, that if I was reading such things I must be about to put it all into practice.

At least the magazines girls are reading today circulate in a public domain, where their content can be discussed and perhaps challenged, rather than furtively exchanged and whispered over in classrooms and playgrounds. Moreover, we cannot assume a direct link between the magazines' representations of sexuality and young women's sexual activities. For example, Elizabeth Frazer (1987) demonstrated that girls reading *Jackie* reflect upon what they are reading and are often critical of it. Teenage girls are even more likely than adult women to be seen as cultural dupes. The assumption is that, as children, they are peculiarly vulnerable to brainwashing, they do not know their own minds and therefore they are in danger of being corrupted. We need to credit young women with some ability to think for themselves. On the other hand, the new emphasis on women and girls as active readers can go too far in denying that particular texts have any effectivity at all. We can see this by means of analogy with the pornography debate: it is far too simplistic to claim that pornography directly causes sexual violence, but at the same time those of us opposed to pornography would want to argue that it contributes to the construction of a form of masculinity which makes sexual violence possible.

> We need to move beyond causal accounts of human actions, and look instead at the resources humans bring to their interpretations and representations, the meanings which shape their desires and constrain the stories they can imagine for themselves. For we are clearly not free to imagine just anything; we work both with and against the grain of the cultural meanings we inherit. (Cameron and Frazer, 1992: 381)

What young people read about sexuality will not *make* them act in particular ways, but it is likely to inform the meanings they construct around their own sexuality. Girls read magazines, in part, for information on how to manage sexual relationships. They do not read uncritically, for the contents of the magazines are discussed among them and mulled over individually. Nonetheless, what they read does feed into the competencies or lack of them that girls bring to relationships, their understanding of and expectations about sexuality. This is not grounds for barring them from reading about sex, but is grounds for being concerned about what sort of sex they are reading about.

The debate around the Bill is framed in terms of whether access to explicit sexual information is a good or a bad thing – rarely is the quality of information discussed, other than in moral terms, and what counts as 'sex' is almost never questioned. Moreover, the 'shock horror' tone of the discussion emphasizes what is new and different rather than considering their content in the light of wider, longer-term trends. The increased sexualization of the magazines' content is seen in isolation, rather than as an aspect of the increased sexualization of femininity in general. Changes in teenage girls' magazines parallel those in adult women's magazines and, in many respects, the boundaries between the two are blurring. There is now far more explicit sexual content in women's magazines in general and far less desexualized romance. Heterosexual love is itself becoming more sexualized, a trend discernible in Western culture as a whole since the early 20th century and visible in girls' magazines since the 1950s. Earlier magazines featured romance and male pin-ups (with their clothes on), now they feature sex and pin-ups (often with most of their clothes off).

One feminist interpretation of this trend is that it is indicative of the increased eroticization of women's subordination. Other feminists take a more optimistic view. Angela McRobbie (1996), for example, sees signs of progress in the newer magazines, a postmodern celebration of plurality. She argues that they represent a potential for less uniform, monolithic modes of femininity, for a more knowing and assertive female sexuality, for the exploration of alternatives to heterosexuality. In some ways the new magazines are an advance on earlier ones, but in many other ways I find it difficult to share McRobbie's optimism – indeed I wonder whether we have been reading the same magazines. We have certainly been reading them differently.

So what's in these magazines?

The content of these magazines offers a predictable diet of fashion, beauty, articles on sex and romance and how to manage relationships (including 'true life' stories on all of these), plus pin-ups of male pop stars, sport stars and models. There are other and serious issues covered, including drugs and bereavement. There is also a fairly strong emphasis on the occult which, since horror stories and movies are popular with young people, is not surprising. There are also, of course, horoscopes, 'self-knowledge' quizzes and problem pages. The main focus is on *boys* – how to attract, please them and get on with them – or what might be called 'compulsive heterosexuality'. (This is a term one of my students accidentally substituted for 'compulsory heterosexuality', but which seems an apt depiction of what is going on in girls' magazines.)

While writing this article I bought a selection of these magazines over a period of about three weeks and asked friends and colleagues with teenage daughters what they read. The most popular ones are either music focused – although their real interest seems to be male stars as objects of female lust – or the fashion and relationships variety. It is the latter which have the most explicitly sexual content and it is these I have looked at most closely – although it was *TV Hits* which sparked off the controversy by printing a problem page inquiry about oral sex.

These magazines have changed from those around in the 1960s and 1970s. Although these earlier magazines, of which *Jackie* is the best remembered, did include fashion, beauty tips, pin-ups, features on relationships and so on, their stock-in-trade was comic-strip romances. These have disappeared and the magazines now look much more like adult women's magazines of the *Cosmopolitan* or *Marie Claire* variety. Even magazines for pre-teens now have a more grown-up look and share some of the content with teenage magazines. *Bunty*, for example, which once featured tales of boarding schools, gymkhanas and ballet classes, now has a more adult look. It still has some of the old stories – the Four Maries are still, nearly 40 years on, trapped in the third form at St Elmo's – but these sit alongside articles with lead-ins like: 'Which holiday hunk is the one for you?' Glossy pictures of fluffy dogs vie for space on the bedroom wall with pinups of Boyzone. And this is where you can still find comic-strip romances – including a tale about a girl who gives up drooling over posters of a TV star when a real boy rescues her dog and then asks her out.

Once past this stage, the next step up is to magazines like *Just Seventeen*, the most popular of this genre among 11–14 year olds – read by 52 per cent of them (Central Statistical Office, 1994). There's also the fortnightly *Mizz* and somewhat glossier monthlies such as *Sugar* and *Bliss* (the latter carrying the message 'a girl's gotta have it' under the title). The monthlies may be intended for slightly older girls, but I know of 12-year-olds who read them regularly. All of those I have mentioned are explicitly aimed at girls still at school – a good indication of this is provided by the problem pages and the quizzes: for example, 'At a school disco, you spot your boyfriend chatting to a girl you don't know, do you ... etc.' (*Sugar* quiz entitled 'Are you a cling-on?').

The barkers on the front of these magazines give an indication of what the fuss is about: 'Sex: should you tell mum or keep schtum'; 'I slept around, but I'm still a virgin'; 'Make him want you bad'; 'He slept with me for a bet'; 'Does sex change your life?'; 'I got pregnant on purpose'; 'Dribble over the sexiest footballer alive', and so on. There are also more serious sexual themes: 'Shock report: why 12 year olds are turning to prostitution'; 'Could I have AIDS?: one girl's scary story'.

The sexual message is more explicit still in the magazines for older teenagers such as *19* and *More!*, the latter being (in)famous for its regular 'position of the fortnight' (with line drawings, full instructions and a 1 to 5 difficulty rating). The May 1996 edition of *More!* and June edition of *19* both featured orgasms: 'Talking about the Big "O": Orgasm stories to get you going and coming'; 'Blissed Out: Treat Yourself to the O to Mmm of Orgasm'. *More!* is the most adult of these magazines in other senses than its sexual explicitness, in that it addresses its readers as young women with jobs living independently of their parents. The biggest clue to its target audience is that it is alone among these magazines in assuming that the objects of its readers' lust are men rather than boys. According to Angela McRobbie (1996), its 415,000 readers are aged on average between 15 and 17.

Mixed messages

Once past the lurid headlines, the contents of these magazines are mixed and often contradictory. Problem page reassurance that all bodies are normal is contradicted by injunctions to improve, disguise or conceal bodily imperfections. Advice on saying no to sex and not rushing into it sits side by side with articles and quizzes which give the impression that the only important thing in life is to attract, keep and please your man. An article in *Bliss* about the joys of being without a boyfriend, which looks at first sight like a positive move, lists among the 'good things about being single' such items as being free to do what you want, to spend time with your mates, but also 'you can eye up any guy you want without feeling guilty'.

It is true that the tone of all this talk of boys, sex and looking good is, as Angela McRobbie says, often ironic and self mocking. Boys are not treated with any great reverence and often they are the butt of jokes. I'm not sure, however, how far this undermines the fairly conventional range of femininities represented in these magazines, although it does suggest a certain distancing from and self-consciousness about the constraints of femininity. Certainly the way readers are addressed implies a more knowing and active sexuality: girls are no longer expected to passively wait until Mr Right makes a move, they are expected to make it happen. This does speak to girls' desires for more equal sexual relationships, in which girls can take the initiative, in which they usurp what was once a male prerogative: objectifying those one desires. But is this progress? Equality seems to be understood within the discourse of these magazines as being like men: girls can look at male bodies just as men have traditionally looked at female bodies. Even some of the language is the same as that used by men, for example: '8 poster prints – top totty for your wall' (*Bliss*). At the same time there is an acknowledgement of persistent difference as in '11 things you should NEVER say to boys' (*Sugar*); 'Dazed and confused: just 17 girly things lads will never understand' (*Just Seventeen*).

Moreover, the old idea that girls' sexuality *is* being attractive and alluring has by no means vanished. The boundaries of what is acceptable in this respect have shifted and behaviour once thought of as that of a 'slag' or 'tart' is now playfully endorsed. Here is the response to those who score highly on a sexiness quiz in *Mizz*:

> Grrrrr! You little tiger! You have the secret of sex appeal all right, right down to wearing slinky black numbers to take the dog for a walk, and flirting with your Headmaster to get out of detention. Stop that wiggle when you walk – you'll do yourself an injury!

Yet alongside this sexualization of traditional femininity are more serious articles about both sexuality and other aspects of life. The same issue of *Mizz* carries articles on teenage prostitution and on a girl coping with her mother's death. The more considered discussions of sexuality in both articles and problem pages are often constructive and informative. The readers of these magazines certainly know far more about coercive sex, sexual exploitation, rape and incest than previous generations and are better informed about avoiding pregnancy and sexually transmitted diseases. Girls also know more about their own bodies and how to derive pleasure from them. This is all to the good. So too, in my view, is the demystification of romantic notions that good sex is something which magically happens once you fall in love. However, this has its down side, in that the idea that sex has to be 'worked at' produces its own anxieties and is itself a form of social regulation.[4]

The advice given on heterosexual sex in the problem pages is often sensible and, in this respect at least, magazines read by younger teenagers cannot be accused of promoting early sexual experimentation. Generally the message is not to rush into early sex and to resist being pressured into it either by friends or boyfriends. Some carry regular explicit warnings on their problem pages on the illegality of underage sex: 'Be sure, be safe and remember sex under 16 is illegal' (*Just Seventeen*); 'It's cool to wait, sex under 16 is illegal' (*Bliss*). Some of the advice on sex is helpful and positive – the sorts of things young heterosexual women need to know but may not find out from other sources, for example, that a condom is ineffective if the guy doesn't withdraw before losing his erection. Sex, however, is still defined in terms of the penetrative norm – 'having sex' means heterosexual coition – even though there are items on problem pages and elsewhere explaining clitoral orgasms and masturbation.

Endorsing heterosexuality

These magazines are relentlessly heterosexual. This is one of the points on which my reading of these magazines differs markedly from Angela McRobbie's. McRobbie says that:

> Gay and lesbian identities now move more freely across the field of popular women's and girls' magazines. These exist as sexual possibilities where in the past they were permitted only a shadowy stigmatized existence. (1996: 183)

This may be more true of magazines for older readers, or it may be that my sample (two copies each of *Bliss* and *More!*, one each of *Sugar*, *Mizz*, *Just Seventeen*, *TV Hits* and *19*) is unrepresentative. In any case, I did not find evidence of 'gay and lesbian sexualities [being] frequently invoked' in the pages of these magazines (McRobbie, 1996: 188) or any great sign of a postmodern plurality of sexualities. It may true that, as McRobbie says, 'teenybopper stars now come out as gay' in teenage magazines, but even in the gossip pages which she sees as a source of representations of alternative sexualities, I found only the odd oblique reference to (male) gay identities. While there is undoubtedly greater openness about lesbian and gay sexualities, in the magazines I read they remain marginalized.

I only found four explicit discussions of lesbianism and homosexuality – all, significantly, on problem pages. The line taken is, on the whole, a liberal one which seeks to present a fairly positive view of homosexuality and lesbianism but without challenging the normality of heterosexuality. For example, a girl writing to *19* has just discovered that her father is gay, is angry that he has not told her before and worried about friends ostracizing both her father and herself. She is encouraged to be understanding, told that she might end up being proud of his courage in coming out and that if her friends can't deal with it 'that's their problem'. A young woman writing to *More!* saying that she is attracted to women but afraid of her parents' reaction is encouraged to ring lesbian line and given some contact numbers. However, where young people are less certain about their sexuality, the reaction seems to be to reassure them that they are 'normal' – that is, heterosexual. A girl was concerned that 'her friend' might be a lesbian because she was 14 and had never had a boyfriend. She was advised not to worry, there was still time, it didn't mean that she was a lesbian – then, as an afterthought, that if she was a lesbian she shouldn't feel bad about it (*TV Hits*). A boy worried that his friends were calling him gay because he had kissed another boy while drunk wasn't told that it was okay to be gay – just that his friends would stop teasing him eventually (*Just Seventeen*). In this last case an opportunity to challenge heterosexism was completely missed.

The problem pages reveal that some boys, at least, read girls' magazines – assuming, that is, that the letters are genuine. It is now common for magazines to have 'agony uncles' as well as 'agony aunts', both to advise on boys' problems and to offer a male point of view on girls' dilemmas. Given that these magazines assume a community of young, heterosexual and primarily female readers and that they focus on heterosexual relationships, one obvious area of concern is ideas about sexuality circulating among teenage boys.

What are boys reading?

In all the public discussion of girls' magazines, there has been a silence around what boys are reading. In part this reflects the lack of magazines aimed at a young male market. Since there are still only a few adult 'men's magazines', aside from pornographic ones, it is not surprising that no one has yet launched a publication aimed at teenage boys – particularly since boys seem to read less than girls. *Viz*, the most popular magazine among young teenage boys, is intended for adult men of a puerile disposition. Its appeal may be that it is a fairly easy progression from the *Beano* (which remains among the top five magazines for boys in the early teens). A large proportion of *Viz* is devoted to cartoons and its entire tone – as well as being overtly misogynist – can best be summed up as lavatory wall humour. (I had already decided on this phrase when I caught sight of the cover of an issue of the magazine in my local newsagent, proudly advertising 'a golden shower of piss-poor cartoons and lavatory humour'.)

Aside from *Viz* and the *Beano*, the other 'top five' publications for boys in their early teens are the *Sun* and two computer game magazines: *Gamesmaster* and *Sega Power* (Central Statistical Office, 1994). It would seem from this list that if boys of this age are engaging with issues of sex and relationships at all, it is at the level of page 3 and 'the fat slags' – hardly promising for young heterosexual women in search of either true love or sensational sex. Most research on young people's access to sexual information suggests that pornography is boys' main source of 'knowledge' on sex.

There is no moral panic about what boys are reading. Sex is not thought of as a threat to boys – they are expected to 'know' about it rather than remaining innocent. Yet what they 'know' is deeply problematic – especially given that male definitions of sex still prevail in the negotiation of heterosex. It is male sexuality which constitutes the major problem young women face – whether manifested as sexual harassment and coercion, male reluctance to engage in safer sex or simply men's inability to understand women's sexual desires and aspirations. Yet it is young women's sexuality which is being constructed, once again, as a social problem. The message is still that young women should remain 'innocent' – in other words ignorant.

Double standards

In the early 1970s, while I was researching teenage girls' ideas about sexuality, I worked in a psychiatric unit for boys aged 11–15. The boys all read pornography and the walls of the unit were covered in photographs of naked women – those with fully exposed genitals were strongly favoured. Some of the staff objected, but the psychiatrist in charge saw the consumption of pornography as a sign of 'healthy development' in the boys and a legitimate part of the therapeutic environment. Meanwhile, the youth club in which I was conducting my research, which claimed to have liberal attitudes to sex, threw me out because I mentioned orgasms to the girls and let on that it was possible for girls to masturbate. I suspect that while more politically correct health and youth workers might no longer endorse quite such gross double standards, they have by no means vanished. I suspect that these double standards are what underpin the concern about explicit sex in teenage magazines.

Whatever reservations I have about the magazines girls are reading, however much I might object to their relentless endorsement of compulsory (or compulsive) heterosexuality, I can't help feeling that girls are better served by these magazines than by those available in the past. The girls I was talking to in the early 1970s all read *Jackie* – still then in its comic-strip romance phase – thought of sex in terms of 'love' and were woefully ignorant about their own bodies, although many were sexually active. Readers of *Bliss*, *Mizz*, *Sugar* and the like are far better informed about safer sex and their own bodies, and are constantly exhorted to assert their own sexual wants and needs – including saying no to sexual practices they don't want.

This knowledge does not, of course, translate easily into more egalitarian sexual relationships. All the evidence we have suggests that whatever girls may know in theory, in practice the power dynamics of heterosexual relationships still work against them. However, ignorance would only make girls more vulnerable. One of the problems girls have in negotiating sex with boys is finding a language in which to discuss sexuality and assert their own sexual desires. At least these magazines begin to provide them with such a language, speak to them in terms which make sense in the light of their everyday experience – even as they simultaneously help construct that experience. The problem is not that girls are exposed to too much, too explicit sex, but the limited, male oriented ways in which sexuality is discussed.

Notes

1 The wit is not mine. Titles of articles in *Trouble & Strife* are decided upon by the editorial collective and this one was supplied by Debbie Cameron.
2 *Editorial note*: the Periodical (Protection of Children) Bill was a Private Member's Bill introduced under the ten-minute rule and never became law.
3 *Editorial note*: the murdered child beauty queen, JonBenet Ramsey was also compared to 'an animated Barbie doll' (Patrick Brogan, *Glasgow Herald*, 13 January 1997: 10).
4 *Editorial note*: see Jackson and Scott (1997) for a further elaboration of this idea.

11 Taking Liberties: Feminism, Gay Rights and the Problem of Heterosexuality

This chapter arises out of, and owes much to, collaborative work with Momin Rahman (see Rahman and Jackson, 1997). While the ideas expressed here derive from my contributions to our joint work, they were developed through our collaboration. The initial impetus behind our critique of the Liberty report (1994) was our shared disquiet about the assumptions underpinning it, and our awareness that these assumptions were by no means confined to this document but underpinned much of the gay rights agenda. Our interests as a heterosexual feminist and a gay man coincided in our concern with the failure of many gay activists to challenge gender divisions and the institution of heterosexuality.

This piece, written for Trouble & Strife, *is polemical in tone. Yet I felt, and still feel, some trepidation about writing about this issue as a straight woman, without the authority I might have were I a lesbian and therefore able to position myself within a shared oppression. However, I am neither trying to preach to gay men nor claiming to speak on behalf of either gay men or lesbians. My views are those of a heterosexual feminist who still believes that women's oppression and the oppression of lesbians and gay men are inter-connected, that both are sustained by the hierarchy of gender, in which male dominance is sustained, in part, through the heterosexual contract. While straight women, lesbians and gay men are located differently in relation to compulsory heterosexuality, its institutionalization is oppressive to us all.*

For a brief period in the early 1970s radical gay activists allied themselves with the women's movement, believing that gay liberation, like women's liberation, required the dismantling of patriarchal structures and insti-tutions. Today large sections of the male dominated gay movement are pursuing goals which are antithetical to feminism – and also counter-productive for gay liberation. This can be illustrated by a report published by Liberty (formerly the National Council for Civil Liberties) in 1994: *Sexuality and the State: Human Rights Violations Against Lesbians, Gays, Bisexuals and Transgendered People.*

While produced by a civil rights organization, the report was compiled in consultation with Stonewall and OutRage, representing respectively the reformist and radical faces of gay politics in Britain. The arguments it presents reflect those widely aired by gay activists and most of the evidence cited in support of these arguments comes from the gay press. The report can, therefore, be taken as representative of male dominated gay politics. It is certainly not representative of lesbian politics.

While claiming to speak for both lesbians and gays, the Liberty report is primarily a defence of the rights of gay men. While there are women in both OutRage and Stonewall, the agenda of these organizations is defined from a gay male perspective and this, unsurprisingly, is reflected in the report. Lesbian feminist perspectives are totally excluded. Among all the references to the gay press there are none to feminist publications and there appears to have been no consultation with those feminist organizations, such as Rights of Women, which have campaigned around the legal rights of lesbians.

Endorsing heterosexuality

The lack of any engagement with feminism not only illustrates the distance between gay male politics and feminist politics, but also leads to some of the fundamental flaws in the arguments Liberty presents. Because the report ignores decades of feminist activism and scholarship on sexuality (as well as the work of more radical gay theorists), it reads as if no one had ever developed critical perspectives on the social construction of gender and sexuality. In particular, it fails to address the ways in which institutionalized heterosexuality reinforces both patriarchal domination and the oppression of lesbians and gays.

Any attempt to further gay rights should recognize that lesbianism and homosexuality exist in opposition to heterosexuality. In the first place, the categories 'homosexual' and 'lesbian' serve to police the boundaries of institutionalized heterosexuality: homosexuals and lesbians are defined as deviant outsiders in order to confirm the 'normality' of heterosexuality. This is central to the oppression of lesbians and gays. Second, in mobilizing around these identities, redefining them as political rather than deviant, lesbians and gays potentially challenge the institutionalization of heterosexuality. Lesbianism, in particular, has been adopted as a political stance in opposition to the appropriation of women within patriarchal societies.

The Liberty report does not recognize the oppositional location of lesbians and gays. Hence it fails to question the structures and ideologies which maintain the distinction between heterosexuality and homosexuality, and which confirm the former as the norm. Nor does it take any critical stance on heterosexuality itself. It considers neither the power relations which exist within heterosexual relationships nor the power relations which operate between heterosexuals and homosexuals. Instead, heterosexuality's normative status is confirmed. It is taken as the standard on which human rights are founded, and hence the issue of rights is posed in terms of equality *with* heterosexuals, leaving heterosexuality itself unchallenged.

The Liberty report aims to expose the ways in which the British state denies the rights of lesbians and gays. The argument is framed in terms of internationally agreed standards for human rights, such as the United Nations (UN) International Covenant on Civil and Political Rights (ICCPR). It is partly because it accepts the terms of such international agreements, themselves formulated on the assumption of a universal heterosexual normality, that the report is problematic. I have no quarrel with the aim of defending civil liberties for lesbians and gay men, but this aim is not furthered by a perspective which treats heterosexuality as the standard for human rights and which does not consider the political consequences of endorsing patriarchal, heterosexual institutions.

'Nature' versus choice: a false opposition

One of the grounds on which Liberty argues that discrimination on the basis of sexual orientation is an abuse of human rights is that 'sexual orientation is an immutable part of every person like their race or gender' (Liberty, 1994: 11). In the very next paragraph, however, it is stated that: 'A debate continues about whether sexual orientation is a biologically innate characteristic or a conscious political choice'.

You cannot have it both ways! If sexual orientation is biological in origin it cannot be a matter of choice. Liberty wants to have it both ways because each of these options can be used to argue for protection against discrimination: 'either similar protection to that which is afforded women and ethnic minorities, or protection from discrimination because of political or other opinions' (1994: 11). This either–or distinction between biology and choice is not confined to this document: it has been a feature of other recent debates and campaigns, such as those around Section 28 and the homosexual age of consent.[1] It relies, as Lynda Birke (1994) argues, on a reductionist view of biology as a single, simple explanation for complex human behaviour. More importantly, it leaves no room at all for social structures and processes. In ruling out the third alternative, that sexuality is socially or culturally constructed, it ignores the social contexts which shape both biological research and the choices we make. In addition to these problems, I am not convinced that either alternative – biology or choice – provides a sound basis for advocating equality.

It is not clear whether the idea of sexuality as a choice is a misunderstanding of social constructionist theories of sexuality or of political lesbianism or both. If the idea of choice derives from political lesbianism, it is a somewhat naive interpretation of it; the slogan may have been that 'any woman can' be a lesbian but, in fact, not every woman could. Lesbian feminist theorists such as Adrienne Rich (1980) had a great deal to say about the material and ideological constraints involved in the maintenance of compulsory heterosexuality. Those who became lesbian for political reasons did so as a result of a particular analysis of sexuality, one which derived from the women's movement: that sexuality was socially constructed within heterosexually ordered patriarchal relations. It was in this context that the possibility of challenging and transforming sexuality opened up, making new choices available. Moreover, although the idea of choice has been important to feminist thinking on sexuality, feminists have also long been aware of the complexity of sexuality and the dangers of a liberal individualistic model of desire and identity (see Stacey, 1991).

Locating oneself as lesbian or gay *is* potentially political, because it entails embracing an identity oppositional to the prevailing norm: it is precisely the *social* significance of homosexuality and lesbianism that creates this political potential. Following the logic of homosexuality as a choice, Liberty argues for gay rights as analogous to the rights of political belief and dissent. What they do not consider is what gays and lesbians are dissenting from if not compulsory heterosexuality. The one thing which a politically motivated lesbian or homosexual does not want is to be just like a heterosexual, yet the aim of the report is precisely that lesbians and gays should be treated just like heterosexuals. They should, it is argued, have the right to form heterosexual style marriages including entitlements to the pensions and tax allowances which derive from the economic inequality underpinning heterosexual marriage. The goal is to be included into heterosexual privilege rather than to challenge it. Political lesbianism, on the other hand, has always been seen as a challenge to institutionalized heterosexuality, a refusal to live within its boundaries.

Even in the absence of such a radical analysis, what freedoms could a posited right to a dissident sexuality guarantee? The right to believe and articulate a political defence of homosexuality or lesbianism is not equivalent to the right to freedom of sexual conduct. There is not, nor can there be, absolute freedom of action for any of us. Liberty's claim that the ICCPR 'protects the right of people to enter into relationships' (Liberty, 1994: 11) is, to say the least, rather vague. None of us is free to enter into any relationship we choose, still less are we free to act as we please within those relationships which are permitted. Many feminists would balk at the extreme libertarianism which such an argument could lead to. We would not, for example, support the right of an adult man to enter into a sexual relationship with a six-year-old child nor the right of a man to abuse his wife.

The return of biological determinism

The alternative strategy offered by Liberty is the claim to rights premised on sexuality as a biologically ordained, immutable characteristic. Their assumption that immutable sexual nature is the only alternative to political choice is not an isolated instance, but part of a more general turn to biological explanations among gay activists. In the absence of a political understanding of sexuality as socially constructed, the idea of being 'born that way' has become attractive to many gays and some lesbians. The cultural legitimacy of 'science' provides individuals with an easily under-standable way of accounting for their own sexual desires and practices. Biological explanations 'ring true' not because they are based on incon-trovertible fact, but because they provide culturally approved ways of making sense of sexuality.

A further reason for the popularity of biological determinism among gay activists is that the political Right sometimes uses a version of social constructionism against lesbians and gays, suggesting that it is possible to 'promote' homosexuality or convert people to it. This, however, is no reason to abandon social and cultural perspectives. If both choice and determinism can be used to defend gay and lesbian rights, they can equally be deployed against those rights – to damn lesbians and gays as genetic freaks on the one hand or moral degenerates on the other.

More importantly, countering the Right's homophobia by resorting to biological determinism concedes political ground. Feminists have long been aware that homosexuality – and more specifically lesbianism – *does* rep-resent a threat to institutionalized heterosexuality and to the hierarchy of gender which is integral to it. It has always been a central tenet of feminism that sexuality is socially constructed and that we can therefore struggle politically to change it. The existence of such a threat, the potential for political change, depends on recognizing that the current ordering of gender and sexuality is social rather than natural.

The notion of an innate sexual orientation offers no challenge to hierarchies of gender and sexuality. This is precisely why biological theories appeal to the less radical wing of the gay rights movement: they render homosexuality unthreatening. If gays are 'born that way', then there is no risk of their ranks being swelled by converted heterosexuals, no challenge to the hegemony of the heterosexual social order. Indeed this is the political stance taken by Simon LeVay (1993), the originator of the 'gay brain' theory.

This position also ignores the continued vitality of lesbian and gay communities, which have managed to reproduce themselves non-biologi-cally. As Sarah Franklin argues:

> There is a distinct political significance to the simple fact that we do not reproduce ourselves biologically. We reproduce ourselves socially, entirely by means of the social, political and cultural struggles that keep lesbian and gay sub-cultures alive. According to every theory of evolution, biological determinism or genetic essentialism we should be extinct. But we are not extinct. (Franklin, 1993: 38).

The implication of biological and genetic theories, that they suggest that lesbians and gays, if not extinct, should be a dying breed, seems to have been missed by those gay activists who endorse such theories. They also ignore the central issue raised by Franklin, the political importance of the social reproduction of lesbian and gay communities. Instead they assume that lesbians and gays constitute a permanent, more or less stable, natural minority. To campaign for equal rights on this basis is misguided. The hope behind this, as voiced by the American gay activist Randy Shilts, is that being gay could have no more significance than being left-handed, that it will therefore cease to be regarded as socially intolerable. Pleas for rights on this basis – we deserve tolerance and protection because we can't help it – hardly seem a promising start for claims to equality.

Such aspirations are founded on a misunderstanding of why homosexuality is socially significant, or why it exists as a meaningful social category at all. Homosexuality is not a natural difference that has become stigmatized through some irrational prejudice, but a category which only exists in relation to normative heterosexuality. It cannot be equal to heterosexuality: it is necessarily in opposition to it. Homosexuality will inevitably be regulated, oppressed and stigmatized while heterosexuality retains its privileged position as the unquestioned, institutionalized cultural norm. Nowhere in the report is this privilege challenged.

The politics of gender and sexuality

It is somewhat ironic that the Liberty report takes the immutability of sexual orientations as analogous to gender (1994: 11), given that the concept of gender has been used by feminists in order to refute the idea that sex differences are natural and unchanging. It also leads to further contradictions. Gender, we are told, is fixed and immutable – but because Liberty wants to defend transgendered individuals it complains that 'the law does not recognize the right of people to have changes to their gender acknowledged' (1994: 58). The argument runs like this: gender can't change but the law should recognize our right to change it! Liberty does not see that the very existence of gender divisions might be part of the problem and that this is linked to the division between hetero- and homosexuality.

Heterosexuality as a system depends upon gender hierarchy and patriarchal domination. Heterosexuality as a sexual practice is legitimated as the 'natural' outcome of equally 'natural' sex differences: to be a woman is to desire men (and vice-versa). At the core of heterosexuality is the gendering of desire – the idea that we should be attracted to 'the opposite sex'. Because homosexuality involves the 'wrong' choice of sexual partner, it has often been seen as a 'gender disorder'. Some recent forms of biological determinism promoted by gay scientists and activists accept this. For example, Simon LeVay's (1993) 'gay brain' theory relies on the idea that the brains of gay men are characteristically feminized, and hence assumes that if men desire other men they must be 'like' women. Thus the patriarchal and heterosexist ideology which identifies gay men as failed men – and lesbians as failed women – is left intact.

The policing of gender divisions and of heterosexuality are intimately interconnected. It is this which the author of the Liberty report fails to appreciate. He also has not noticed that heterosexuality is necessarily a gendered institution: a man plus a woman equals a heterosexual relationship. Heterosexuals are not a genderless category. Moreover, men and women do not share equally in heterosexual privilege since heterosexual marriage has historically institutionalized women's subordination to their husbands. It is a nonsense to claim equality with heterosexuals when the condition of being heterosexual, by definition, differs for women and men.

Pretended families?

Major problems arise when Liberty demands rights in areas which are central to the institutionalization of heterosexuality, notably 'the right to form a family' (1994: 18, 37–44). The well-worn example of Section 28 of the Local Government Act 1988 demonstrates that the family, by definition, is heterosexual: gays and lesbians can only have 'pretended family relationships'. This, however, only served to underline what was already the case. However diverse family forms are becoming, a variety of state social policies reinforces the institutionalized heterosexuality and male dominance on which families are still founded. Why would lesbians and gays want to be included in an institution which has served to perpetuate heterosexuality and patriarchal domination? Liberty mobilizes the idea of family diversity to argue that the ICCPR's provision on family rights could be extended to lesbians and gays, but the rights it argues for do not rely at all on ideas about diversity, but rather on the closest possible mimicry of conventional heterosexual domesticity. Rather than looking for ways of enhancing diversity, Liberty simply wants to give lesbians and gays rights modelled precisely on the heterosexual family. It would seem that Liberty is indeed advocating rights enabling lesbians and gays to establish 'pretended (heterosexual) family relationships'.

Demands for the recognition of gay marriage are now, of course, widely heard throughout the Western world. Liberty's call for legal recognition of same-sex relationships includes the 'benefits' accruing to heterosexual couples, such as wives' pension rights and the 'married man's tax allowance' (1994: 37).[2] The report's author seems curiously oblivious of the implications of this. Taxation and social security provisions have evolved in the context of a hierarchical system in which husbands are economic heads of households and wives are their dependants. Again we might ask why lesbians and gays should want to replicate the patterns of support and dependency which have typified patriarchal marriage.

The right to parent is potentially of a different order from the right to marriage, in that rearing children outside conventional families could pose a more radical challenge to institutionalized heterosexuality. This, however, is played down in the Liberty report. Liberty's defence of the rights of lesbians and gays to parent and, especially, to foster and adopt, is couched in terms of the difficulties faced by lesbian and gay *couples* (1994: 43). This presupposes the normality and desirability of monogamous coupledom.

Presumably the aim is to appear respectable and reasonable – but it also reflects an insensitivity to issues of gender.

Although the report mentions the specific problems faced by lesbian mothers – loss of custody of their children and barriers to access to assisted conception – it assumes a generalized opposition to lesbian/gay parents. This is not the case, since that opposition is clearly related to the gender of the parent as well as their sexuality. The work that has been done on lesbian mothers by organizations such as Rights of Women suggests that one of the reasons why they lose custody of children is that their children are growing up without being subject to the proper patriarchal authority. Similarly, the 'virgin mothers' scare around Artificial Insemination by Donor in 1991 entailed publicly expressed outrage that women should dare to become pregnant without men, without being 'possessed' by a man, without ful-filling conventional feminine obligations to men (see Radford, 1991).

The gender division underpinning heterosexuality means that gays and lesbians are not simply commonly oppressed through their homosexuality, but are located differently in relation to compulsory heterosexuality. Rights pursued by gay men may not, therefore be rights for lesbians. Aside from the (very) limited recognition of gender difference in relation to the specific problems faced by lesbian mothers, the report largely ignores differences between lesbians and gay men.

The problem of consent

Another obviously gender specific issue is the campaign for an age of consent which applies equally to heterosexuals and homosexual men.[3] What is not widely recognized, and is not mentioned in Liberty's coverage of the issue, is that the age of consent is a gendered concept – it applied initially only to heterosexual women. The law encodes a model of hetero-sexual acts as something men do and women merely consent to (or not). Feminists have long been aware that this derives from a history in which male sexual access to a woman's body was an act of appropriation whereby a man gained rights over a woman's person, property and labour. This history should not be ignored, for we do not yet live beyond its influence.

The extension of the concept of the age of consent to gay men has been a result of the partial decriminalization of homosexuality. The only model available for the enforcement of age-limits was one developed through heterosexist assumptions of sexual activity and passivity, effectively posi-tioning (*sic*) gay men in an analogous situation to straight women: consent-ing to have 'it' done to them. This model of sexual relations is clearly absurd since, in practice, both active and passive partners are equally liable to prosecution for sex with someone under the age of consent. Yet the assumption of an active older man and a passive younger man certainly shapes the thinking of some of those who oppose lowering the age of consent, who see it as a licence for men to bugger young boys. I am not suggesting that the age of consent campaign is misguided, merely that it should be recognized that it does not render gay men formally equal to heterosexual men but to heterosexual women. This holds true whether one regards the age of consent for women as repressive discriminatory legislation or a necessary protection against male sexual exploitation.

The lack of attention given to these issues is surprising since the NCCL (now Liberty) argued in the early 1980s for the removal of the age of consent on the grounds of sex discrimination – an argument controversial at the time since many feminists felt (and still feel) that it was necessary to protect young women from sexual violence and exploitation. The history of heterosexual age of consent legislation has also been much debated among feminists, particularly in terms of whether its protective intent was progressive for women or repressive of their sexuality. This has been ignored despite the fact that it was the same piece of legislation – the Criminal Law Amendment Act of 1885 – which both raised the heterosexual age of consent to 16 and outlawed 'acts of gross indecency' between men.

Whose rights?

The issue of consent serves to underline, yet again, that the pursuit of rights 'equal' to those of heterosexuals is far from unproblematic, that the way in which heterosexuality has been constructed and institutionalized should be questioned. Throughout Liberty's report, the social construction of heterosexuality remains unexamined. Moreover, the focus on individual rights diverts attention away from social inequalities which are not amenable to change simply through legal reform. We cannot even begin to challenge heterosexual hegemony while limiting our concept of equality to formal, individual rights. The fact that women have gained many such rights without attaining social equality should demonstrate the limitations of a politics of rights which ignores the structural bases of social inequality.

To whom, in any case, do the lesbians and gays of the 'rights' lobby want to be equal: heterosexual women or heterosexual men? I suspect that many gay men are seeking equality with heterosexual men and are quite happy to leave lesbians the less enviable goal of equality with heterosexual women. Lesbian feminists, of course, have continued to fight for equality for all women and an end to gender hierarchy. This does not mean equality with men, or being like men, for 'if women were the equals of men, men would no longer equal themselves' (Delphy, 1993: 8). The same logic can and should be extended to the division between homo- and heterosexualities. If real equality existed heterosexuality would no longer be what it is today. To seek equality with heterosexuals is a logical absurdity since it cannot happen without displacing heterosexuality from its status as privileged, institutionalized norm. Rather, the goal should be to make the anatomical contours of one's chosen sexual partners socially irrelevant. This itself requires that gender ceases to be a significant factor in the way we organize our sexual and social lives.

Notes

1 Section 28 of the Local Government Act 1988 prohibited local authorities in Britain from 'promoting homosexuality' and forbade the teaching, in any state school, of 'the acceptability of homosexuality as a pretended family relationship' (Weeks, 1991: 216; see also Stacey, 1991; Cooper, 1995).
2 The demise of the married man's tax allowance was announced in the 1999 budget – and with it one form of discrimination against lesbian and gay couples (although this was not the intent behind this measure, which was designed to shift resources from childless couples to parents).
3 In Britain the age of consent for homosexual males was set at 21 when homosexuality was decriminalized in 1967. In 1994, after decades of campaigning for parity with the heterosexual age of consent, the homosexual age of consent was reduced to 18, the House of Commons having rejected the more radical alternative of setting it at 16 (see Waites, 1998). Britain, in line with most of the rest of Europe, may finally achieve parity between heterosexual and male homosexual ages of consent. In January 1999 the House of Commons voted to reduce the age of consent for gay men to 16. A similar move in the previous year was knocked back by the House of Lords, but this time its chances of success looked good, primarily because the Sexual Offences (Amendments) Bill included a new 'abuse of trust' offence. This was designed to protect young people (of both sexes) between 16 and 18 years of age who are under the supervision of adults. This was intended to allay the fears of those concerned about young men being 'corrupted' by older men and thus lessen the opposition to the lowering of the age of consent. However, the House of Lords still voted it down.

12 Heterosexuality, Heteronormativity and Gender Hierarchy: Some Reflections on Recent Debates

As I indicated in the Introduction and in Chapter 9, there is currently a renewed interest in problematizing heterosexuality on the part of feminists. At the same time we have witnessed the development of queer theory, which also seeks to question the normative status of heterosexuality. For the most part these interrogations of heterosexuality have been going on in two quite separate arenas, each with its own theoretical and political agendas, although some feminists are engaging with both sets of arguments. Hence, although Queer is among the perspectives which have been drawn upon in recent feminist debates on heterosexuality (Smart, 1996a, 1996b; Wilton, 1996), it has a life of its own separate from those debates and unconnected with them.

In Britain the impetus for the revival of feminist debate came, as in the past, from radical lesbian feminists. Amid fears that old wounds would be reopened, that the bitter arguments of the early 1980s would be rehearsed all over again, some commentators on the debate detected signs of the old defensiveness and guilt on the part of heterosexual feminists. Yet on the whole the response from heterosexual feminists has been more positive, with many evincing a willingness to engage in a critique of heterosexuality as institution and practice. They have certainly contested the terms of this critique with radical lesbian feminists, but have done so more constructively and with less antagonism than was the case in the past; witness, for example, Carol Smart feeling that she cannot disagree with some of Sheila Jeffreys' arguments (Smart, 1996b: 168). On the other side, radical lesbians are showing greater readiness to listen to those who challenge their position and are no longer damning their heterosexual sisters as collaborators. The new rapprochement is not, however, true of all. Lynne Segal (1994), for example, responded to the reopening of debate by retreating to the old battle lines – although with some new weapons in her theoretical armoury. While I share with Segal a vested interest in affirming the possibility of heterosexual feminist politics and pleasurable heterosexual sex, these goals are not, in my view, best served by refusing to engage with the critique of male domination within heterosexual relations.

Whereas feminist critiques of heterosexuality took the oppression of women as their point of departure, Queer has developed from gay political and theoretical priorities. Queer theory is not particularly easy to define; it is not a single unified perspective and most of its founding canonical texts (for instance Butler, 1990a; Dollimore, 1991; Fuss 1991; Sedgwick, 1991) do not announce themselves as such by their titles. Some feel that it has had its day, or at least that the term has outlived its usefulness. One of those credited with originating the idea of queer theory, Teresa de Lauretis (1991), soon claimed that it had become 'a conceptually vacuous creature of the publishing industry' (1994: 297). The term, however, has refused to die and, if nothing else, serves as a convenient shorthand for an approach to dissident sexualities framed from deconstructionist, poststructuralist or postmodernist perspectives informed by the ideas of Lacan, Derrida and, above all, Foucault.

One area of potential confusion here is the distinction between queer politics, arising from AIDS activism, and queer theory with its roots in the academy. In some respects they converge. Both are inclusive in scope, incorporating not only gays and lesbians, but bisexuals, transsexuals and, indeed, anyone or anything not one hundred per cent conventionally heterosexual. Both emphasize the transgression and subversion of conventional heterosexual and gender norms which, in the case of queer politics, entails an unapologetic 'in your face' activism which departs from the reformist wing of the gay rights movement. They differ in that, politically, Queer often becomes an affirmation of identity, whereas queer theory seeks to destabilize all identities. Steven Seidman, for example, sees the central tenet of queer theory as being 'its challenge to what has been the dominant foundational concept of both homophobic and affirmative homosexual theory: the assumption of a unified homosexual identity' (1997: 93). Where a queer identity is mobilized, it is for strategic purposes (see, for example, Butler, 1991) and is thus provisional and contingent, defined in relation to the heterosexual presumptions it seeks to unsettle:

> Those who knowingly occupy ... a marginal location, who assume a de-essentialized identity that is purely positional in character, are properly speaking not gay but *queer*. (Halperin, 1995: 62; emphasis in the original)

Queer theory's project, then, entails disturbing and troubling heterosexuality. This, and its emphasis on interrogating the binary opposites of gay/straight, man/woman, and destabilizing the boundaries between them, suggests points of convergence with feminism. Feminist responses to Queer have, however, been mixed. Lynne Segal (1994), for example, is far more willing to embrace this form of critique than that mounted by lesbian feminists. At the other end of the spectrum are those such as Sheila Jeffreys, who have always seen heterosexuality as pivotal to women's oppression and lesbianism as a form of resistance. For Jeffreys, Queer is a means of 'disappearing' lesbians, denying both their specific oppression and their resistance to patriarchal control (1994b, 1997). Others, too, suspect that it is yet another manifestation of white male dominance in radical guise (see

Smyth, 1992: 31–3). Some lesbian feminists, however, see in Queer powerful analytical tools with which to explore the interconnection between the oppression of women and the maintenance of heterosexual hegemony (Wilton, 1996, 1997). Finally, some straight feminists have drawn on it to rethink heterosexual desire and practice (Smart, 1996a).

My own response to Queer – in the theoretical sense – can best be described as one of sceptical interest. Part of my scepticism arises from concerns I aired in the first chapter, that some of what is perceived as radical in queer theory is simply a reinvention of the sociological wheel. Moreover, queer theorizing is limited to the extent that it takes place at the level of culture and discourse, paying little attention to social structures and material social practices.[1] I remain interested, however, because Queer does provide some new insights into the deployment of discourses around sexuality. Insofar as it is possible to accommodate the concept of discourse within a materialist frame of analysis, it may be possible to draw on Queer's strengths while avoiding its weaknesses. Queer has played a central role in placing sexuality firmly on the theoretical map, and this is to be cautiously welcomed by those of us who have been working in this field, and thus at the margins of academic respectability, for decades. Yet this fashionability is itself a cause for suspicion; if it can so easily be rendered academically respectable, and so much more respectable than many feminist perspectives, might this not be a sign that it is not as subversive as it pretends to be? Might Queer be nothing more than a smart career move on the part of an ambitious younger generation of theorists? It certainly has been the means of making certain individuals into academic stars (see Grant, 1994/5). Even for those who strongly oppose the Queer enterprise, its very existence as something to react against has had the effect of renewing critical attention to sexuality. In sum, I believe that we have more to gain than to lose by contemplating possible intersections between queer and feminist agendas.

What both queer and feminist approaches have in common is that they call into question the inevitability and naturalness of heterosexuality, its normative status. Furthermore, feminists and queer theorists, to a greater or lesser extent, link the heterosexual/homosexual divide with gender. Whatever theoretical differences exist within and between these two diverse and overlapping constituencies, the common assumption is that neither gender boundaries nor the boundary between heterosexuality and homosexuality/lesbianism are fixed by nature. Queers and feminists both take an oppositional relationship to a social and cultural order which enshrines male dominated heterosexuality as a largely unquestioned norm. Their critique of heterosexuality is a political response to oppression and exclusion, fuelled by a belief in the possibility of resistance and the hope – at least for most feminists – of radical change. In bringing this book to a close I want to reflect on some of the themes emerging from this recent work and their potential for taking the critique of heterosexuality forward.

But first I want to register a note of caution. The renewal of radical critiques of heterosexuality is in sharp contrast with some of what is going on in the world of activist gay politics, where we have seen a retreat to biological determinism accompanied by demands to be included into heterosexual privileges (see Rahman and Jackson, 1997 and Chapter 11). Meanwhile, male dominance in heterosexual relations persists. All this appears to have gone unnoticed by many of those commentating on the contemporary sexual scene, seduced by signs of trendy gender ambiguity into thinking that there has been a cultural shift towards sexual diversity (McRobbie, 1996). While some changes are occurring, we need to be aware these may be accommodated within mainstream culture without much threat to heterosexual hegemony. We might also do well to remember that such gender ambiguity has also been in vogue in the past, in the era of gay liberation with its radical drag and the popularity of such icons as David Bowie. While academic theorists busily deconstruct 'the compulsory order of sex/gender/desire' (Butler, 1990a: 6), at a street level apparent challenges to gender and sexual conformity are often about style rather than politics (Maddison, 1995). Style may, in some circles, have been politicized, particularly through the theatricalization of gay politics (Butler, 1993), but a large and vocal segment of gay (mainly male) activists does not support the central tenets of feminism and Queer: that gender and sexuality are socially constructed and hence mutable. Halperin's (1995) vision of queer activists with Foucault in their pockets may be true of certain intellectuals (and, to be fair, he is aware of the limits of some self-styled queer activism), but not of gay, or even queer, activists in general.

I wonder sometimes whether the theoretical hyperreality inhabited by some of these writers, where the representations they have constructed come to constitute the only 'reality' they acknowledge, might indeed be a separate 'queer planet'. They certainly do not inhabit the same planet on which I live my daily life and struggle constantly to shake my students' belief in crass biological determinism – and where some of those defending this position most vociferously are gay.[2] My students are often willing to accept that aspects of our sexualities are socially constructed, but insist that sexual identity (or, as they would see it, orientation) is fixed at birth. More generally, the views of reformist, anti-social constructionist writers such as Simon LeVay (1993) and Andrew Sullivan (1995) are given immense media publicity, as are other gay writers and activists pleading that they are a small, fixed and finite minority who will not corrupt or convert anyone. In this context Halperin's citing of a gay disco named 'Club Hypothalamus' (which appeared in San Francisco after the publication of LeVay's gay brain thesis) as an example of 'creative appropriation and resignification' may be wishful thinking. We cannot know whether this is a queer, parodic reclamation of 'a word which had contributed to ... scientific objectification' as 'a badge of gay identity and a vehicle of queer pleasure' (Halperin, 1995: 48), or simply an endorsement of that very scientific objectification as the basis for identity.[3]

The idea of being 'born that way' shapes not only narratives of self constructed by gays and lesbians, but also political strategies. This story concedes ground to the heterosexual majority, treats that majority as given and undercuts the radical potential of homosexuality (Whisman, 1996). Of course, both biological determinism and forms of social constructionism can be used as sticks to beat lesbians and gays with, as a means of rendering them intolerable (see Sinfield, 1994). One of the contributions of Queer has been its highlighting of the ways in which the strategic deployment of homophobic discourse might be as important as its content (Halperin, 1995), since its content is often contradictory. We used to think that if we could lay bare the contradictions of ruling ideologies we could demolish them. Now it seems that the contradictions are part of their strength, enabling them to shift and be redeployed to accommodate to new political moments. This is one reason why the concept of ideology gave way to discourse. However, at the danger of being overly repetitive, I would like to reiterate the point that discourses remain ideological, or at least hegemonic, in their effects (see Chapters 1 and 8).

Preconditions for an effective critique of heterosexuality

I now want to turn my attention to the necessary foundations for a more rigorous critique of heterosexuality, bearing in mind what I have already argued about the various levels at which sexuality is socially constructed (see Chapter 1). One cause for greater optimism is that I think we are now capable of a more effective critical analysis than has been possible in the past – but only if we are prepared to listen to each other, to engage in genuine dialogue and retreat from the entrenched positions which are the legacy of the 'sex wars'. Moreover, feminists cannot be expected to make all the running. I continue to be disturbed by the degree of ignorance about feminism evinced by most male queer theorists, including those whose work I admire.

An effective critique of heterosexuality – at the levels of social structure, meaning, social practice and subjectivity – must contain two key elements. The first of these is a critique of heteronormativity, of the normative status of heterosexuality which renders any alternative sexualities 'other' and marginal. The second is a critique of what some have called 'hetero-patriarchy' or 'hetero-oppression' (although I dislike both these terms), in other words heterosexuality as systematically male dominated. It follows that a critical stance on heterosexuality should pay attention to its interlinkage with gender, as both division and hierarchy. This is a clear implication of my second point, but also of my first: the hetero/homo binary makes no sense without the existence of gender divisions since, as I have argued in Chapter 9, desiring 'the same sex' or 'the opposite sex' requires gender as a social, cultural and subjective reality.

The various critiques which have so far been developed often fall short of including both elements, although there is a long feminist tradition of trying to do so, going back at least to Adrienne Rich (1980), for whom compulsory heterosexuality both kept women *in* (within its confines) and kept them *down*, subordinated. Yet feminists – myself included – have often concentrated on one side of heterosexuality at the expense of the other. We have analysed in great detail the myriad ways in which the institutions and practices associated with heterosexuality oppress women and sustain that oppression – but we have not always made it clear that heterosexuality is what we are talking about (see Chapter 1). Lesbian feminists, rarely guilty of this oversight, have addressed both male domination within heterosexuality and heteronormativity – but their analyses of the latter have been partial as a result of their wariness of male gay and queer agendas. Queer, on the other hand, is centrally concerned with destabilizing the heterosexual norm, but not with heterosexuality as patriarchal. Where Queer takes gender seriously, it is usually as division without hierarchy.

The preconditions I have outlined are applicable not only to heterosexuality as an institution, but also as an identity and as it is practised and experienced. It cannot, however, be assumed that heteronormativity and male domination always articulate with each other in predictable ways at all four levels, that it is possible to 'read off' identity, practice and experience from what is institutionalized. It is essential that we pay attention to the complexities of these different facets of heterosexuality. I have argued that problems arise when heterosexuality as institution, identity, practice and experience are conflated, when heterosexuality is treated as a monolithic, unitary entity (see Jackson 1996a, 1996b; see also Chapter 9). This, unfortunately, is common, not only among those radical or revolutionary lesbian feminists seeking to condemn all heterosexual practices as inherently oppressive, but also among those who celebrate a plurality of sexualities outside heterosexuality. The former deny heterosexuality any complexity at all: it simply *is* eroticized power (see, for example, Jeffreys, 1990). For the latter, heterosexuality is often represented as a singular norm against which diversity must be defended. As a sexual practice it is simply boring, unless it is redefined by virtue of the ambiguity of sexual acts and actors as 'queer'. Lying inside Rubin's (1984) 'charmed circle' of acceptable sexuality, heterosexuality escapes scrutiny. In Judith Butler's work, for example, for all her efforts to destabilize both gender and heterosexuality, the latter never appears as anything other than merely normative (M. Evans, 1994).

I am not alone in noticing this. Carol Smart has also been 'struck by how, at this time of recognition of diversities, heterosexuality is always presented as a unitary concept' (1996b: 170). Smart suggests that we need to recognize 'that heterosexuality may be many things', but that at times we need to collectivize these differences – as when recognizing heterosexual privilege and its naturalization; I would add, also when talking about the institutionalization of gender hierarchy within heterosexuality. When talking about the system, the institution, then, we need a unitary concept; but when talking about identities, practices and experience we can afford to – indeed must – address diversity. Not only does this avoid the dangers of turning a critique of heterosexuality into an attack on heterosexual women, it also enables us to address intersections between different identities, social locations and patterns of dominance and subordination. Importantly, it also enables us to see heterosexuality as a site of struggle and contested meanings for those who *are* heterosexual as well as those who are not, making heterosexual feminism a tenable position rather than a contradiction in terms.

False starts in recent feminist debates

The credit for reopening the feminist debate goes to Sue Wilkinson and Celia Kitzinger, editors of a 1992 special issue of *Feminism & Psychology* and a subsequent book (1993). Although critics, notably Segal (1994), have accused them of wanting to impose the same old guilt trip on hapless heterosexual feminists, others have welcomed the chance to re-engage with old issues from new perspectives.[4] Now, while I think there are certainly problems in the way the debate was initially set up, that it was reopened at all is, as Carol Smart says, immensely significant (Smart, 1996a: 232). Many of the initial contributors did find it difficult to talk about their heterosexuality, in part, no doubt, because of the old controversies (detailed in Chapter 1) and in part because we heterosexual feminists have for so long remained silent on the subject. The way the debate was framed, however, contributed to some of the difficulties initially entailed in participating in it.

One of the problematic aspects of Wilkinson and Kitzinger's agenda was that they overemphasized the issue of political identity. Not only did this mean that other, equally crucial, aspects of heterosexuality did not at first get the attention they deserved, but the question they posed to those they invited to contribute was difficult to answer. 'How' they asked, 'does your heterosexuality contribute to your feminist politics?' (Kitzinger and Wilkinson, 1993: 5). Implicit in this question, and in much of the Editorial Introduction which explored the responses, is the assumption that heterosexuality can be a political identity and that heterosexual feminists are at fault for not making it one. Now, heterosexuality *cannot* in my view form the basis of a political identity – and certainly not an *oppositional* political identity – precisely because it represents conformity with the institutionalized norm. This does not mean that heterosexuality cannot be politicized; it can be, but only by making it visible in such a way as to problematize it and question its privileged status. Just as being white in a racist society can only be a political rallying point for the racist Right, being heterosexual cannot become a positively affirmed political identity except to preserve heterosexual privilege – as in the invocation of the 'heterosexual community' in discourses around AIDS (Grover, 1991). It is hardly surprising, then, that many women resisted the idea of defining their feminism by their heterosexuality (Swindells, 1993).

A second problem was that, in their initial introduction, Kitzinger and

Wilkinson (1993) misrepresented or misunderstood many of their contributors. Kitzinger's later (1994) essay, in particular, depicted heterosexual feminists' desires and practices as monolithic and static. For example, she cites both Bartky (1993) and Gill and Walker (1993) to support her contention that many heterosexual women are not attracted to 'nice guys' or 'new men' (1994: 202–3). Not only does this form the basis for generalizations about *all* heterosexual attraction, but it misrepresents both of the articles cited. While these authors do admit to 'deeply unsound fantasies' in which they are swept off their feet by strong men (Gill and Walker, 1993) and being attracted to 'arrogant' and 'tyrannical' men (Bartky, 1993), that is not all they say. Gill and Walker make it clear that the men they are actually involved with are 'nice guys' with whom they are trying to negotiate egalitarian practices. Bartky discusses how, over time, she has struggled to modify her desires and change her sexual relationships so that she now avoids the 'sadists' she once found irresistible. There is, however, no real basis in the accounts collected for Kitzinger's assumption that all heterosexual women, and still less all heterosexual feminists, are looking for macho, granite-jawed romantic heroes.

It is not only Kitzinger and Wilkinson who are guilty of such misrepresentation, but sometimes those critical of their whole enterprise. While accusing Kitzinger and Wilkinson of treating those who responded to their call for papers with condescension, Lynne Segal herself treats these contributors with contempt. She refers to those 'feminists sufficiently foolhardy to reply to their one-sided questions' and to Kitzinger and Wilkinson's 'selected sample of victims' (1994: 215). She, too, treats Bartky's narrative of changes in her desires as just another heterosexual feminist wallowing in guilt in response to attempts to provoke just that. She cites Bartky's wish that our sexualities be released 'from the prison house of necessity to the free space of choice' to back her arguments. But is this such a terrible goal? I read Bartky's account as more optimistic (if poignant), as indicating that, even if we remain heterosexual, other aspects of our desires are not fixed and unchanging over the span of our lives.

The terms of the debate, as originally set, were contested and other issues emerged – especially the need to disentangle heterosexuality as an institution from the experience and practice of it and to distinguish between structural bases of male sexual power and micro-practices of power within specific (hetero)sexual encounters. Kitzinger and Wilkinson themselves later clarified (modified?) their position, partially admitting the potential complexity of heterosexuality:

> Any particular sexual identity carries a *range* of political meanings; there is no one lesbian identity; no one 'heterosexual' identity to serve as its illusory polar opposite; nor any single 'bisexual' identity. (1994: 332)

Yet, as this quotation indicates, they continued to think primarily in terms of identity. It was the issue of pleasure, however, which preoccupied many participants in the debate. At the same time, and sometimes unconnected with the ongoing feminist debate, issues of pleasures and practices have also featured in queer circles.

The politics of pleasure

Can straight sex be pleasurable? Can it, perhaps, even be queer?

Even while engaging with these questions, I should make it clear that I consider debates on sexual practices to be somewhat limited in their political scope. However successful heterosexual feminists are in creating space for sexual pleasure, or for 'queer' and transgressive sexual activities, this does not necessarily challenge anything beyond our personal lives. It may well be possible to demonstrate that heterosex is not inevitably an expression of male dominance, that it can potentially be practised in novel ways, but making this potential actual and available to most of the population requires that the politics of the personal does not end at the bedroom door – or at the edge of whatever other space where one might choose to have more interesting and innovative sexual encounters. Also, the room for manoeuvre which we have is limited by heterosexual hegemony and male domination.

For many women heterosexual pleasure is not easily attained, as has been demonstrated by the Women Risk and AIDS project. Not only sexual coercion but also an inability to find a language in which to discuss and assert their own pleasures serve as obstacles to the practice of safer sex among young women (Holland et al., 1990, 1991, 1998; Thomson and Scott, 1991). The young women who participated in this research disciplined their own bodies and pleasures to suit men in ways their partners were unlikely even to be aware of. In so doing they concede to men's definitions of what was pleasurable and acceptable, continuing to define sex as 'penetration for men's pleasure in which women find fulfilment primarily in the relationship, in giving pleasure' (Holland et al., 1994: 31). This attribute of femininity is not confined to erotic encounters. As I argued in Chapter 9, the ethic of service to men is integral to other aspects of heterosexuality and should alert us to the dangers of ignoring the wider context in which our sexual lives are played out.

As Caroline Ramazanoglu (1994) argues, we 'need to distinguish between the undoubted possibilities of heterosexual pleasure, and the extremely powerful social forces which constrain these possibilities from being more widely realized' (1994: 321). We academic feminists are relatively privileged compared with most other women – we have access both to economic independence and to feminist ideas and support networks – hence we are better able to dictate the terms under which we enter into heterosexual relationships. Even so, we share some of the problems faced by women in general. As we struggle for change in our sexual lives, we are fighting on terrain which is not of our own choosing in a world where what sex *is* continues to be defined in very conventional terms. We may find that, in each individual relationship or encounter, we have to begin all over again. Like the young women interviewed by the WRAP team, our 'strategies of resistance' may prove 'unstable and elusive' (Holland et al., 1998: 171).

Undeterred by such considerations, some heterosexual feminists have insisted on the pleasures, here and now, of sex with men. They have even committed the ultimate heresy in terms of past debates, of writing in praise of penetrative sex. I have made it clear in Chapter 1 that I do not think that what is pleasurable should be beyond critique, as if erotic delights lie outside the boundaries of the social. On the other hand, it is equally unhelpful to assume that the dominant meanings of heterosexual penetration are fixed, unassailable and beyond the reach of alternative feminist reconceptualizations. To say that penetration is irredeemably patriarchal is to reduce a social relation of dominance and subordination to a physical act – an essentialist move (see Chapter 9). While I would wish to join those asserting the possibility of heterosexual pleasure, I find myself deeply dissatisfied with the ways in which others have described it.

Lynne Segal (1994, 1997) has been a staunch defender of heterosexual eroticism. She is not unaware of inequalities in heterosexual relations, of sexual coercion and violence, but she treats these less savoury aspects of heterosexuality as incidental to it. In part this is because her perspective is a psychological one, and she thus tends to individualize sexual experiences and abstract them from their social context. She is also, in my view, unduly optimistic about the degree of equality currently existing in heterosexual relations. This leads her, for example, to dismiss the evidence of the WRAP project.[5] She sees male power in heterosexual relations as unstable (see Chapter 9) and believes that 'sex easily *threatens* rather than confirms gender polarity' (Segal, 1997: 86; her emphasis). It is a mistake to confuse emotional responses during sex (vulnerability, loss of self, loss of control) with the social relations within which sex takes place. Yet Segal seems to feel that sexual passion is capable of transforming, even dissolving, gender:

> In consensual sex, when bodies meet, the epiphany of that meeting – its threat and excitement – is surely that all the great dichotomies (activity/passivity, subject/object, heterosexual/homosexual) slide away. (1997: 86)

It is as if these 'bodies' are untenanted, or as if the biographies, social locations and social identities of their inhabitants have somehow been left behind. There is no history, no context. It is also a highly romanticized view of sex as magical, raising us above mundane quotidian realities. Consensual sex does not have to be passionate and ecstatic – it can be boring and routinized. It might also be playful or cuddly or simply pleasant without being earth-shattering.

Yet I can see what Segal is trying to convey here – conditions which, in my view too, make for exceptionally good, passionate sex: a sense of total absorption in the act and the other, a sense of nothing existing beyond immediate emotion and sensation, a fluid shifting from active to passive, a mutuality of pleasures given and received. Perhaps Segal has been luckier with her lovers than most of us; while I can recall (and certainly imagine) encounters which approximate to this ideal, much (indeed most) heterosexual sex does not. Some recent research on marital sex suggests that if women in long-term relationships still find it pleasurable in any way, they are doing well (Duncombe and Marsden, 1996). The romanticism of Segal's language, however, intrigues me, since it also features in the account of another heterosexual feminist's intimate desires.

Wendy Hollway, in one of the first responses to the agenda set by Wilkinson and Kitzinger, displayed, I think, enormous courage in offering a very personal account of the pleasures of sex with her lover. Like Segal's more abstract rendition, it is highly romantic. She talks of penetrative sex in terms of the 'experience of having someone you love and trust inside you', that it can 'signify as the ultimate in closeness' which 'breaches the separation from the other'. She eulogizes the virtues of feeling 'safe, protected and loved' when wrapped in her lover's 'strong arms' and speculates on the parallel significance to him of her 'cradling breasts' (1993: 413–14). What strikes me about this account, aside from the psychoanalytic framework which underpins it, is that any sense of physical pleasure is absent: there is no sensuality, no mention of the feeling of flesh on flesh. While she takes Kitzinger and Wilkinson to task for their inadequate representation of the pleasures of penetration as 'the sensation of a full vagina', she herself says almost nothing about sensation. Sexual practices are valued for what they 'signify', not for how they, physically, feel.

Two further points emerge from these attempts to articulate heterosexual pleasure, both of which may be worth exploring further. The first of these is my own sense of distance from these accounts, particularly Hollway's. While I can identify with what Segal defines as pleasurable, Hollway's account, frankly, repels me. Yet the fact that what turns Hollway on turns me off may be significant: it is one more indicator that, at the level of practice and experience, heterosexuality is not monolithic.[6] Those women who remain within the boundaries of heterosexuality do not necessarily experience the same forms of desire. In opposing heterosexuality and homosexuality we forget that there might be many other variations in our desires within and between these two forms of sexual practices. If we did not so privilege the binary divides of gender and sexuality then there might be many other ways of classifying sexuality.[7]

The other feature of these accounts is their limited language of erotic pleasure, so that the only alternative to the cool and clinical seems to be a register borrowed from Mills and Boon (or potentially the vocabulary of pornography). It is not that such languages do not exist – in literary contexts they do – but what is available for both everyday and academic use seems to be restricted to very predictable conventions, to the extent that I find myself sliding into these modes in attempting to describe my own sexuality. This lack of a language of eroticism has been noted in relation to lesbian sex, particularly in Marilyn Frye's much quoted comparison with the language available to gay men. Gay men, says Frye, have at their disposal 'a huge lexicon of *words*: words for acts and sub-acts, preludes and denouements, their stylistic variations, their sequences.' Gay sex is therefore 'articulate' to a degree that 'lesbian "sex" does not remotely approach' (Frye, 1990: 310–11). This lack of articulateness may apply also to heterosexual women and is certainly evident in the WRAP research and in the safer sex advice available to heterosexual women (Wilton, 1997). Some do not see this as a problem. Elizabeth Grosz, for example, perceives advantages in female sexuality, and specifically lesbian sexuality, being unrepresentable, incapable of containment within language (1995: 220–21). The problem for heterosexual women, however, is that their sexuality frequently *is* represented, but within a male-defined discourse which gives them no easy way of finding an alternative voice of their own, no means of asserting what they want within actual heterosexual encounters (see Holland et al., 1998).

Given these constraints of language it perhaps unsurprising that discussions of pleasures and practices have largely been monopolized by those writing from within libertarian or, more recently, queer perspectives which, whether lesbian or gay, have drawn on the language of gay male sexuality. It is within this tradition, too, that we can find some of the earliest reflections on what might constitute ways of rethinking the classification of sexual desires outside the hetero/homo binary. Even here, however, there are linguistic absences. As Frye noted, the lexicon of gay male sex refers primarily to *acts*. It is not a language of feeling, of sensation and emotion. Moreover, those who have advanced modes of classifying sexual desires which are not restricted by the categories heterosexual, homosexual or lesbian have often simply reproduced binary divides in a new form, as in the S/M terminology of 'tops and bottoms' (see, for example, Hollibaugh and Moraga, 1984). Once more we are limited to thinking in opposites rather than envisaging more fluid, open sexual desires and practices which are not constrained by the polarity of activity–passivity.

This polarity, however, is frequently seen as unstable to the extent that it is not gender specific and can therefore be used to question gendered assumptions about heterosexuality. It is within libertarian and queer writing that we find an emphasis on the potentially subversive effects of transgressive sexual acts. It is here, too, that some have found inspiration for 'queering' heterosexual sex. Yet rendering Queer so inclusive that it can encompass even heterosexuals must surely undercut its claims to radicalism. Moreover, equating the sexually transgressive with the progressive ignores the extent to which the heterosexual status quo can incorporate and defuse individualistic challenges.

An example of heterosexual practices being identified as 'queer' is Clare Hemmings' citation of the following:

Heterosexual behaviour does not always equal 'straight'. When I strap on a dildo and fuck my male partner, we are engaged in 'heterosexual' behaviour, but I can tell you that it feels altogether queer, and I'm sure my grandmother and Jesse Helms would say the same. (Carol Queen, quoted in Hemmings, 1993: 132)

Hemmings argues that, in the context of bisexuality, such performances may serve to destabilize the hierarchical ordering of heterosexuality. I have my doubts about this and would concur with Elizabeth Wilson's interpretation of the same passage. She suggests that such acts are not necessarily transgressive, that they are perfectly capable of being incorporated into a conventional, albeit 'kinky', heterosexual couple's repertoire without having any such destabilizing consequences (Wilson, 1993: 113). In a context where heterosexual sex has come to be seen as something to be worked at in producing ever more skilled and varied performances, where the market in 'how to do it' manuals is huge (Jackson and Scott, 1997), heterosexual couples who expand their repertoire to include a few 'queer' practices are hardly radical subversives. They are also not necessarily transforming heterosexuality at any other level: there is nothing very queer, and certainly nothing at all radical, about a man who gets fucked in bed but still expects his wife to wash the sheets.[8]

I have already suggested, in Chapter 9, that the social significance of sexual acts is in no way reducible to the conjunction of particular body parts. There is nothing intrinsically 'queer' about a man being penetrated; the act is capable of being defined as such because of the symbolic meanings which penetrative sex has acquired. Carol Smart has reflected upon the implications of acknowledging that 'penetration is as heterosexual as kissing', that 'men penetrate men, women penetrate women and women can penetrate men' (1996a: 236), suggesting that it might help us to challenge both penetration's privileged place as the essential heterosexual act and its meaning as an 'invasion and colonization' of women's bodies:

> This diversity of practices allows for penetration to have various meanings, not the exclusive meaning of dominance and subordination which is endlessly mapped onto the binary of male and female. Wrenching penetration out of a heterosexual matrix of meanings deprives it of its symbolic power. (Smart, 1996a: 236)

What Smart is suggesting is that, in disengaging penetration from heterosexuality and re-coding it as more sexually ambivalent, we may be able to move in the direction of a 'post-heterosexual' desire. In effect she is arguing for a 'queering' of heterosexual sex through the recognition that it is not particular acts which define sex *as* heterosexual and, conversely, that heterosexual sex can encompass a wide range of desires and practices. I would agree that transforming heterosex entails redefining penetration – but in the old feminist sense of dissociating it from the active(male)/ passive(female) dichotomy, as well as in the newer queer sense of recasting it as no longer definitively heterosexual. I would also add that we should not lose sight of the long-standing feminist goal of deprioritizing penetrative sex, dislodging it from its privileged place as what sex *is*.

The potential for redefining penetrative sex within our existing, heterosexually ordered, society and culture is limited. In the first place, it is still used as a weapon, mobilizing its symbolic meaning as 'invasion and colonization' of women's bodies – and sometimes men's – in the real, material practice of rape.[9] Even in consensual sex, most straight men are decidedly queasy about the very idea of being penetrated. The unease and revulsion this activity provokes is precisely because it is generally still read within the 'heterosexual matrix of meanings'. For most straight men being fucked means being 'unmanned'.[10] Most are not particularly receptive, either, to the idea of giving up the idea that sex with women equates with penetrating them. The average straight man still operates a single non-negotiable script for sex: foreplay, following by intercourse, followed by his orgasm (although there is considerable variation in the way these stages are enacted). The idea that there is any alternative to this pattern has little currency outside feminist and queer circles. Only a tiny minority of the women interviewed by the WRAP team, for example, had any idea that there might be other ways of doing sex, and these were also the ones best able to assert their own sexual desires in practice (Holland et al., 1998).

After more than two decades of feminist attempts to redefine sex, more recent queer interventions and the challenge posed by HIV and AIDS, conventional heterosexual definitions of sex remain entrenched. We may have begun to erode them, but we still have a long way to go. For the here and now, we must be content with whatever pleasures are attainable, but remember to keep our critical faculties honed in the process and not assume that pleasure is anything more than a personal indulgence. We certainly should not kid ourselves that anything we do in bed (or in other erotic settings) will have any impact on the sexual lives of the majority of women – however radical it seems to us.

There are limits, then, to the extent to which straight sex can be 'queered'. Insofar as Queer entails being located as oppositionally marginal to straight culture, it is doubtful whether heterosexuals can aspire to this location while still inevitably enjoying the privilege of their presumed 'normality'. Moreover, as I have already suggested, however innovatory we are in our erotic practices, these may either remain private to us or, alternatively, simply be reappropriated by mainstream, straight erotic culture. If Queer is about destabilizing what counts as sex and subverting the normative status of heterosexuality and the binary divide of gender, then heterosexuals can be involved in the project – but at a political and theoretical level, rather than through our sexual practices per se. In other words, what we say about sex is more important than what we do in our own sexual lives, but even that will have little effect unless our ideas are heard beyond feminist and queer circles.

In my view, we should be aiming higher than simply destabilizing heterosexual erotic conventions – we should be working towards transforming them. This is unlikely to be achieved without a parallel transformation in heterosexuality as a social institution and the erosion of the gender hierarchy it entails. To think about this it is necessary to move beyond the narrow scope of the politics of pleasure and consider the ways in which heterosexuality is sustained. This brings me back to the two faces of heterosexuality which I outlined at the beginning of this chapter, hetero-normativity and male domination, and to the centrality of gender.

Sustaining heterosexuality

> For heterosexuality to achieve the status of the 'compulsory', it must present itself as a practice governed by some internal necessity. The language and law that regulates the establishment of heterosexuality as both an identity and an institution, both a practice and a system, is the language and law of defence and protection: *heterosexuality secures its self-identity and shores up its ontological boundaries by protecting itself from what it sees as the continual predatory encroachments of its contaminated other, homosexuality.* (Fuss, 1991: 2; my emphasis)

Aside from its personification of heterosexuality, this classically queer statement could be read as a simple reiteration of the old sociological truism that deviance functions to police the boundaries of normality. But more than this, Fuss is drawing our attention to ways in which homosexuality and heterosexuality serve to define each other, that the one can only exist in relation to the other, that neither makes sense without its other: they are co-constructed in a reciprocal, but hierarchical, relationship. Heterosexuality in these terms is sustained by silencing and marginalizing dissent, by naming the other as the outsider. Yet the presence of the other always threatens to undermine the heterosexual norm. It is the potentially destabilizing potential of this other which has preoccupied many queer theorists. This is what informs their deconstruction of literary texts, which provides queer readings suggestive of the outsider within. In terms of Fuss's inside/outside trope, the outsider is part of the inner workings of heterosexuality; in defining itself in relation to its 'outside', it thus incorporates the outside within itself, including it in its self-definition (Fuss, 1991: 3).

But heterosexuality also, and very importantly, is sustained by maintaining a silence about itself. It dare not speak its name,[11] for in so doing it makes evident what it keeps hidden, that it is only one form of sexuality. Hence heterosexuality is named by straights only when it is felt to be under threat, as in the case of the infamous Section 28, by the 'promotion' of homosexuality by local authorities (see Cooper, 1995; Weeks, 1991). Homosexuality, constituted as 'perversion', existed as a concept before heterosexuality and the latter still does not have the same currency as the former. 'Homosexuality' (or its more pejorative synonyms) is often mentioned in everyday straight talk, whereas the term heterosexuality is sometimes not even understood. Hence heterosexuals often do not know what they are; they do not need to know; they are simply 'normal'.

An example of this is provided by an HIV/AIDS worker quoted in Julia Brosnan's *Lesbians Talk Detonating the Nuclear Family*:

> The amount of times I've spoken to groups and discussed heterosexuality and homosexuality, only to have people ask what heterosexuals are. This happens all the time, from straight people of course. They see themselves as normal – they don't even know that there is a word to describe them. (Charles Irvine, in Brosnan, 1996: 14)

This brought to mind a memory from some time in the late 1970s or early 1980s. There was a badge much in vogue among feminists at that time which read 'How dare you presume I'm heterosexual'. Picture a group of women in a pub, some of them wearing this badge, and a man asking them what the badge meant. The word heterosexual had to be explained. He was still perplexed until one woman, exasperated, burst out: 'It means I'm a dyke!' A slogan intended to challenge the heterosexual norm failed because the norm was so deeply entrenched that it wasn't named and, even when the name was understood, the idea of not presuming heterosexuality was too alien to be comprehended.

But heterosexuality does not sustain itself only by particular patterns of speaking and silence, nor just by keeping outsiders penned within their deviant enclosures. Fuss draws a parallel with gender, and I am sure she is well aware that both heterosexuality and homosexuality depend for their definition on gender. What she does not say – and this is indicative of Queer's preoccupation with heteronormativity alone – is that what is fundamental to heterosexuality, to what sustains it 'as an identity and an institution, both a practice and a system', is gender hierarchy. Its 'inside' workings are not simply about guarding against the homosexual other, but about maintaining male domination: and these two sides of heterosexuality are inextricably intertwined.

I have argued that the intersection between gender and sexuality is a critical element in the analysis of heterosexuality, hence exploring the workings of this intersection is important. In Chapter 9, as in much of my recent work, I have argued for the logical priority of gender (see Jackson, 1996a, 1996b; Rahman and Jackson, 1997). There are several reasons why I have consistently taken this position. Initially, I wanted to challenge the undue emphasis given to sexuality by feminists and non-feminists alike and to oppose those arguments which reduced women's oppression to any single cause, whether that be sexuality or any other. For that reason I would distance myself, for example, from MacKinnon's argument that sexuality should occupy the same place in feminism that labour does in Marxism, and her assertion that gender is a product of sexuality, of men's (hetero)sexual appropriation of women (MacKinnon, 1982). It has always seemed to me that this misses the many other ways in which women's subordination and the gender division itself are sustained: through, for example, divisions of paid and unpaid labour.

I would take the same view of more recent arguments which seek to challenge the concept of gender, replace it with 'sex', and then focus on its intersection with sexuality. Elizabeth Grosz, for example, deals with the blurring of the distinction between sex and gender in recent feminist theory by declaring the concept of gender redundant. She then defines 'sex' as referring to 'the domain of sexual difference, to questions of the *morphologies of bodies*' (1995: 213; her emphasis) and sexuality as 'sexual impulses, desires, wishes, hopes, bodies, pleasures, behaviours and practices.' Gender is redundant because 'all its effects, the field that it designates, are covered by the integration of and sometimes the discord between sexuality and sex' (1995: 213). All the differences between women and men are reduced to 'morphologies of bodies' and relations between them to the sexual. Almost the entire field of gender, as I would understand it, is erased. Who is doing the housework and raising children? Are wage differentials between women and men to be reduced to bodily morphologies? How are we to understand how bodies and sexualities figure in patterns of employment and workplace cultures, for example, when the whole social world has been reduced to bodies?[12]

I have also held that, at the level of our individual subjectivities, gender is temporally prior to sexuality since we acquire a sense of ourselves as gendered long before we become reflexively aware of ourselves as sexual (see Chapter 2). Moreover, I have also argued that our sexualities are gendered in that the ways in which we express our sexualities reflect other aspects of gender (for example, the feminine ethic of serving men's needs and tending to their egos; see Chapters 2 and 9). This is not determined by the mere fact of an anatomical woman relating to an anatomical man, but indicates that sexuality is part of a wider pattern of gender relations. In my more recent work, as in Chapter 9, I have argued that the very distinction between heterosexuality and homosexuality depends upon the prior existence of gender categories without which it would be meaningless to construct sexual categories on the basis of 'object choice'.

Part of the problem we have in thinking through the connections between gender, sexuality in general and heterosexuality in particular is that we do not all mean the same thing by these terms and are often talking about different objects at different levels of analysis. How the intersection works depends on precisely what we are talking about. The term 'heterosexuality' can be used in relation to the erotic or to denote an institution involving a much wider social relation between women and men. 'Sexuality' itself is sometimes understood primarily in terms of the hetero/homo binary, or the straight, gay or lesbian identities deriving from it, while others take it to encompass a fuller range of desires, practices and identities. 'Gender' can mean the division or distinction between women or men, whether this is seen as primarily a bodily difference or a social hierarchy, but also refers to the content of these categories, to what we understand as femininity or masculinity.

I would always opt for the broader senses of these terms because to narrow them down risks losing sight of significant portions of social life. Hence, for example, I have been critical of Elizabeth Grosz (above) and Judith Butler (in Chapter 9) because they both, despite the differences between them, concentrate almost exclusively on bodily aspects of gender (or sex) and, in Butler's case, only the erotic aspect of heterosexuality. As I use the term gender, then, it covers both the division itself and the social, subjective and embodied differences which give it everyday substance. Heterosexuality, as I have repeatedly argued, is not a simple monolithic thing, but a complex of institution, identity, experience and practice, all of which intersect with gender, which is similarly sustained at a variety of levels. Moreover, heterosexuality is not only a means of ordering our sexual lives but also of structuring domestic and extra-domestic divisions of labour and resources. Sexuality itself is not just a question of the maintenance of the heterosexual/homosexual binary, but of the multitude of desires and practices which exist on both sides of that divide. Hence the intersections between gender and heterosexuality are exceedingly complex and require much more thorough exploration than is possible here.[13]

Some recent accounts have challenged the priority given to gender from perspectives which do incorporate broad definitions of both gender and heterosexuality, for example those of Tamsin Wilton (1996, 1997) and Chrys Ingraham (1996). Wilton's argument is that gender and heterosexuality are mutually defined and constituted to such an extent that neither can be accorded priority over the other. While she draws heavily on queer theory, and is therefore concerned with the issue of heteronormativity, she never loses sight of heterosexuality as an institution implicated in the subordination of women. Hence the 'disciplinary regimes of gender and the erotic are intrinsically co-dependent and foundational to the super-ordination of men to women' (Wilton, 1996: 126).

Wilton takes issue with Judith Butler for implicitly giving precedence to gender in saying that 'it seems crucial to retain a theoretical apparatus that will account for how sexuality is regulated through the policing and shaming of gender' (Butler, 1994: 27; see also Butler, 1993: 238). The policing and shaming of gender, the damning of gay men as failed men and lesbians as not proper women, is clearly crucial to the maintenance of heterosexuality. Wilton's point is that there is an equally strong relationship the other way round, the regulation of gender through 'the policing and shaming of sexuality', through, for example, sexual harassment (Wilton, 1996: 137, 1997: 13). She develops her argument through the concept of 'heteropolar-ity', the socially constructed difference that positions men and women as complementary opposites, which is crucial for the maintenance of hetero-sexuality. Thus far I have no quarrel with any of this.

Wilton also draws attention to the ways in which heterosexuality is often reduced to the purely sexual, thus occluding many aspects of its intersection with gender. However, her suggested solution to this problem is to 'speak instead of heteropolarity', a term which she says 'resists being reduced to the erotic', but 'saturates and structures the social fields of gender and the erotic, and renders them indivisible' (1996: 138). I doubt that this term does resist reduction to the erotic, since this is how it is most often justified – through the 'vive la différence' idea (see Chapter 5) which legitimizes sexual difference as necessary for sexual attraction – and for species survival. In this latter sense it has been fundamental to biological determinism. More importantly, I do not think the problem of the interrelationship between gender and heterosexuality can be resolved by collapsing both into one term – 'heteropolarity' – covering both gender difference and the ideologies and practices which tie that difference into heterosexuality. While gender and sexuality are so closely intertwined that it is not easy to unravel the connection, we need to retain the analytical capacity to tease out the tangled connections between them.

For me, Wilton's argument holds in terms of the mutual reinforcing of gender division and normative heterosexuality, where each is policed in relation to the other. I am not sure whether it works beyond this point. It is certainly the case that our individual sexualities – our erotic identities, desires and practices – are profoundly gendered and, conversely, that our sense of ourselves as gendered is imbued with sexual significance and validated, at least in part, by our sexual activities and relationships. Yet this is only one way in which gender is sustained, albeit an important one. If heterosexuality is defined so broadly as to encompass the entire field of gendered social relations, then it might be logically possible (if not desirable) to argue that all aspects of gender are reducible to it. However, it would then be necessary to argue that even the gender of those who live outside heterosexual relations is ultimately heterosexual. Now Wilton, if I read her correctly, is resistant to the idea that everyone's gendered and sexual lives are governed by heterosexuality. She is certainly opposed to the idea that lesbian and gay sexual practices which re-enact divisions of roles or hierarchies can be termed 'heterosexual' (*pace* Jeffreys, 1990).

I would agree that such activities cannot be conceptualized as precisely analogous to heterosexual sex, but lesbian and gay sexuality – whatever it entails – is nonetheless gendered. There *are* differences between gay male and lesbian sexualities – and these differences in many respects parallel those between masculine and feminine sexualities. Moreover, gender can be sustained through lesbian and gay lifestyles and practices (albeit in unconventional form). Gay macho, for instance, may in some ways be a parody of 'real' masculinity, but is also a reaction against the idea of the effeminate gay. It does have a relationship to conventional masculinity which is not entirely subversive. Similarly, new styles of lesbianism, especially the emergence of a distinctly femme identity, may be seen as parodic, but they still have a relationship with conventional femininity. The femme might still be 'read' by straight culture as simply a feminine woman; she can 'pass' whether she wants to or not.[14] We do not escape our gender by withdrawing from compulsory heterosexuality. Lesbians, despite Wittig's (1992) claim to the contrary, are still women, are still socially located as such – and gay men are still men and can enjoy at least some aspects of patriarchal privilege, notably economic ones.

Wilton's argument, in the end, does not convince me that we should collapse gender and heterosexuality together, nor does it shift me from my conviction that the distinction between hetero- and homosexualities depends on the prior division between women and men. If sexuality as a field of enquiry entails more than the homo/hetero binary, then it is crucial to retain a means of analysing the ways in which all sexualities are gendered. If, as I believe, all aspects of social life are also gendered, then we need to be able to think about how this gendering process is related to heterosexuality without deciding the issue in advance. If heterosexuality as an institution is not merely about specifically sexual relations, we should consider whether the term should be confined to the actualities of social relations between heterosexual couples (in and out of marital and monogamous relations) or should be extended to cover wider aspects of social life. For example, are gendered labour markets and wage differentials heterosexual in themselves or are they simply related to the social organization of heterosexual life?

These questions are crucial to an evaluation of Ingraham's (1996) argument that heterosexuality should displace gender as the central category of feminist analysis. Of all the analyses I have read which challenge my belief in the primacy of gender, it is Ingraham's which I find most convincing and hence difficult to contest. This is because, despite the almost opposite conclusions we come to, she is working within a sociological and materialist feminist framework very similar to my own. From this perspective she shares my scepticism about the sex–gender distinction (see Chapter 1) and defines heterosexuality as an institution which regulates more than merely our erotic lives. Her concern is with the 'heterosexual imaginary' that masks the ways in which gender has consistently been defined from a heteronormative perspective. Like Wilton, she draws attention to the construction of 'women' and 'men' as mutually attracted 'opposite sexes', and argues that sociologists (including feminists) have failed to see the heterosexual ends to which this gender divide is directed.

As Ingraham points out, the definitions of gender employed by feminist sociologists indicate that it is a binary 'organizing relations *between* the sexes' (1996: 186; her emphasis). She goes on to suggest that heterosexuality 'serves as the organizing institution and ideology ... for gender' (1996: 187). She sees heterosexuality implicated in the operation of all social institutions at all levels of society, from family to workplace to the state, and reasons thus:

> Without institutionalized heterosexuality – that is, the ideological and organizational regulation of relations between men and women – would gender even exist? If we make sense of gender and sex as historically and institutionally bound to heterosexuality, then we shift gender studies from localized examinations of

individual behaviours and group practices to critical analyses of heterosexuality as an organizing institution. (Ingraham, 1996: 187)

Ingraham's question cannot be conclusively answered, but I find it possible to imagine a male dominated society which is not ordered around the heterosexual contract.[15] Aside from this, I take Ingraham's point that heterosexuality is *an* organizing principle of many aspects of social structure and social life; this has, for example, emerged from some recent studies of workplace cultures (Adkins, 1995; Hearn et al., 1989), but I still have my doubts about according it primacy. Defining heterosexuality so broadly that it encompasses all aspects of gendered relations and then substituting it (or Ingraham's alternative, 'heterogender') for gender, raises some of the same difficulties as Wilton's conceptualization of heteropolarity – although Ingraham's argument is far more internally consistent. It seems to me that it is necessary to maintain an analytical distinction between gender, as the hierarchical relation between women and men, and heterosexuality, as a specific institutionalized form of that relation, and that not all gender relations are specifically heterosexual.

Accepting that we need to challenge the 'heterosexual imaginary' and subject heterosexuality to rigorous feminist and sociological inquiry, why is Ingraham so sure that, for this to happen, gender must give way to heterosexuality? A clue resides in the quotation above, in Ingraham's characterization of gender studies as being concerned with 'individual behaviours and group practices'. This may be an accurate depiction of gender studies in the USA, but it would not apply to the ways in which feminist sociologists have operationalized the concept on this side of the Atlantic. Here gender studies have sometimes focused on localized settings, but there is a strong tradition of materialist sociological work which has concerned itself with the structuring of gender within major institutions and at the level of the social totality. It may be that, working in a US context, Ingraham has had access to materialist analyses of heterosexuality without materialist analyses of gender. When British and French feminist sociologists talk of gender in terms of relations between women and men, we do not generally mean only personal, or face to face, relations but wider, structural, social relations (see Delphy, 1993). In the end, the differences between Ingraham and myself may come down to a difference of emphasis attributable to our differing national and sexual locations. Whatever the significance of these differences, I can certainly endorse Ingraham's call for 'a critique of institutionalized heterosexuality as a formal area of inquiry within sociology' (1996: 188).

Doing and undoing gender and sexuality

Heterosexuality is sustained not only at the institutional level, but through our everyday sexual and social practices, which indicates that, in some sense, it requires our continual reaffirmation for its continuance. Most of the population 'do' heterosexuality every day without reflecting critically on that doing. Moreover, it is clear from the above discussion that whatever view we take on heterosexuality and gender, they are interrelated. Hence 'doing heterosexuality' is also about 'doing gender'. This is accomplished through talk and action, through the embodied practices of dress and demeanour, through active participation in formal institutional settings, through the mundane activities through which our everyday lives are ordered. If we 'do heterosexuality' and 'do gender' in our everyday lives, to what extent can we 'undo' them?

Those who live their lives outside compulsory heterosexuality are, of course, not complicit in its maintenance to the same extent as heterosexuals, and some are politically committed to undoing, or at least unsettling, it. The subversive potential of dissident sexualities has primarily been asserted from a queer perspective. Recently, too, bisexual theorists have used their ambiguous location to reflect on the possibility of undoing both gender and sexuality. Consider, for example, Elizabeth Däumer's musings:

> What if, by mistake, one forgot that the person holding one's hand was a man – or a woman – and if one, equally by mistake, were to slip into a heterosexual relationship with a woman, a lesbian relationship with a man? (1992: 97)

Presumably Däumer refers here to some momentary lapse of concentration since, if she is imagining the possibility of forgetting gender more permanently, this is a profoundly illogical thought. If gender were forgotten, there would no longer be 'men' or 'women' to have any sort of relationships with, and the terms 'lesbian' and 'heterosexual' would no longer have any meaning.

Although there has been a great deal of emphasis in recent theory on destabilizing gender and heterosexuality, there is a reluctance to think about the possibility of thoroughly undoing them: doing away with them. The currently fashionable ideas of performative subversions of gender and sexual binaries, deriving from the work of Judith Butler, are not so much undoing gender as doing it in new ways. Butler's reflections on a lesbian femme's claim that she likes her 'boys to be girls' may serve to illustrate this:

> ... 'being a girl' contextualizes and resignifies 'masculinity' in a butch identity. As a result, that masculinity, if that it can be called, is always brought into relief against a culturally intelligible 'female body.' It is precisely this dissonant juxtaposition and the sexual tension that its transgression generates that constitute the object of desire. In other words, the object of lesbian-femme desire ... [is] neither some decontextualized female body nor a discrete yet superimposed masculine identity, but the destabilization of both terms as they come into erotic interplay. (Butler, 1990a: 122)

Formulations such as these do reveal the artificiality of gender, its status as a construction with no necessary relationship to particular bodies or sexualities. I find Butler's idea of gender as a performance, of drag as a parody without an original to imitate, interesting and productive. I also welcome her later emphasis on the constraining effects of gender (Butler, 1993). But, quite apart from the absence of the social (beyond the simply normative) in her work, the destabilizing effects she envisages for such transgressive performances are limited. If Butler has a utopian vision, it is a world of multiple genders and sexualities, not a world without gender or heterosexuality. This she shares with many others writing from a queer position.

Lurking somewhere beneath the postmodern posturing of Queer is the old assumption that the whole of human potential equals the sum of its gendered parts – but reformulated in a new way. Where androgynists aimed to weld the two incomplete 'halves' of masculinity and femininity into a complete whole, queer theorists seek to destabilize both and create more 'genders' by jumping between them or recombining their elements in innovative or parodic forms. They still, therefore, have a stake in 'doing gender', which is radical only to the extent that the performance, the act of 'doing' is made more visible. Some combination of femininity and masculinity, and same gender or other gender desire, is not the only human possibility. If men and women are products of a hierarchical relation, in the absence of that relation very different subjectivities and desires might emerge.

I find it depressing that much of what passes as radical these days does not envisage the end of gender hierarchy or the collapse of institutionalized heterosexuality, but simply a multiplying of genders and sexualities or movement between them. It might be argued that this would ultimately have the effect of rendering the difference between women and men as simply part of a fluid continuum of differences and of divesting heterosexuality of its privileged location. But seeking to undo binary divisions by rendering their boundaries more permeable and adding more categories to them ignores the hierarchical social relations on which the original binaries were founded. It fails to address the ways in which heterosexuality and gender are sustained at the macro level of structures and institutions as well as the micro level of our everyday social practices.

Our capacity to undo gender and heterosexuality is constrained by the structural inequalities which sustain them. Our ability to conceptualize their undoing is limited to the extent that our sense of ourselves has been constructed within a heterosexual, patriarchal social order. It may be this which accounts for the lack of vision which, in my view, underpins much queer writing, the failure to imagine a world without gender, without heterosexuality (and without other systematic inequalities deriving from a social order which remains capitalist and imperialist as well as patriarchal). Concern with material inequalities has given way to a preoccupation with difference as something to be valued and affirmed.

In my view there are dangers in endorsing too wholeheartedly 'the doxa of difference' (Felski, 1997) which has gained such a hold in feminist and queer circles. Certainly we should be cautious of affirming sources of difference which are themselves products of systematic inequalities. The theoretical impetus for this preoccupation with differences derives from postmodernism's scepticism about grand narratives purporting to reveal the 'truth' of historical, social conditions. The political impetus came from the realization that such truth claims were generally made from male, white, Western, heterosexual locations. Yet, as Rosemary Hennessy (1993) has argued, there are some totalities – capitalist, patriarchal, imperialist, racist – which continue to have pervasive, real and often brutal effects. Affirmation of 'difference' can simply lead to the acceptance of social divisions produced by these totalities. In the present context, I do not want hetero-sexuality to be treated as simply one difference among many, nor masculi-nity and femininity 'appreciated' as differences which could be rendered harmless if only we valued them equally, permitted fluid movement be-tween them or admitted the possibility of other genders. Why not think instead of the end of gender, the end of the hetero/homosexual division? This idea is often interpreted as making everyone the same. But why should it? Might it not open up the possibility that differences other than the ones we know today might flourish, differences that are not founded on hier-archy?

Such utopian visions are no longer fashionable; most radical intellectuals have abandoned those metanarratives, such as Marxism, which once promised a better future, and have taken to heart Foucault's view that power is inescapable. We can resist, subvert and destabilize, but nothing much will change; or, if it does, there will be new deployments of power to be resisted, subverted and destabilized. This is a politics of resistance and transgression, but not a politics of radical transformation; its goal is permanent rebellion but never revolutionary change. It is ultimately a pessimistic politics. Of course, optimism is difficult to sustain in the political climate prevailing at turn of the millennium. Holding on to utopian ideals may be more than a little crazy when there seems little prospect of their ever being realized. Yet I believe that it is crucially important, both politically and analytically, that we are at least able to *imagine* social relations being radically other than they are. If we cannot do this we lose the impetus even to *think* critically about the world in which we live.

Notes

1 There is beginning to be some concern with the material world in queer theory, and a move away from purely textual analysis (see, for example, Seidman 1996a, 1997), insofar as it is recognized that the policing of sexual identities has real social and political consequences. Yet in most queer theory, even that which addresses the material, economic and social structures, relations and everyday practices are conspicuously absent. Judith Butler (1993), for example, discusses the ways in which bodies are 'materialized' almost purely in terms of norms –

but with no sense of where these norms come from or how they are constituted (see Jackson, 1998a). More recently, Butler (1997) has conceded the importance of political economy, in the Marxist sense, to our understanding of sexuality. However, she does this by a return to Lévi-Strauss's (1969) notion of 'the exchange of women' drawn upon, among others, by Rubin (1975) in her conceptualization of the sex/gender system . This, however, brings us back to an ahistorical notion of kinship which avoids confronting the historical and cultural specificity of the various social practices through which gender and sexuality are produced (see Hennessy, 1998). In fact, this formulation was crucial to the 'cultural turn' (Barrett, 1992) whereby many feminists turned their backs on materialist analysis (see Jackson, 1998d; Ramazanoglu, 1995). Butler, in her search for a more material grounding to her theory, returns to this precise point in our theoretical history, where structuralism paved the way for poststructuralism. While she distances herself from the universalism under-pinning Lévi-Straussian notions, I remain unconvinced of her willingness to look more closely at material, social and economic relations.

2   A couple of anecdotes might serve to illustrate my everyday reality. A straight male colleague was astounded at being confronted by a group of young gay students berating him for his reactionary views – he had suggested in a lecture that sexuality was socially constructed. He, like me, came to political awareness in an era when it was taken as axiomatic that biological determinism was the reactionary stance. A younger, more knowing gay colleague set up a formal debate on this issue at the university lesbian, gay and bisexual society (which has embraced diversity enough to admit bisexuals); few of the gay men were willing to consider that they might not be 'born that way', that the heterosexuality of the majority might be normative rather than natural.

3   Maybe Halperin does know, in having some local knowledge about those who so named the club or about the readings of it in circulation among the San Francisco gay community, but this is by no means obvious in the information he supplies.

4   A cynic might also say that they have obtained a lot of mileage – and publications – from both inviting heterosexual feminists to contribute to edited collections and using those contributions as data for further publications.

5   In *Straight Sex* Segal (1994) accuses the WRAP researchers of simply finding what they were looking for, having decided in advance that women could not enjoy heterosex. Yet the WRAP team's analysis of its data was thorough and meticulous; moreover the team coded for, and expected, more evidence of pleasure than in fact it found.

6   It might also help explain why Hollway believes in psychoanalysis and I do not. It clearly has personal resonance for her, makes sense in terms of her own desires and experiences, in a way which it does not for me (see Chapter 1).

7   In reflecting on this, I have thought about discussions with close friends about sexual desire and the fact that the friend whose feelings I can identify with most is a life-long lesbian.

8   There are other problems with the idea that sexual transgression is, in itself, in some way radical or destabilizing of the status quo. As I indicated in Chapter 1, such claims avoid the question of where particular desires come from and thus can end up reproducing an erotic of domination and subordination which replicates heterosexual norms. I also suggested that the appeal of the Foucaul-dian emphasis on practices rather than desires is that such questions no longer have to be posed. Practices can be valorized as liberatory without having to ask why people want to engage in them in the first place.

9   Rape is still endemic to most of the world's societies and still reaches epidemic proportions in times of war (see Chapter 3). We shouldn't need reminding of this in the context of the rape which has accompanied genocide in Rwanda and

former Yugoslavia: this often entails men being forced to watch the raping of 'their' women before being killed, to emphasize their impotence in the face of the aggressor. Here rape is both a brutal physical act and a symbolic act whereby men demonstrate their power over women and over conquered men. In the week before this passage was written there was a great deal of media coverage of rape in men's prisons in the USA, where weaker men – younger, more 'effeminate' men – are singled out for brutalization.

10 To link this back to Clare Hemmings' invocation of Carol Queen, I do not think straight women are going to solve this problem by rushing out to buy strap-on dildos and insisting on using them (even supposing we had the power to insist). Not only am I sceptical about claiming widespread social effects for individual acts of sexual transgression, but I am extremely wary of elevating any sexual practice into a form of political rectitude – especially one whose power to transgress or to shock relies merely on reversing the conventional gendered pattern of heterosexual sex. More radical assertions of the transformative power of sexual transgression often come from gay men. David Halperin, for example sees fisting as an activity which challenges the goal oriented, end driven practice of sexual intercourse in that it takes hours, may or may not involve orgasm and its key values are 'intensity and duration of feeling'. This may be so, and it certainly disturbs conventional ideas about sex far more than a simple hetero-sexual role reversal does, but I doubt his claim that fist-fucking 'as both a sexual and a subcultural phenomenon ... has the potential to contribute to redefining both the meaning and practice of sex' (1995: 91). It may well have that potential within gay communities, and perhaps among those supportive of them, but in the current climate it is unlikely to have any impact anywhere else other than to confirm, in the eyes of the straight majority, the 'queerness' – in the pejorative sense – of those practising it.

11 I was somewhat disappointed to find that David Halperin (1995) had already said this – although it is not a strikingly original thought.

12 This critique of Grosz was developed in recent collaborative work with Sue Scott, in a paper entitled 'Putting the body's feet on the ground', presented at the British Sociological Association's Annual Conference in 1998. This will ultimately appear in a collection from the conference edited by Kathryn Backett-Milburn and Linda Mackie, due for publication by Macmillan in April 2000. Until then, copies of the paper are obtainable, for a small handling fee, from the BSA offices, Unit 3F/G, Mountjoy Research Centre, Stockton Road, Durham DRI 3UR, UK.

13 I am hoping to do more work on this area in a book I am preparing for the Open University Press under the working title of *Women, Gender and Sexual Differ-ence*, presently scheduled for publication in 2000.

14 Waiting at a cash point queue on a major Edinburgh thoroughfare on a busy Saturday afternoon, a little drama of gender and sexual ambiguity was played out in front of me. I was standing behind a group of young femmes, dressed up and made up to the nines. I am probably au fait enough with the dress codes to have read these women as femme lesbians even had I not been close enough to them to hear their conversation (which left me in no doubt). Heterosexual men on the street, however, clearly did not see them as anything other than a group of attractive, available young women. The men reacted with the usual barrage of whistles and appreciative or crude comments – or simply looks from the more timid (or politically correct) – which make up the everyday sexual harassment we are all so familiar with. The young women were enjoying themselves at the men's expense: flaunting themselves while withholding themselves (which some have seen as the radical edge of femme). But would any of them have had the same bravado had she been alone? And could any of them have resisted any

more effectively than a straight woman if at another, quieter, time in another, less public, place one such man had decided that she was 'asking for it'?

15 If we take a leap of the imagination, it is possible to envisage a male dominated society without heterosexuality being the privileged form of sexual relationship, a society in which men used women as slave labour and producers of children but not as sexual partners within a personal relationship. This is the dystopian vision presented by Suzy McKie Charnas in *Walk to the End of the World* (1989). However, I find it impossible to imagine a heterosexually ordered society without gender inequality. That is to say, if the division of gender did not exist, I do not think that the majority of anatomical females would freely choose to have sexual relations only or primarily with anatomical males – rather our sexual partners would be chosen by criteria other than their genitals.

Bibliography

Abu-Lughod, L. (1990) 'Shifting politics in Bedouin love poetry', in C. Lutz and L. Abu-Lughod (eds) *Language and the Politics of Emotion*. Cambridge: Cambridge University Press, pp. 1–23.

Abu-Lughod, L. and Lutz, C. (1990) 'Introduction: emotion, discourse and the politics of everyday life', in C. Lutz and L. Abu-Lughod (eds), *Language and the Politics of Emotion*. Cambridge: Cambridge University Press, pp. 24–45.

Adkins, L. (1995) *Gendered Work: Sexuality, Family and the Labour Market*. Buckingham: Open Univeristy Press.

Allen, S and Leonard, D. (1996) 'From sexual divisions to sexualities: changing sociological agendas', in J. Weeks and J. Holland (eds), *Sexual Cultures: Communities, Values and Intimacy*. Basingstoke: Macmillan, pp. 17–33.

Amir, M. 1967. 'Victim precipitated forcible rape', *Journal of American Law, Criminology and Police Science*, 58: 493–502.

Amir, M. 1971. *Patterns in Forcible Rape*. Chicago, IL: University of Chicago Press.

Barnes, K. (1958) *He and She*. London: Darwin Finlayson.

Barrett, M. (1980) *Women's Oppression Today*. London: Verso Books.

Barrett, M. (1992) 'Words and things: materialism and method in contemporary feminist analysis', in M. Barrett and A. Phillips (eds), *Destabilizing Theory*. Cambridge: Polity, pp. 201–19.

Barrett, M. and McIntosh, M. (1991) *The Anti-Social Family*, 2nd edn. London: Verso.

Barthes, R. (1978) *A Lover's Discourse*. New York: Hill and Wang.

Bartky, S. (1990) *Femininity and Domination*. New York: Routledge.

Bartky, S. (1993) 'Hypatia unbound: a confession', in S. Wilkinson and C. Kitzinger (eds), *Heterosexuality*. London: Sage, pp. 41–52.

Baruch, E.H. (1991) *Women, Love and Power*, New York: New York University Press.

Becker, H. (1966) *Social Problems: A Modern Approach*. New York: Wiley.

Bernstein, B. (1971) 'On the classification and framing of educational knowledge', in M. Young (ed.), *Knowledge and Control*. London: Collier Macmillan, pp. 47–69.

Bertilsson, M. (1986) 'Love's labour lost? A sociological view', *Theory, Culture & Society*, 3 (1): 19–35.

Birke, L. (1994) 'Interventions in hostile territory', in Gabriele Griffin, Marianne Hester, Shirin Rai and Sasha Roseneil (eds), *Stirring It: Challenges for Feminism*. London, Taylor and Francis, pp. 185–94.

Bologh, R.W. (1987) 'Max Weber on erotic love: a feminist inquiry', in Sam Whimster and Scott Lash (eds), *Max Weber, Rationality and Modernity*. London: Allen and Unwin, pp. 242–58.

Brake, M. (1982) *Human Sexual Relations*. Harmondsworth: Penguin.

Brodribb, S. (1992) *Nothing Mat(t)ers: A Feminist Critique of Postmodernism*. Melbourne: Spinifex.

Brogan, P. (1997) 'Murder stalks the queasy realm of child pageants', *Glasgow Herald*, 13 January 1997: 10.

Brosnan, J. (1996) *Lesbians Talk Detonating the Nuclear Family*. London: Scarlet Press.

Broverman, I.K. et al. (1970) 'Sex-role stereotypes and clinical judgements of mental health', *Journal of Consulting and Clinical Psychology*, 34: 1–7.

Brownmiller, S. (1975) *Against Our Will: Men, Women and Rape*. London: Secker and Warburg.

Brunt, R. (1988) 'Love is in the air', *Marxism Today*, February: 18–21.

Butler, J. (1990a) *Gender Trouble: Feminism and the Subversion of Identity*. New York: Routledge.

Butler, J. (1990b) 'Gender trouble, feminist theory and psychoanalytic discourse', in L. Nicholson (ed.), *Feminism/Postmodernism*. New York: Routledge, pp. 324–40.

Butler, J. (1991) 'Imitation and gender insubordination', in D. Fuss (ed.), *Inside/Out*. New York: Routledge, pp. 13–31.

Butler, J. (1993) *Bodies that Matter*. New York: Routledge.

Butler, J. (1994) 'Critically queer', *GLQ: A Journal of Lesbian and Gay Studies*, 1 (1): 17–32.

Butler, J. (1997) 'Merely cultural', *Social Text*, 52/53: 265–78.

Califia, P. (1981) 'Feminism and sadomasochism', *Heresies*, 12: 30–4.

Cameron, D. (1993) 'Telling it like it wasn't: how radical feminism became history', *Trouble & Strife*, 27: 11–15.

Cameron, D. and Frazer, E. (1987) *The Lust to Kill*. Oxford: Polity.

Cameron, D. and Frazer, E. (1992) 'On the question of pornography and sexual violence: moving beyond cause and effect', in C. Itzen (ed.), *Pornography: Women, Violence and Civil Liberties*. Oxford University Press, pp. 359–83.

Campbell, B. (1980) 'Feminist sexual politics', *Feminist Review*, 5: 1–18.

Cancian, F. (1990) *Love in America*. Cambridge: Cambridge University Press.

Caplan, P. (ed.) (1987) *The Cultural Construction of Sexuality*. London: Tavistock.

Central Statistical Office (1994) *Social Focus on Children*. London: HMSO.

Charnas, S. McKie (1989) *Walk to the End of the World/Motherlines*. London: The Women's Press.

Chodorow, N. (1978) *The Reproduction of Mothering*. Berkeley: University of California Press.

Christian-Smith, L. (1991) *Becoming a Woman through Romance*. London: Routledge.

Clark, L. and Lewis, D. (1977) *Rape: The Price of Coercive Sexuality*. Toronto: The Women's Press.

Cleaver, E. (1970) *Soul on Ice*. London: Panther Books.

Comer, L. (1974) *Wedlocked Women*. Leeds: Feminist Books.

Connell, R.W. and Dowsett, G.W. (1992) ' "The unclean motion of the generative parts": frameworks in Western thought on sexuality', in R.W. Connell and G.W. Dowsett (eds), *Rethinking Sex*. Melbourne: University of Melbourne Press, pp. 49–75.

Cooper, D. (1995) *Power in Struggle: Feminism, Sexuality and the State*. Buckingham: Open University Press.

Coward, R. (1978) 'Re-reading Freud: the making of the Feminine', *Spare Rib*, May: 43–46.

Coward, R. (1982) *Female Desire*. London: Paladin.

Coward, R. and Ellis, J. (1977) *Language and Materialism*. London: Routledge and Kegan Paul.

Coward, R., Cowie, E. and Lipshitz, S. (1976) 'Psychoanalysis and patriarchal structures', in Women's Publishing Cooperative (eds) *Papers on Patriarchy*. Lewes: Lewes Women's Publishing Co-operative, pp. 6–20.

Däumer, E. (1992) 'Queer ethics: or, the challenge of bisexuality to lesbian ethics', *Hypatia*, 7(4): 91–105.

Davies, B. (1989) *Frogs and Snails and Feminist Tales*. Sydney: Allen and Unwin.

Dawkins, J. (1967) *A Textbook of Sex Education*. Oxford: Blackwell and Mott.

de Beauvoir, S. (1972) *The Second Sex*. Harmondsworth: Penguin.

de Lauretis, T. (1991) 'Queer theory: lesbian and gay sexualities, an introduction', *differences*, (5) 3: iii–xviii.

de Lauretis, T. (1994) 'Habit changes', *differences*, 6 (2 & 3): 296–313.

Delphy, C. (1977) *The Main Enemy*. London: Women's Research and Resources Centre.

Delphy, C. (1984) *Close to Home: A Materialist Analysis of Women's Oppression*. London: Hutchinson.

Delphy, C. (1992) 'Mothers' union?', *Trouble & Strife*, 24: 12–19.

Delphy, C. (1993) 'Rethinking sex and gender', *Women's Studies International Forum*, 16 (1): 1–9.

Delphy, C. (1994) 'Changing women in a changing Europe: is "difference" the future for feminism?', *Women's Studies International Forum*, 17 (2/3): 197–201.

Delphy, C. (1995) 'The invention of French Feminism: an essential move' *Yale French Studies*, 87: 190–221.

Delphy, C. and Leonard, D. (1992) *Familiar Exploitation: A New Analysis of Marriage in Contemporary Western Societies*. Oxford: Polity.

Dollimore, J. (1991) *Sexual Dissidence*. Oxford: Oxford University Press.

Douglas, J. and Atwell, F.C. (1988) *Love, Intimacy and Sex*. London and Beverly Hills: Sage.

Doyal, L., Naidoo, J. and Wilton, T. (eds) (1994) *AIDS: Setting a Feminist Agenda*. London: Taylor and Francis.

DuBois, E. and Gordon, L. (1984) 'Seeking ecstasy on the battle field: danger and pleasure in nineteenth century feminist thought', in C. Vance (ed.), *Pleasure and Danger: Exploring Female Sexuality*. London: Routledge and Kegan Paul, pp. 31–49.

Duchen, C. (ed.) (1987) *French Connections: Voices from the Women's Movement in France*. London: Hutchinson.

Duncombe, J. and Marsden, D. (1993) 'Love and intimacy: the gender division of emotion and "emotion work" ', *Sociology*, 27 (2): 221–41.

Duncombe, J. and Marsden, D. (1996) 'Whose orgasm is this anyway? "Sex work" in long-term heterosexual couple relationships', in J. Weeks and J. Holland (eds), *Sexual Cultures*. Basingstoke: Macmillan.

Dworkin, A. (1987) *Intercourse*. London: Secker and Warburg.

Echols, A. (1984) 'The taming of the id: feminist sexual politics 1968–83', in C. Vance (ed.), *Pleasure and Danger*. London: Routledge, pp. 50–72.

Edwards, S. (1981) *Female Sexuality and the Law*. Oxford: Martin Robertson.

Edwards, T. (1993) *Erotics and Politics: Gay Male Sexuality, Masculinity and Feminism*. London, Routledge.

Engels, F. (1891) *The Origin of the Family, Private Property and the State*. Moscow: Foreign Language Publishing.

Ennew, J. (1986)*The Sexual Exploitation of Children*. Cambridge: Polity,

Epstein, S. (1992) 'Gay politics, ethnic identity: the limits of social constructionism', in E. Stein (ed.), *Forms of Desire*. New York: Routledge, pp. 239–93.

Epstein, S. (1996) 'A queer encounter: sociology and the study of sexuality', in S. Seidman (ed.), *Queer Theory/Sociology*. Oxford: Blackwell, pp. 145–67.

Errington, F. and Gewertz, D. (1987) *Cultural Alternatives and a Feminist Anthropology*. Cambridge: Cambridge University Press.

Esland, G. (1971) 'Teaching and learning as the organization of knowledge', in M. Young (ed.), *Knowledge and Control*. London: Collier Macmillan, pp. 70–115.

Ettorre, E.M. (1980) *Lesbians, Women and Society*. London: Routledge and Kegan Paul.

Evans, D.T. (1993) *Sexual Citizenship: the Material Construction of Sexualities*. London: Routledge.

Evans, D.T. (1994) 'Sexual Citizenship', unpublished paper, University of Glasgow.

Evans, M. (1994) 'Desire incarnate: review of Judith Butler's *Bodies that Matter'*, *The Times Higher Education Supplement*, 18 February: 241.

Faderman, L. (1982) *Surpassing the Love of Men*. London: Junction Books.

Faraday, A. (1981) 'Liberating lesbian research', in K. Plummer (ed.), *The Making of the Modern Homosexual*. London: R.K.P., pp. 112–39.

Felski, R. (1997) 'The doxa of difference', *Signs*, 23 (1): 1–22.

Finn, G. (1988) 'Women, fantasy and popular culture: the wonderful world of Harlequin romances' in R.P. Gruneau (ed.), *Popular Cultures and Political Practices*. Toronto: Garamond, pp. 51–67.

Firestone, S. (1972) *The Dialectic of Sex*. London: Paladin.

Ford, C. S. and Beach, F.A. (1952) *Patterns of Sexual Behaviour*. London: Eyre and Spottiswood.

Foucault, M. (1979) *The History of Sexuality, Vol. 1*. London: Allen Lane.

Foucault, M. (1980) 'Truth and power', in C. Gordon (ed.), *Michel Foucault: Power/ Knowledge*. Brighton: Harvester, pp. 109–33.

Foucault, M. (1981) *The History of Sexuality, Vol. 1*. Harmondsworth: Penguin.

Foucault, M. (1988) 'Technologies of the self', in L.H. Martin, H. Gutman and P.H. Hutton (eds), *Technologies of the Self*. London: Tavistock, pp. 16–49.

Fowler, B. (1991) *The Alienated Reader: Women and Popular Romantic Literature in the Twentieth Century*. Hemel Hempstead: Harvester Wheatsheaf.

Franklin, S. (1993) 'Essentialism, which essentialism? Some implications of reproductive and genetic techno-science' in J.P. DeCecco and J.P. Elia (eds), *If You Seduce a Straight Person, Can You Make Them Gay? Issues in Biological Essentialism Versus Social Constructionism in Gay and Lesbian Identities*. New York: Harrington Park Press, pp. 27–40.

Fraser, N. (1989) *Unruly Practices: Power, Discourse and Gender in Contemporary Social Theory*. Oxford: Polity.

Fraser, N. and Bartky, S.L. (eds) (1992) *Revaluing French Feminism*. Bloomington and Indianapolis: Indiana University Press.

Frazer, E. (1987) 'Teenage girls reading *Jackie'*, *Media Culture & Society*, 9 (4): 407–25.

Freud, S. (1905) 'Three essays on sexuality' in *The Standard Edition of the Complete Works of Sigmund Freud*, Vol. 7. London: Hogarth Press, pp. 123–245.

Freud, S. (1912) 'On the universal tendency to debasement in the sphere of love', in *The Standard Edition of the Complete Works of Sigmund Freud*, Vol. 11. London: Hogarth Press, pp. 177–90.

Freud, S. (1925) 'Some psychical consequences of the anatomical distinction between the sexes' *The Standard Edition of the Complete Works of Sigmund Freud*, Vol. 19. London: Hogarth Press, pp. 241–58.

Freud, S. (1931) 'Female sexuality', in *The Standard Edition of the Complete Works of Sigmund Freud*, Vol. 21. London: Hogarth Press, pp. 221–43.

Freud, S. (1933) 'Femininity', in *The Standard Edition of the Complete Works of Sigmund Freud*, Vol. 22. London: Hogarth Press, pp. 576–99.

Frye, M. (1990) 'Lesbian "sex"', in J. Allen (ed.) *Lesbian Philosophies and Cultures*. New York: New York University Press.

Fuss, D. (1989) *Essentially Speaking: Feminism, Nature and Difference*. New York and London: Routledge.

Fuss, D. (1991) *Inside/Out: Lesbian Theories, Gay Theories*. New York: Routledge.

Gagnon, J.H. (1965) 'Sexuality and sexual learning in the child', *Psychiatry*, 28: 212–28.

Gagnon, J.H. (1973) 'The creation of the sexual in early adolescence', in S. Groubard (ed.), *From Twelve to Sixteen*. New York, W.W. Norton.

Gagnon, J. and Simon, W. (1974) *Sexual Conduct*. London: Hutchinson.

Gagnon, J.H. and Simon, W. (1987) 'The sexual scripting of oral genital contacts', *Archives of Sexual Behaviour*, 16: 1–25.

Gallop, G. (1982) *Feminism and Psychoanalysis: The Daughter's Seduction.* London: Macmillan.

Gatens, M. (1983) 'A critique of the sex/gender distinction', in J. Allen and P. Patton (eds), *Beyond Marxism? Interventions After Marx.* New South Wales: Intervention Publications, pp. 143–60.

Geertz, C. (1984) ' "From the native's point of view": on the nature of anthropological understanding', in R.A Shweder and R.A LeVine (eds), *Culture Theory: Essays in Mind, Self and Emotion.* Cambridge: Cambridge University Press, pp. 123–36.

Gergen, M. (1993) 'Unbundling our binaries – genders, sexualities, desires', in S. Wilkinson and C. Kitzinger (eds), *Heterosexuality.* London: Sage, pp. 62–4.

Giddens, A. (1991) *Modernity and Self-Identity.* Oxford: Polity.

Giddens, A. (1992) *The Transformation of Intimacy.* Oxford: Polity.

Gill, R. and Walker, R. (1993) 'Heterosexuality, feminism, contradiction: on being young, white heterosexual feminists in the 1990s', in S. Wilkinson and C. Kitzinger (eds), *Heterosexuality.* London: Sage, pp. 68–72.

Gill, D.G., Reid, G.D.B. and Smith, D.M. (1974) 'Sex education: press and parental perceptions', in R. Rogers (ed.), *Sex Education, Rationale and Reaction.* Cambridge: Cambridge University Press.

Goode, W. (1959) 'The theoretical importance of love', *American Sociological Review*, 24 (1): 38–47.

Goode, W. (1974) 'The theoretical importance of love', in R.L. Coser (ed.), *The Family: Its Structure and Functions.* London: Macmillan.

Goodison, L. (1983) 'Really being in love means wanting to live in a different world', in S. Cartledge and J. Ryan (eds), *Sex and Love: New Thoughts on Old Contradictions.* London: Women's Press, pp. 48–66.

Graham, A. (1996) 'Made up, dressed up, fed up (and she's only five)', *Radio Times*, 17 January–2 February: 22–4.

Grant, C. (1994/5) 'Queer theorrhea and what it might mean for feminists', *Trouble & Strife*, 29/30: 37–43.

Gray, A. (1992) *Video Playtime: The Gendering of a Leisure Technology.* London: Routledge.

Greer, G. (1970) *The Female Eunuch.* London: Paladin.

Griffin, C. (1982) 'Cultures of femininity: romance revisited', Centre for Contemporary Cultural Studies Occasional Paper, University of Birmingham.

Griffin, C. (1987) *Typical Girls.* London: Routledge and Kegan Paul.

Grosz, E. (1995) *Space, Time and Perversion.* New York: Routledge.

Grover, J.Z. (1991) 'AIDS: keywords', In D. Crimp (ed.), *AIDS: Cultural Analysis/ Cultural Activism.* Cambridge, MA: MIT Press, pp. 17–30.

Guillaumin, C. (1981) 'The practice of power and belief in nature. Part 1: The appropriation of women', *Feminist Issues* 1 (2): 3–28.

Guillaumin, C. (1987) 'The question of difference', in C. Duchen (ed.), *French Connections.* London: Hutchinson. pp. 64–77.

Guillaumin, C. (1995) *Racism, Sexism, Power and Ideology.* London: Routledge.

Halperin, D.M. (1995) *Saint Foucault: Towards a Gay Hagiography.* Oxford: Oxford University Press.

Harne, L. (1984) 'Lesbian custody and the new myth of the father', *Trouble & Strife*, 3: 12–14.

Harris, A. (1974) 'Sex education in schools', in R. Rogers (ed.), *Sex Education, Rationale and Reaction.* Cambridge: Cambridge University Press.

Haug, F. et al. (1987) *Female Sexualization.* London: Verso.

Hearn, J. et al. (eds) (1989) *The Sexuality of Organization.* London: Sage.

Heath, S. (1982) *The Sexual Fix.* London: Macmillan.

Hemmings, C. (1993) 'Resituating the bisexual body', in J. Bristow and A.R. Wilson (eds), *Activating Theory: Lesbian, Gay, Bisexual Politics*. London: Lawrence and Wishart, pp. 118–38.

Hennessy, R. (1993) *Materialist Feminism and the Politics of Discourse*. New York: Routledge.

Hennessy, R. (1998) 'Disappearing capital: the queer material of sexual identity', paper presented at the Centre for Interdisciplinary Gender Studies, University of Leeds.

Herdt, G. (1981) *Guardians of the Flutes*. New York: McGraw Hill.

Herschberger, R. (1970) *Adam's Rib*. New York: Harper and Row.

Hite, S. (1976) *The Hite Report*. New York: Dell.

Hite, S. (1988) *Women and Love: A Cultural Revolution in Progress*. London: Viking.

Hochschild, A. (1983) *The Managed Heart*. Berkeley: University of California Press.

Hoffman, M. (1975) 'Assumptions in sex education books', *Educational Review*, 27 (3): 211–20.

Holland, J., Ramazanoglu, C., Scott, S., Sharpe, S. and Thomson, R. (1990) ' "Don't die of ignorance" – I nearly died of embarrassment': Condoms in Context*. London: Tufnell Press.

Holland, J., Ramazanoglu, C., Sharpe, S. and Thomson, R. (1991) *Pressure, Resistance, Empowerment: Young Women and the Negotiation of Safer Sex*. London: Tufnell Press.

Holland, J., Ramazanoglu, C., Sharpe, S. and Thomson, R. (1994) 'Power and desire: the embodiment of female sexuality', *Feminist Review*, 46: 21–38.

Holland, J., Ramazanoglu, C., Sharpe, S. and Thomson, R. (1998) *The Male in the Head: Young People, Heterosexuality and Power*. London: Tufnell Press.

Hollibaugh, A. (1984) 'Desire for the future: radical hope in passion and pleasure,' in C. Vance (ed.), *Pleasure and Danger: Exploring Female Sexuality*. London: Routledge, pp. 401–10.

Hollibaugh, A. and Moraga, C. (1984) 'What we're rolling around in bed with', in A. Snitow et al. (eds), *Desire: The Politics of Sexuality*. London: Virago.

Hollway, W. (1984a) 'Gender difference and the production of subjectivity', in J. Henriques et.al., *Changing the Subject*. London: Methuen, pp. 227–63.

Hollway, W. (1984b) 'Women's power in heterosexual sex', *Women's Studies International Forum*, 7 (1): 63–8.

Hollway, W. (1989) *Subjectivity and Method in Psychology*. London: Sage.

Hollway, W. (1993) 'Theorizing heterosexuality: a response', *Feminism & Psychology*, 3 (3): 412–17.

Ingraham, C. (1996) 'The heterosexual imaginary', in S. Seidman (ed.), *Queer Theory/Sociology*. Oxford: Blackwell, pp. 168–93.

Irigaray, L. (1985) *This Sex Which is Not One*. Ithaca: Cornell University Press.

Irigaray, L. (1993) *Je, tu, nous: Toward a Culture of Difference*. New York: Routledge.

Jackson, S. (1978a) *On the Social Construction of Female Sexuality*. London: Women's Research and Resources Centre.

Jackson, S. (1978b) 'The social context of rape' *Women's Studies International Quarterly*, 1(1): 27–38.

Jackson, S. (1978c) 'How to make babies: sexism and sex education', *Women's Studies International Quarterly*, 1 (4): 341–52.

Jackson, S. (1982a) *Childhood and Sexuality*. Oxford: Basil Blackwell.

Jackson, S. (1982b) 'Masculinity, femininity and sexuality', in S. Friedman and E. Sarah (eds), *On the Problem of Men*. London: Women's Press, pp. 21–8.

Jackson, S. (1983) 'The desire for Freud: psychoanalysis and feminism', *Trouble & Strife*, 1: 32–41.

Jackson, S. (1990) 'Demons and innocents: Western ideas on children's sexuality in historical perspective', in M.E. Perry *Handbook of Sexology Volume 7: Childhood and Adolescent Sexology*. Amsterdam: Elsevier, pp. 23–50.

Jackson, S. (1992a) 'Towards an historical sociology of housework: a materialist feminist analysis', *Women's Studies International Forum*, 15 (2): 153–72.

Jackson, S. (1992b) 'The amazing deconstructing woman: the perils of postmodern feminism', *Trouble & Strife*, 25: 25–31.

Jackson, S. (1993a) 'Even sociologists fall in love: an exploration in the sociology of emotions', in *Sociology*, 27 (2): 201–20.

Jackson, S. (1993b) 'Love and romance as objects of feminist knowledge', in K. Lubelska, M. Kennedy and M. Walsh (eds), *Making Connections: Women's Studies, Women's Movements, Women's Lives*. London: Taylor and Francis, pp. 39–50.

Jackson, S. (1993c) 'Childhood and sexuality in historical perspective', *Child and Adolescent Clinics of North America*, 20 (3): 355–67.

Jackson, S. (1994) 'Theorizing heterosexuality: gender, power and pleasure', Strathclyde Papers on Sociology and Social Policy, University of Strathclyde.

Jackson, S. (1995a) 'Women and heterosexual love: complicity, resistance and change', in L. Pearce and J. Stacey (eds), *Romance Revisited*. London: Lawrence and Wishart, pp. 49–62.

Jackson, S. (1995b) 'Theorising heterosexuality: towards a materialist feminist analysis', in M. Maynard and J. Purvis (eds) *(Hetero)sexual Politics*. London: Taylor and Francis, pp. 11–26.

Jackson, S. (1995c) 'Heterosexuality, power and pleasure', *Feminism & Psychology*, 5 (1): 131–5.

Jackson, S. (1996a) 'Heterosexuality as a problem for feminist theory', in L. Adkins and V. Merchant (eds), *Sexualising the Social*. Basingstoke: Macmillan, pp. 15–34.

Jackson, S. (1996b) 'Heterosexuality and feminist theory', in D. Richardson (ed.), *Theorising Heterosexuality: Telling it Straight*. Buckingham: Open University Press, pp. 21–39.

Jackson, S. (1996c) 'Récents débats sur l'héterosexualité: une approche féministe matérialiste', *Nouvelles Questions Féministes*, 17 (3): 5–25.

Jackson, S. (1996d) 'Ignorance is bliss when you're just seventeen', *Trouble & Strife*, 33: 50–60.

Jackson, S. (1998a) 'Theorising gender and sexuality', in S. Jackson and J. Jones (eds), *Contemporary Feminist Theories*. Edinburgh: Edinburgh University Press, pp. 131–46.

Jackson, S. (1998b) 'Telling stories: memory, narrative and experience in feminist theory and research', in C. Griffin, K. Henwood and A. Phoenix (eds), *Standpoints and Differences*. London: Sage, pp. 45–64.

Jackson, S. (1998c) 'Lesbian politics, gay politics and the problem of heterosexuality', in T. Carver and V. Mottier (eds), *Politics of Sexuality*. London: Routledge, pp. 68–78.

Jackson, S. (1998d) 'Feminist social theory', in S. Jackson and J. Jones (eds), *Contemporary Feminist Theories*. Edinburgh: Edinburgh University Press, pp. 12–33.

Jackson, S. and Scott, S. (1996) 'Sexual skirmishes and feminist factions: twenty-five years of debate on women and sexuality', in S. Jackson and S. Scott (eds), *Feminism and Sexuality*. Edinburgh: Edinburgh University Press; New York: Columbia University Press, pp. 1–31.

Jackson S. and Scott S. (1997) 'Gut reactions to matters of the heart: reflections on rationality, irrationality and sexuality', *Sociological Review*, 45 (4): 551–75.

Jackson, S. and Scott, S. (1998) 'Putting the body's feet on the ground: towards a sociological rconceptualisation of gendered and sexual embodiment', paper delivered to the British Sociological Association Annual Conference, University of Edinburgh.

Jagger, A. (1989) 'Love and knowledge: emotion in feminist epistemology', in A. Jagger and S. Bordo (eds), *Gender/Body/Knowledge: Feminist Reconstructions of Being and Knowing*. New Brunswick, NJ: Rutgers University Press, pp. 145–72.

Jardine, A. and Smith, P. (eds) (1987) *Men in Feminism*. New York: Methuen.

Jeffreys, S. (1985) *The Spinster and her Enemies*. London: Pandora.

Jeffreys, S. (1990) *Anticlimax: a Feminist Critique of the Sexual Revolution*. London: Women's Press.

Jeffreys, S. (1994a) *The Lesbian Heresy: a Feminist Perspective on the Lesbian Sexual Revolution*. London: Women's Press.

Jeffreys, S. (1994b) 'The queer disappearance of lesbian sexuality in the academy', *Women's Studies International Forum*, 17 (5): 459–72.

Jeffreys, S. (1997) 'The queer disappearance of lesbians', in B. Mintz and E.D. Rothblum (eds), *Lesbians in Academia*. New York: Routledge, pp. 269–78.

Johnson, R. (1986) 'The story so far: and further transformations?' in D. Punter (ed.), *Introduction to Contemporary Cultural Studies*. London: Longman, pp. 217–313.

Kaplan, C. (1986) *Sea Changes*. London: Verso.

Kappeler, S. (1986) *The Pornography of Representation*. Oxford: Polity.

Keddie, N. (1971) 'Classroom knowledge', in M. Young (ed.), *Knowledge and Control*. London: Collier Macmillan pp. 133–60.

Kelly, L. (1988) *Surviving Sexual Violence*. Cambridge: Polity.

Kinsey, A.C. et al. (1953) *Sexual Behavior in the Human Female*. Philadelphia, PA: W.B. Saunders.

Kirkpatrick, C. and Kanin, K. (1957) 'Male sex aggression on a university campus', *American Sociological Review*, 22: 52–8.

Kitzinger, C. (1994) 'Problematizing pleasure: radical feminist deconstructions of sexuality and power', in H.L. Radtke and H.J. Stam (eds), *Power/Gender: Social Relations in Theory and Practice*. London: Sage, pp. 194–209.

Kitzinger, C. and Wilkinson, S. (1993) 'Theorizing Heterosexuality', in S. Wilkinson and C. Kitzinger (eds), *Heterosexuality: A 'Feminism and Psychology' Reader*. London: Sage, pp. 1–32.

Kitzinger, C. and Wilkinson, S. (1994) 'Re-viewing heterosexuality', *Feminism & Psychology*, 4 (2): 330–6.

Kitzinger, J. (1988) 'Defending innocence: ideologies of childhood', *Feminist Review*, 28: 77–87.

Klein, V. (1946) *The Feminine Character*. London: Routledge and Kegan Paul.

Koedt, A. (1972) 'The myth of the vaginal orgasm', in A. Koedt (ed.), *Radical Feminism*. New York: Quadrangle, pp. 198–207.

Kollontai, A. (1972) *Sexual Relations and the Class Struggle*. Bristol: Falling Wall Press. (Orig. pub. 1919.)

Komarovsky, M. (1962) *Blue Collar Marriage*. New York: W.W Norton.

Lacan, J. (1977) *Écrits*. London: Tavistock.

Landry, D. and MacLean, G. (1993) *Materialist Feminisms*. Oxford: Blackwell.

Langford, W. (1992) 'Gender, power and self-esteem: women's poverty in the economy of love', unpublished paper presented to the Women's Studies Network (UK) Conference, University of Central Lancashire.

Langford, W. (1999) *Revolutions of the Heart: Gender, Power and the Delusions of Love*. London: Routledge.

Lawson, A. (1988) *Adultery*. Oxford: Blackwell.

Leeds Revolutionary Feminists (1981) 'Political lesbianism: the case against heterosexuality', in Onlywomen Press (eds), *Love Your Enemy: The Debate Between Heterosexual Feminism and Political Lesbianism*. London: Onlywomen Press, pp. 5–10.

Lees, S. (1986) *Losing Out*. London: Hutchinson.

Lennhoff, F.G. (1971) 'In the classroom', in F.G. Lennhoff, *Honesty to Children.* Shrewsbury: Shotton Hall.

Leonard, D. (1980) *Sex and Generation.* London: Tavistock.

LeVay, S. (1993) *The Sexual Brain.* Cambridge, MA: MIT Press.

Lévi-Strauss, C. (1969) *The Elementary Structures of Kinship.* Boston: Beacon Press.

Liberty (1994) *Sexuality and the State: Human Rights Violations Against Lesbians, Gays, Bisexuals and Transgendered People.* London: National Council for Civil Liberties.

Liddington, J. (1998) *Female Fortune. Land, Gender and Authority: The Anne Lister Diaries and Other Writings 1833–36.* London: Rivers Oram Press.

Light, A. (1984) ' "Returning to Manderley" – romance fiction, female sexuality and class', *Feminist Review*, 16: 7–25.

Lindemann, G. (1997) 'The body of sexual difference', in K. Davis (ed.), *Embodied Practices: Feminist Perpsectives on the Body.* London: Sage, pp. 73–92.

Luhmann, N. (1986) *Love as Passion.* Cambridge: Polity.

Lutz, C. (1986) 'Emotion, thought and estrangement: emotion as a cultural category', *Cultural Anthropology*, 1: 287–309.

Lutz, C. (1990) 'Engendered emotion: gender, power and the rhetoric of emotional control in American discourse', in C. Lutz and L. Abu-Lughod (eds), *Language and the Politics of Emotion.* Cambridge: Cambridge University Press, pp. 69–91.

McCall, M.M. (1966) 'Courtship as social exchange', in B. Farber (ed.), *Kinship and Family Organization.* London: Wiley, pp. 190–200.

Macfarlane, A. (1978) *The Origins of English Individualism.* Oxford: Blackwell.

Macfarlane, A. (1987) *The Culture of Capitalism.* Oxford: Basil Blackwell.

McIntosh, M. (1968) 'The homosexual role', *Social Problems*, 16 (2): 182–92.

McIntosh, M. (1992) 'Liberalism and the contradictions of oppression', in L. Segal (ed.), *Sex Exposed.* London: Virago, pp. 155–69.

MacKinnon, C.A. (1982) 'Feminism, Marxism, method and the state: an agenda for theory', *Signs*, 7 (3): 515–44.

McNay, L. (1992) *Feminism and Foucault.* Oxford: Polity.

McRobbie, A. (1982) '*Jackie*: an ideology of adolescent femininity', in Bernard Waites et al. (eds) *Popular Culture Past and Present.* London: Croom Helm, pp. 263–83.

McRobbie, A. (1991) *Feminism and Youth Culture.* London: Macmillan.

McRobbie, A. (1996) '*More!*: new sexualities in girls' and women's magazines', in J. Curran, D. Morley and V. Walkerdine (eds), *Cultural Studies and Communications.* London: Edward Arnold, pp. 172–94.

Maddison, S. (1995) 'A queered pitch', *Red Pepper*, February: 27.

Malinowski, B. (1929) *The Sexual Life of Savages in North-Western Melanesia.* London: Routledge and Kegan Paul.

Mansfield, P. and Collard, J. (1988) *The Beginning of the Rest of Your Life.* London: Macmillan.

Marks, E. and de Courtivron, I. (eds) (1981) *New French Feminisms: An Anthology.* Brighton: Harvester.

Martin, E. (1989) *The Woman in the Body.* Milton Keynes: Open University Press.

Masters, W.H. and Johnson, V. (1966) *Human Sexual Response.* Boston, MA: Little, Brown.

Mathieu, N.C. (1977) *Ignored by Some, Denied by Others: The Social Sex Category in Sociology.* London: Women's Research and Resources Centre.

Mathieu, N.C. (1996) 'Sexual, sexed and sex-class identities: three ways of conceptualising the relationship between sex and gender', in D. Leonard and L. Adkins (eds), *Sex in Question.* London: Taylor and Francis, pp. 72–108.

Matza, D. (1964) *Delinquency and Drift.* London: Wiley.

Matza, D. (1969) *Becoming Deviant.* Englewood Cliffs, NJ: Prentice Hall.

Mead, G.H. (1934) *Mind, Self and Society.* Chicago, IL: University of Chicago Press.

Mead, M. (1935) *Sex and Temperament in Three Primitive Societies*. New York: William Morrow.

Medea, A. and Thompson, K. (1974) *Against Rape*. New York: Farrar, Straus and Giroux.

Millett, K. (1972) *Sexual Politics*. London: Abacus.

Millett, K. (1970). 'Sexual politics in literature', in R. Morgan (ed.), *Sisterhood is Powerful*. New York: Random House, pp. 349–76.

Mills, C.W. (1940) 'Situated actions and vocabularies of motive', *American Sociological Review*, 5: 439–52.

Mills, C.W. (1970) *The Sociological Imagination*. Harmondsworth: Penguin.

Mitchell, J. (1972) 'Female Sexuality', Marie Stopes Memorial Lecture, University of York.

Mitchell, J. (1975) *Psychoanalysis and Feminism*. Harmondsworth: Penguin.

Mitchell, J. (1982) 'Introduction I' in J. Mitchell and J. Rose (eds), *Feminine Sexuality: Jacques Lacan and the École Freudienne*. London: Macmillan, pp. 1–26.

Mitchell, J. and Rose, J. (eds) (1982) *Feminine Sexuality: Jacques Lacan and the École Freudienne*. London: Macmillan.

Modleski, T. (1984) *Loving With a Vengeance*. London: Methuen.

Modleski, T. (1991) *Feminism Without Women*. New York: Routledge.

Moi, T. (1982) 'Jealousy and sexual difference', *Feminist Review*, 11: 53–69.

Money, J. (1963) 'Developmental differentiation of masculinity and femininity compared', in S. Farber and R. Wilson (eds), *The Potential of Woman*. New York: McGraw Hill.

Montgomery, M. (1991) 'Our tune: a study of a discourse genre', in P. Scannel (ed.), *Boadcast Talk*. London: Sage, pp. 138–77.

Moss, G. (1989) *Unpopular Fictions*. London: Virago.

Newton, E. (1979) *Mother Camp: Female Impersonators in America*, 2nd edn. Chicago, IL: University of Chicago Press.

Oakley, A. (1972) *Sex, Gender and Society*. Oxford: Martin Robertson.

Oakley, A. (1984) *The Sociology of Housework*, 2nd edn. Oxford: Blackwell.

Onlywomen Press (eds) (1981) *Love Your Enemy: The Debate between Heterosexual Feminism and Political Lesbianism*. London: Onlywomen Press.

Pateman, C. (1988) *The Sexual Contract*. Oxford: Polity.

Pearce, L. and Stacey, J. (1995) *Romance Revisited*. London: Lawrence and Wishart.

Person, E.S. (1988) *Love and Fateful Encounters: The Power of Romantic Passion*. New York: W.W. Norton.

Plummer, K. (1975) *Sexual Stigma*. London: Routledge and Kegan Paul.

Plummer, K. (1995) *Telling Sexual Stories*. London: Routledge.

Questions Féministes Collective (1981) 'Variations on common themes', in E. Marks and I. de Courtivron (eds), *New French Feminisms*. Brighton: Harvester, pp. 212–30.

Radford, J. (1991) 'Immaculate conceptions', *Trouble & Strife*, 21: 8–12.

Radway, J. (1987) *Reading the Romance*. London: Verso.

Rahman, M. and Jackson, S. (1997) 'Liberty, equality and sexuality: essentialism and the discourse of rights', *Journal of Gender Studies*, 6 (2): 117–29.

Ramazanoglu, C. (ed.) (1993) *Up Against Foucault*. London: Routledge.

Ramazanoglu, C. (1994) 'Theorizing heterosexuality: a response to Wendy Hollway', *Feminism & Psychology*, 4 (2): 320–21.

Ramazanoglu, C. (1995) 'Back to basics: heterosexuality, biology and why men stay on top', in M. Maynard and J. Purvis (eds), *(Hetero)sexual Politics*. London: Taylor and Francis, pp. 27–41.

Ramazanoglu, C. and Holland J. (1993) 'Women's sexuality and men's appropriation of desire', in C. Ramazanoglu (ed.), *Up Against Foucault*. London: Routledge, pp. 239–64.

Rich, A. (1980) 'Compulsory heterosexuality and lesbian existence', *Signs*, 5 (4): 631–60.

Richardson, D. (1993) 'Sexuality and male dominance', in D. Richardson and V. Robertson (eds), *Introducing Women's Studies*. London: Macmillan, pp. 74–98.

Richardson, D. (ed.) (1996) *Theorising Heterosexuality: Telling it Straight*. Buckingham: Open University Press.

Rights of Women (1984) *Lesbian Mothers on Trial*. London: Community Press.

Riley, D. (1988) *'Am I that Name?' Feminism and the Category of 'Women' in History*. London: Macmillan.

Robinson, V. (1993) 'Heterosexuality: beginnings and connections', in S. Wilkinson and C. Kitzinger (eds), *Heterosexuality*. London: Sage, pp. 80–2.

Rosaldo, M. (1980) 'The use and abuse of anthropology: reflections on feminism and cross-cultural understanding', *Signs*, 5 (3): 389–417.

Rosaldo, M. (1984) 'Towards an anthropology of self and feeling', in R.A. Shweder and R.A. Levine (eds), *Culture Theory*. Cambridge: Cambridge University Press, pp. 137–57.

Rose, J. (1982) 'Introduction II', in J. Mitchell and J. Rose (eds), *Feminine Sexuality*. London: Macmillan, pp. 27–58.

Rose, N. (1989) *Governing the Soul: The Shaping of the Private Self*. London: Routledge.

Rowland, R. (1993) 'Radical feminist heterosexuality: the personal and the political', in S. Wilkinson and C. Kitzinger (eds), *Heterosexuality: A 'Feminism and Psychology' Reader*. London: Sage, pp. 75–9.

Rubin, G. (1975) 'The traffic in women', in R. Reiter (ed.), *Toward an Anthropology of Women*. New York: Monthly Review Press, pp. 157–210.

Rubin, G. (1984) 'Thinking sex: notes for a radical theory of the politics of sexuality', in Carole S. Vance (ed.), *Pleasure and Danger: Exploring Female Sexuality*. London: Routledge and Kegan Paul, pp. 267–319.

Rubin, G. and Butler, J. (1994) 'Sexual Traffic', *differences*, 6 (2/3): 62–99.

Rubin, L. (1976) *Worlds of Pain*. New York: Basic Books.

Rubin, L. (1983) *Intimate Strangers*. New York: Harper and Row.

Sarsby, J. (1983) *Romantic Love and Society*. Harmondsworth: Penguin.

Sayers, J. (1979) 'Anatomy is destiny: variations on a theme', *Women's Studies International Quarterly*, 2: 19–32.

Schill, E. (1971) 'Looking towards marriage', in F.G. Lennhoff (ed.), *Honesty to Children*. Shrewsbury: Shotton Hall.

Schofield, M. (1965) *The Sexual Behaviour of Young People*. London: Longman.

Schofield, M. (1973) *The Sexual Behaviour of Young Adults*. London: Allen Lane.

Scott, S., Jackson, S. and Backett-Milburn, K. (1998) 'Swings and roundabouts: risk anxiety and the everyday worlds of children', *Sociology*, 32 (4): 689–705.

Scully, D. (1990) *Understanding Sexual Violence*. London: Unwin Hyman.

Searles, P. and Berger, R.J. (1995) *Rape and Society: Readings on the Problem of Sexual Assault*. Oxford: Westview Press.

Sedgwick, E.K. (1991) *The Epistemology of the Closet*. Hemel Hempstead: Harvester Wheatsheaf.

Segal, L. (1994) *Straight Sex: The Politics of Pleasure*. London: Virago.

Segal, L. (1997) 'Feminist sexual politics and the heterosexual predicament', in L. Segal (ed.), *New Sexual Agendas*. Basingstoke: Macmillan, pp. 77–89.

Segal, N. (1992) 'Why can't a good man be sexy? Why can't a sexy man be good?', in D. Porter (ed.), *Between Men and Feminism*. London: Routledge, pp. 35–47.

Seidman, S. (1991) *Romantic Longings: Love in America 1830–1980*. New York: Routledge.

Seidman, S. (1992) *Embattled Eros: Sexual Politics and Ethics in Contemporary America*. New York: Routledge.

Seidman, S. (1996a) *Queer Theory/Sociology*. Oxford: Blackwell.

Seidman, S. (1996b) 'Introduction', in S. Seidman, *Queer Theory/Sociology*. Oxford: Blackwell, pp. 1–29.

Seidman, S. (1997) *Difference Troubles: Queering Social Theory and Sexual Politics*. Cambridge: Cambridge University Press.

Shorter, E. (1976) *The Making of the Modern Family*. London: Collins.

Simon, W. (1996) *Postmodern Sexualities*. New York: Routledge.

Simon, W. and Gagnon, J.H. (1969) 'On psychosexual development', in D.A. Goslin (ed.), *Handbook of Socialization Theory and Research*. Chicago, IL: Rand McNally, pp. 733–52.

Sinfield, A. (1994) *The Wilde Century*. London: Cassell.

Smart, C. (1976) *Women, Crime and Criminology*. London: Routledge.

Smart, C. (1992) 'Disruptive bodies and unruly sex: the regulation of reproduction and sexuality in the nineteenth century', in C. Smart (ed.), *Regulating Womanhood: Historical Essays on Marriage, Motherhood and Sexuality*. London: Routledge.

Smart, C. (1996a) 'Desperately seeking post-heterosexual woman', in Janet Holland and Lisa Adkins (eds), *Sex, Sensibility and the Gendered Body*. Basingstoke: Macmillan, pp. 222–41.

Smart, C. (1996b) 'Collusion, collaboration and confession: on moving beyond the heterosexuality debate', in D. Richardson (ed.), *Theorising Hetrosexuality: Telling it Straight*. Buckingham: Open University Press, pp. 161–77.

Smith-Rosenberg, C. (1975) 'The female world of love and ritual', *Signs*, 9 (1): 1–29.

Smyth, C. (1992) *Lesbians Talk Queer Notions*. London: Scarlet Press.

Snitow, A., Stanstell, C. and Thompson, S. (eds) (1984) *Desire: The Politics of Sexuality*. London: Virago.

Stacey, J. (1991) 'Promoting normality: Section 28 and the regulation of sexuality', in Sarah Franklin, Celia Lury and Jackie Stacey (eds), *Off Centre: Feminism and Cultural Studies*. London: Harper Collins, pp. 284–304.

Stanley, L. (1982) ' "Male needs": the problems and problems of working with gay men', in S. Friedman and E. Sarah (eds), *On the Problem of Men: Two Feminist Conferences*. London: Women's Press, pp. 190–213.

Stein, A. and Plummer, K. (1996) ' "I can't even think straight": "queer" theory and the missing sexual revolution in sociology', in S. Seidman (ed.), *Queer Theory/Sociology*. Oxford: Blackwell, pp. 129–44.

Stoller, R.J. (1968) *Sex and Gender: On the Development of Masculinity and Femininity*. New York: Science House.

Stone, L. (1977) *The Family, Sex and Marriage in England 1500–1800*. London: Weidenfeld & Nicolson.

Sullivan, A. (1995) *Virtually Normal: An Argument About Homosexuality*. New York: Alfred A. Knopf.

Svalastoga, K. (1962) 'Rape and social structure', *Pacific Social Review*, 5: 48–53.

Swindells, J. (1993) 'A straight outing', *Trouble & Strife*, 26: 40–4.

Sykes, G. and Matza, D. (1957) 'Techniques of neutralization: a theory of delinquency', *American Sociological Review*, 22: 667–70.

Szasz, T. (1973) *The Manufacture of Madness*. London: Paladin.

Taylor, H. (1989a) 'Romantic readers', in H. Carr (ed.), *From My Guy to Sci-Fi*. London: Pandora, pp. 58–77.

Taylor, H. (1989b) *Scarlett's Women: Gone With The Wind and its Female Fans*. London: Virago.

Thompson, S. (1984) 'Search for tomorow: on feminism and the reconstruction of teen romance', in C. Vance (ed.), *Pleasure and Danger: Exploring Female Sexuality*. London: Routledge, pp. 350–84.

Thomson, R. (1994) 'Moral rhetoric and public health pragmatism: the recent politics of sex education', *Feminist Review*, 48: 40–60.

Thomson, R. and Scott, S. (1991) *Learning About Sex: Young Women and the Social Construction of Sexual Identity*. London: Tufnell Press.

Toner, B. (1977) *The Facts of Rape*. London: Arrow.

Trouble & Strife Collective (1983) 'Editorial', *Trouble & Strife*, 1: 2–3.

Van Every, J. (1996) 'Heterosexuality and domestic life', in D. Richardson (ed.), *Theorising Heterosexuality: Telling it Straight*. Buckingham: Open University Press, pp. 39–54.

Vance, C.S. (1984) (ed.) *Pleasure and Danger*. London: Routledge.

Vance, C.S. (1989) 'Social construction theory: problems in the history of sexuality', in D. Altman et al., *Which Homosexuality?* London: Gay Men's Press, pp. 13–34.

Waites, M. (1998) 'Sexual citizens: legislating the age of consent in Britain', in T. Carver and V. Mottier (eds), *Politics of Sexuality*. London: Routledge.

Walby, S. (1990) *Theorizing Patriarchy*. Oxford: Blackwell.

Walkerdine, V. (1984) 'Some day my prince will come', in Angela McRobbie and Mica Nava (eds), *Gender and Generation*. London: Macmillan, pp. 162–84.

Walkowitz, J. (1980) 'The politics of prostitution', in Catherine R. Stimpson and Ethel Spector Person (eds), *Women, Sex and Sexuality*. Chicago, IL: University of Chicago Press, pp. 145–57.

Wallace, C. (1987) *For Richer For Poorer: Growing Up In and Out of Work*. London: Tavistock.

Watney, S. (1987) *Policing Desire*. London: Routledge.

Weale, S. (1996) 'Publishers fight curb on "explicit sex" in teenagers' magazines', the *Guardian*, 6 February: 2.

Weber, M. (1948) *From Max Weber*, ed. by Hans Gerth and C. Wright Mills. London: Routledge and Kegan Paul.

Weedon, C. (1987) *Feminist Practice and Poststructuralist Theory*. Oxford: Blackwell.

Weeks, J. (1981) 'Discourse, desire and sexual deviance: some problems in a history of homosexuality', in K. Plummer (ed.), *The Making of the Modern Homosexual*. London: Routledge and Kegan Paul, pp. 76–111.

Weeks, J. (1985) *Sexuality and its Discontents*. London: Routledge.

Weeks, J. (1990) *Sex, Politics and Society: The Regulation of Sexuality Since 1800*. 2nd edn. London: Longman.

Weeks, J. (1991) 'Pretended family relationships', in D. Clark (ed.), *Marriage, Domestic Life and Social Change*. London: Routledge, pp. 214–34.

Weiss, K. and Borges, S. (1973) 'Victimology and rape: the case of the legitimate victim', *Issues in Criminology*, 8: 71–115.

Westwood, S. (1984) *All Day, Every Day*. London: Pluto Press.

Whisman, V. (1996) *Queer by Choice: Lesbians, Gays and the Politics of Identity*. New York: Routledge.

Whiting, P. (1972) 'Female sexuality: its political implications', in M. Wandor (ed.), *The Body Politic*. London: Stage 1, pp. 189–213.

Wilkinson, S. and Kitzinger, C. (eds) (1993) *Heterosexuality: A 'Feminism and Psychology' Reader*. London: Sage.

Wilson, E. (1981) 'Psychoanalysis: psychic law and order', *Feminist Review*, 8: 63–78.

Wilson, E. (1983) 'A new romanticism?', in E. Phillips (ed.), *The Left and the Erotic*. London: Lawrence and Wishart, pp. 37–52.

Wilson, E. (1988) *Halllucinations*. London: Hutchinson.

Wilson, E. (1993) 'Is transgression transgressive?', in J. Bristow and A. Wilson (eds), *Activating Theory*. London: Lawrence and Wishart, pp. 107–17.

Wilton, T. (1996) 'Which one's the man? The heterosexualisation of lesbian sex', in D. Richardson (ed.), *Theorising Heterosexuality: Telling it Straight*. Buckingham: Open University Press, pp. 125–42.

Wilton, T. (1997) *Engendering AIDS: Deconstructing Sex, Text and Epidemic*. London: Sage.

Wittig, M. (1992) *The Straight Mind and Other Essays*. Hemel Hempstead: Harvester Wheatsheaf.

Wood, J. (1984) 'Groping towards sexism: boys' sex talk', in A. McRobbie and M. Nava (eds), *Gender and Generation*. London: Macmillan, pp. 54–84.

Young, A. (1993) 'The authority of the name', in S. Wilkinson and S. Kitzinger (eds), *Heterosexuality*. London: Sage, pp. 37–8.

Young, I.M. (1990) *Throwing Like a Girl and Other Essays*. Bloomington and Indianapolis: Indiana University Press.

Subject index

Author index